Harvie's Dyke

HARVIE'S DYKE

The People, their Liberty and the Clyde

CHRISTOPHER A. WHATLEY

First published in Great Britain in 2025 by
John Donald, an imprint of Birlinn Ltd

West Newington House
10 Newington Road
Edinburgh
EH9 1QS

www.birlinn.co.uk

ISBN: 978 0 85976 730 9

British Library Cataloguing-in-Publication Data
A catalogue record for this book is available on request from the British Library

MIX
Paper | Supporting responsible forestry
FSC® C011748

Typeset by Hewer Text UK Ltd, Edinburgh
Printed and bound in Britain by Ashford Colour Ltd, Gosport

Contents

Plates

Preface: Pride Comes Before a Fall

This book is about one of the most dramatic episodes in Glasgow's history. It tells the story of the remarkable rise and subsequent ruin of Thomas Harvie, who in the early nineteenth century had become the city's leading whisky distiller and supplier of spirits. But Harvie, ruthless in his business dealings, was not content simply to make money. He aspired to the lavish lifestyle Glasgow's scarlet-cloaked, cane-carrying, silver-wigged tobacco lords had enjoyed during their golden age in the eighteenth century. Lacking any sense of decorum, he spared no effort in ostentatiously displaying his new-found prosperity, rubbing his good fortune in the faces of those less fortunate. He purchased an estate in the countryside some three miles beyond the eastern edge of the overcrowded centre of what had been Glasgow's medieval core. He extended and improved the grand mansion house that went with the property – Westthorn – sparing no expense in furnishing it.

Harvie, however, had no intention of sharing his newly acquired assets. Instead, he erected imposing boundary walls to keep out the general public, mainly his working-class neighbours in the scatter of fast-growing frontier villages that lay close to his house and grounds.

The larger of his two walls – known locally as Harvie's Dyke – blocked a time-honoured, much-frequented and greatly loved walkway along the north bank of the river Clyde. Such was the outrage felt by the handloom weavers, coal miners, cotton spinners and other workers from Calton and the villages of what would become the eastern fringe of the sprawling city of Glasgow, that they rose in protest. In June 1823 hundreds of them marched towards the Dyke, to which Harvie had added an armed watchtower.

This book describes in vivid detail what happened next. It is revealed in the first-hand testimonies of most of the main actors, along with witnesses to the confrontation. For two centuries their silent voices have been secured in bundles of dusty and grime-covered legal case papers held in store among Scotland's national records in Edinburgh. These tell a story of community action, and of the solidarity of working-class communities in defence of what they considered to be their inalienable rights. The same sources tell too of meetings, marches, violent explosions, of the dyke's destruction (and reconstruction), of dragoons, mass arrests, courtroom drama and the imprisonment of those few individuals the authorities managed to convict.

There followed an outpouring of sympathy across the city for those jailed for their part in the assault on Harvie's property. His grimly determined attempts to block public access along the walkway inspired a six-year-long campaign for the 'liberty of the banks of the Clyde'. In an alliance that challenges simplistic notions of class antagonisms, the lead was now taken by reformers from the ranks of Glasgow's emerging middle class – professional men, small merchants and manufacturers, and even poets. They deliberately shunned physical force and instead fought tirelessly by legal means supported by public subscriptions. The campaign, which began in the low-lying cottages, subdivided houses, workshops, change houses (inns) and streets of Bridgeton, Camlachie, Dalmarnock, Parkhead, Shettleston and Tollcross, moved to the law courts of Edinburgh and, eventually, Britain's highest court of appeal, the House of Lords.

David – Glasgow's people – took on Goliath. It was a rare occasion when in a dispute over access to land the poor did have their lawyers. And won.

Harvie was humiliated. He had spent a large part of his wealth on legal fees and related costs, assuming that the weight of his gold would crush the opposition from the little people, who had few financial resources and whom he considered to be beneath contempt. He miscalculated, badly.

In one sense, this is a simple moral tale, of good overcoming evil against all the odds; of the people's rights against those of an arrogant Glaswegian who had committed the cardinal sin of getting above himself. Infusing their outrage was the thriving spirit of Presbyterian egalitarianism.

But the book is about more than this. The Harvie's Dyke protest was not simply a one-off isolated incident. It represents a strand in the story of Scottish radicalism that has so far been largely overlooked.

The French Revolution more than thirty years before had ignited serious social and political unrest in Scotland. The old order was no longer secure. Disorder and rioting carried on even after the momentous victory of British forces under the command of the Duke of Wellington at Waterloo in 1815 where some 4,000 of his soldiers had lost their lives. In Scotland as elsewhere in Europe there was anger among ordinary people that the sacrifices made in support of monarchies, and then the pain of re-adjustment as soldiers in their thousands were discharged, had not been recognised by their rulers. Demands for political and social change intensified.

In Manchester, post-war protest peaked in 1819 with the bloody massacre by the military of eighteen innocent people and the infliction of injuries to hundreds more at St Peter's Field, where thousands had assembled to listen to political reformers. It was a tragedy on British soil that almost immediately became known as the battle of 'Peterloo'.

In Scotland, radical activity and plotting with their counterparts in England had carried on until Easter 1820, partly as a response to the horrors of Peterloo. This culminated in an armed rising that commenced in and around Glasgow and Paisley on 4 April. Yet Scotland's much discussed, hotly debated and still celebrated 'Radical War', which was accompanied by a massive strike of workers in the west of Scotland, was effectively over in little more than a week. In August, lifelong advocate of reform sixty-three-year-old James Wilson was hanged and beheaded in Glasgow. His crime: treason. A week later, John Baird and Andrew Hardie suffered the same fate, in Stirling. Nineteen of the other individuals charged with treason were ordered to be transported to Botany Bay, seven of them for the rest of their lives.

The provost and magistrates of Glasgow thought they could breathe more easily. Peace had been restored. They conveyed their heartfelt thanks to the departing soldiers who in unprecedented numbers had been stationed in and around the militarised city during 1819 and 1820.

But their valedictions were premature. Within months Glasgow was the scene of further outbreaks of popular violence. The army was recalled, and a new cavalry barracks erected.

The defeat of the radicals in 1820 had been a major blow for those concerned, but not everyone who participated had given up the struggle for liberty and social justice. In the succeeding years former activists necessarily kept a low profile, but they and the causes for which they fought lived on.

One of these was land rights, which were under threat from increasingly property-conscious, commercially minded landowners. Battles over land were not confined to the Highlands. In Lowland Scotland, even in the towns, the engorgement by private individuals of what had formerly been considered to be common land and rights of way was a profoundly important and much-contested issue.

This book uncovers – for the first time – the links between the reformers of the 1790s, the angry radicalism of the distressed years that followed the wars with France that ended with the Treaty of Vienna in 1815, the Radical War of 1820 and the campaign against Harvie's Dyke. It also sheds new light on the culture and attitudes to authority of the communities in which radical activists lived and worked. The aims of those initially involved in the Harvie's Dyke affair may have been less ambitious in their scope and significance than those of 1820. But liberty is a rich feast. The right to perambulate freely on tracks and pathways that had been regularly used 'beyond memory of man' was arguably a more tangible gain than the somewhat vague and hopelessly ambitious aspirations announced by the radicals in April 1820, who sought a provisional government to replace the much-hated Tory regime in London.

Freedom of access to familiar pathways, and the liberty to delight in the flora and fauna of the countryside and breathe fresh air, were not the concerns of a single class. They mattered to Glasgow's rising place-proud middle class, as well as to working people. This book highlights the extent to which the classes were at one in their affection for the river Clyde, its 'bonny banks' and the natural delights they offered. The people's affection for all of this was palpable, as was the unity of purpose evinced in the firmness of their demand to walk along the banks of the Clyde at will. Indeed, so momentous was the struggle over the Dyke that it featured prominently in Glasgow's public memory for many decades thereafter. On the ground, its legacy was more substantial than 1820. The once contested pathway is still open, on the Glasgow–Cambuslang stretch of the 40-mile-long (65-kilometre) Clyde Walkway which runs from Partick in Glasgow's west end out to New Lanark.

But Glasgow has forgotten what had been won, despite Glasgow being where Scotland's rights of way movement commenced. It would be another twenty years before what later became the Scottish Rights of Way Society would be founded, in the capital (in 1845), to protect public roadways around Edinburgh. Scotland has also forgotten, even though what began as a local fight had national ramifications. It was the first major legal challenge in defence of the people's right to walk along long-established paths in Britain. It is an early instance of environmental activism, of green consciousness long before the Greens.

The story has never been fully told. But it deserves to be.

Acknowledgements

In researching for and writing this book I have been assisted by many individuals and organisations. Without their substantial help my task would have been much harder and the result far less satisfactory.

Much of the material I have used is held in Glasgow. Anthony Lewis from Kelvingrove Art Gallery and Museum searched for and found in the Glasgow Life collections medals that were made for and awarded to the committee that led the legal campaign against Thomas Harvie's attempts to obstruct the Clyde pathway. Tony was also an early enthusiast for the project. He introduced me to Susan Pacitti at Glasgow Life. who made available some of the images used in the book. Glasgow's Mitchell Library houses a vast store of primary materials including newspapers, pamphlets and popular poetry and song. I am indebted to Clare Thomson and her colleagues in Special Collections as well as the Glasgow Collection for their guidance and friendly assistance. In Glasgow City Archives, also housed in the Mitchell, I have been assisted by Barbara McLean, Nerys Tunnicliffe, Irene O'Brien and others. Thanks are due too to David Kenning, Archives and Special Collections, University of Glasgow. Pam McNicol and Neil Dickson in Stirling Council Archives kindly sent me transcriptions of materials in their care. Clare Harrison, Library and Heritage Manager, Royal College of Physicians and Surgeons of Glasgow, took time to find information for me about Dr William Lyon and kindly arranged for me to acquire a picture of this important but little-known Glasgow physician. John Moore, formerly Collections Manager at the University of Glasgow, and the leading authority on Glasgow's maps, kindly alerted me to the existence of the papers and drawings of the surveyor William Kyle, held in Glasgow City Archives. The 'Statistical Account of the Barony Parish of Glasgow' (1826) the original copy of which is held by the University of Glasgow, and which he and Professor John Hume transcribed, edited and published as *A City Made for Commerce* (2023) has been an invaluable source.

Anne Cameron of the University of Strathclyde's Archives and Special Collections was instrumental in obtaining for me a contemporary image of Glasgow Fair. Margaret McGinty at North Lanarkshire Heritage Centre in Motherwell was also obliging in directing me to the whereabouts of an invaluable weather report for Airdrie in the early nineteenth century, which I used as a proxy for the eastern end of Glasgow.

It is difficult to overstate the value of Scotland's two national repositories – both of which are in Edinburgh – for Scottish historians. At the National Records of Scotland, I have been helped by Heike Vieth, Emma Filshie and their colleagues in finding and accessing the voluminous court records which have been one of the foundations of this project. Generally, the Historical Search Room staff have been both efficient and polite. Staff at the National Library of Scotland (NLS) including Peter Findlay and Carmen Hesketh have been tireless in their endeavours on my behalf, always prepared to go that little bit extra, and with good grace. The same applies to Louise Speller in the Map Library. The National Library is a model of first-class public service provision. Morag Ferguson of the Advocates Library co-operated with NLS in making available to me some printed Court of Session productions. Further afield, I am indebted to Mari Takayanagi of the Parliamentary Archives for identifying and arranging for me to obtain digital copies of key House of Lords papers. For pointing me in this direction, I am grateful to David Torrance, in the House of Commons Library. Professor Murray Pittock of the University of Glasgow has been supportive throughout and, typically generously, gifted me a copy of an invaluable source for anyone conducting research on Glasgow, *Glasgow Past and Present* by Robert Reid, or 'Senex'. By inviting me to deliver the John Galt Society's annual lecture in Irvine in 2023 Professor Rhona Brown, of Glasgow University, provided me with an opportunity to test some of my ideas about the Harvie's Dyke episode in a public forum. I benefited from email correspondence about poetry of the period with Professor Nigel Leask, also at the University of Glasgow. His colleague Craig Lamont's innovative work on Glasgow's history has been enormously helpful.

The illustrations have been drawn from the following collections: Archives and Special Collections, University of Glasgow; Archives and Special Collections, University of Strathclyde; Glasgow Life Photo Library; Glasgow Museums and Libraries Collections; the National Library of Scotland; the National Records of Scotland; the Royal College of Physicians and Surgeons of Glasgow; the Scottish National Portrait Gallery; the National Portrait Gallery.

Hugh Andrew, both a friend and managing director of Birlinn Ltd, has been an enthusiastic supporter of this project from the outset. In preparing the book for publication I have had the pleasure, not for the first time, of working with Mairi Sutherland, the scrupulous managing editor of the John Donald imprint under which this book appears, the punctilious copy editor Susan Milligan and the cover designer Jim Hutcheson, whose patience as we debated which of his several design ideas to use, must have been tested to its limits. I am also grateful to Nicola King, who prepared the index.

I owe a special thanks to two people who are much more familiar with and able to use Scotland's People and similar databases than I am. Dr Stephen Mullen, from the School of Humanities at the University of Glasgow, the historian of Glasgow's slave trade, was able to find crucial information about Thomas Harvie, in particular his business background. Dr David Abercrombie, a long-standing friend from our time as PhD students at Strathclyde University, has, since his early retirement, become an assiduous family history researcher. Although trained as a mathematician and statistician, David has now acquired the skills of the most diligent historian. These he applied to Thomas Harvie and was able to uncover information unknown to me about Harvie's family background, and the circumstances in which he died. This has made the book much more complete than it would have been otherwise. David also read through two of the most relevant chapters and pointed out an embarrassingly high number of mainly typographical slips.

Last but certainly not least I must thank my partner Dr Catriona Macdonald who from the outset has sustained me in this investigation. At an early stage in the gestation of the project we parked her bright blue car outside the Celtic Social Club in London Road, and searched out, behind the undergrowth down by the river Clyde nearby, the remaining traces of Harvie's Dyke. Subsequently she has patiently listened as I dug deeper into my subject and kindly read and commented on initial drafts of the chapters as I turned them out. Her frank comments, astute observations and searching questioning have vastly improved my text and made this a far better book. Her presence in general has been life affirming. Any flaws and failings in what follows, however, are entirely my own responsibility.

I

Drumming up a Storm: Early Summer 1823

The dull tap and muffled rattle of a drum beating interrupted the relative quiet of a late Saturday afternoon in Glasgow's east end in June 1823. It was the 21st, midsummer's day, the longest of the year. Like the two previous days it was sunny and dry. Most works in this part of Glasgow's sprawling Barony parish, the most populous in Scotland, had shut down a few hours earlier. The workpeople at several collieries, cotton mills, a corn mill, brickworks, tanneries and dyeworks were relieved from their daily toil for the remainder of what would be a weekend unlike any other. Even the district's numerous handloom weavers had stepped aside from the weary monotony of operating their looms, many leaving webs unfinished. The days when working people such as weavers in Glasgow could rest idle from Saturday afternoon through to Wednesday morning and spend at least some of their time drinking or otherwise enjoying themselves had long gone, for most a memory from the later eighteenth century.[1]

Short silences, when the drumming stopped, were filled with the sonorous sound of a man's voice. He wasn't quite shouting, but speaking loudly and deliberately, and only briefly at each place he halted before moving on. The orator was Thomas John Fraser, a handloom weaver, aged around fifty-four, who lived with his wife Ann Christie in Browns Land, Parkhead. 'Land' usually referred to a discrete property, a large house or tenement, subdivided into smaller living and working spaces. Like most ageing, bent-backed weavers Fraser was less active than he had once been at the loom and had taken on the role of 'bellman' (so-called as in former times a bell was rung to attract the inhabitants' attention), or drummer and public crier for 'the villages betwixt Camlachie Bridge and Baillieston Toll'. These separate communities of mainly handloom weavers, coal miners, cotton mill operatives and tradesmen such as tailors and shoemakers were strung along the sides of the rough-made roads in what until only a handful of decades earlier had been farmland and small settlements of sub-tenants and cotters. Built up or old Glasgow was still some distance to the west, with the vast bulk of its inhabitants concentrated on ten principal streets and seventeen wynds, or lanes. Especially crowded were the backlands which ran off at right angles from the High Street that ran from the medieval Cathedral past the college or university and down to Glasgow Cross and the Saltmarket.

To the east beyond the burgh boundary only Camlachie and Shettleston were recognised as distinct entities in the mid eighteenth century – both being depicted by the military surveyor William Roy on his monumental map of Scotland of 1753–4 as having a few houses. As more and deeper coal mines were sunk and industrial activity took root, the rural character of the area around them began to change. It became increasingly populated as the overwhelmingly working-class weaving communities of Calton and Bridgeton grew. Glasgow's better-off residents preferred to move westwards to the fashionable newly built terraces and townhouses of George Square and Blythswood Square, or south over the river Clyde at Hutchesontown and Laurieston.

By the end of the century Tollcross and Westmuir also had a presence on maps of Glasgow and its eastern suburbs. So too did a Cameronian meeting house to the east of Tollcross and a church at Shettleston.[2] Small knots of houses that would later become discrete communities such as Barrowfield, Dalmarnock and Jeanfield also began to appear. But they lay beyond the bounds of the Royalty of Glasgow, unplanned and unchecked as they expanded, and largely outwith the authority of the city's town council and magistracy.

Glasgow was spreading, but it had not yet become the expansive conurbation it was to become in the Victorian age and is nowadays. Before 1800 Glasgow comprised less than 2,000 acres; by 1900 this had risen to slightly more than 12,600 acres; by the end of the twentieth century this had extended to just under 40,000 acres, or around 62 square miles.

But in 1800 still there was no Parkhead, at least not marked on maps. However, it was there by 1823. Nearby was a collection of coal miners' houses that sat small and squat around the three tall furnaces of Colin Dunlop's Clyde Iron Works, which dominated the local skyline. The Clyde works had been founded in 1786, a harbinger of Scotland's industrial revolution. To the west lay Henry Monteith's world-renowned and much-visited dyeworks, founded by David Dale and George Mackintosh in 1785, and a similar plant operated by Thomas Lancaster and Company. Some cotton mills were also to be seen. Even so, the area was still largely rural in appearance. Some of the most striking features were grand detached mansion houses and carefully laid out tree-lined avenues and enclosures.[3]

We don't know exactly the route taken by Fraser as he tapped his drum and read out his proclamation. If, as seems most likely, he walked along what was the main road from Glasgow to Edinburgh, he may have by-passed the settlements at Shettleston and Mid Quarter on the Airdrie road a little to the north, although we can't be sure. One way or other the people there would have heard the drum, albeit less loudly than those in the low-lying irregular rows of cramped, single-room cottages on the Edinburgh road.

Call to arms

Perhaps as he was in the open air, John West, a sixteen-year-old weaver from Camlachie who had been to Shettleston to collect a pair of shoes being made for him, was able to hear 'the drum going about for the purpose of assembling a meeting'. This was to be held that very evening, at the 'sheddings' at Parkhead cross, where the main road to the east divided.

This was a meeting with a purpose. Fraser the bellman had been handed a piece of paper that morning by an unnamed individual, upon which the words of what he was to proclaim had been written (see Plate 2).

They were scratched in a hesitant hand, as if the writer was unfamiliar with using a pen and ink. Fraser's instructions were to address the inhabitants of Parkhead and Westmuir, Camlachie, Tollcross 'and adjacent places', and request them to attend a public meeting at the cross of Parkhead at seven o'clock to take into consideration 'measures for taking away the obstruction on the banks of Clyde'.[4] Sometime after five o'clock this is more or less what Robert Dunsmore, a collier who was in the house at Tollcross he rented from Colin Dunlop of the Clyde Iron Works, heard. Fraser's proclamation, he recalled, was to the effect that 'the object of the meeting was business of importance concerning the banks of the Clyde'. Others, however, interpreted the call slightly differently. John Williamson, a forty-year-old teacher, understood that the purpose of gathering a large number of people together was 'to make a way or passage along the side of the river which had formerly been in use, and which had been interrupted by the wall that Mr Harvie had built'. William Lyon, a young, recently licensed surgeon in Parkhead, thought the objective was even more ambitious. It was 'to pull down the walls which had been erected by Mr Harvie'. Thomas Robertson, a young weaver by trade, was of the same opinion: the reason for Fraser's call was 'to pull down the dykes'. This was confirmed by Alexander Whyte, a sixty-four-year-old mason who had been employed by Harvie to assist in building the walls. After an early-evening visit to the barber's at Parkhead cross for a shave, Whyte noted that a 'considerable' crowd had begun to gather, to consider 'measures for taking down the walls erected on Mr Harvie's property'.

The walls in question were on the land of Thomas Harvie (sometimes given as Harvey), the owner of the 115-acre Westthorn estate, one of several located in the eastern end of Glasgow's Barony parish, and in its immediate neighbour, the Lanarkshire parish of Old Monkland. Harvie had acquired this for £20,500 in February 1822, at a roup of the possessions of James Sword, junior, a Glasgow coal merchant, coal dealer, wine and grain dealer and shipowner. Sword, who had acquired the estate in 1809, for £18,000, had overstretched himself. He had debts of over £52,000, the largest of them owing to the Royal Bank.[5]

With Sword having spent some £36,000 on improving the estate, it was an attractive proposition. Westthorn lay to the south of the villages of Parkhead and Tollcross. The property was bounded on the south and west by the river Clyde, across from the royal burgh of Rutherglen (see Plate 1). The lands were described as being 'all arable' other than those areas planted with trees. Not only were they 'fit for bearing any crops', but according to the *Glasgow Herald* they were also 'judiciously subdivided and enclosed' and protected by a 'strong embankment against the river, constructed at great expense'. From here and on the strip of his property that bordered the Clyde, the owner had the right to fish salmon. Usefully for a man of business in Glasgow, the gates at the northern edge of the estate opened onto the main road from Glasgow to London. Indeed, for landowners nearby, the proximity of their estates to Glasgow gave them 'a great advantage'. Harvie's business premises were but a short horse-ride distant.

Thomas Harvie: drink and be merry, and rich

Glaswegians knew Thomas Harvie as 'Lang Tam Harvie'. Born around 1774, he was probably in his thirties when he began to make his mark in the city's commercial circles. He was tall, 'muscular' and 'large-sized'. Helping to give him height too was his habit of holding his head 'as high as if he had been the Lord of the Isles'. Vain, on the streets Harvie 'endeavoured to assume the manners of a mighty gentleman . . . with all the airs of the old Virginian grandees who previously held sway in Glasgow'. His distinctive appearance was compounded by his 'ruddy' whiskers and close-cropped hair. Even more noticeable was how he dressed, so much so that one of his contemporaries described him as 'the very *Beau* Brummel of the city'.[6] It was alleged – almost certainly exaggeratedly – that he ordered a new suit of clothes more or less weekly from Glasgow's two most fashionable tailors, Donald Macdonald and Mr J. S. Stubbs, in Miller Street. He had little regard for the hodden grey worn by country folk and handloom weavers, or the dark clothing favoured by the many devout Presbyterians in the city, but delighted in wearing modish bright colours, such as a '*light blue* superfine coat, with glittering buttons', and 'white and embroidered vests of every shape and variety'. Tight pantaloons covered his legs, along with silk stockings and 'polished Hessian or nice top boots'. These were prepared by his groom, a small smart boy who rode behind his master in his 'elegant tandem with two mettled horses . . . one behind the other'.

Socially ambitious, Harvie was an enthusiastic member of various hunting and coursing clubs, the most prestigious being the Glasgow Hounds or Roberton Hunt, for which he dressed in a scarlet coat and velvet cap. The event, which encompassed both Lanarkshire and Renfrewshire, had first been held in 1771, and was patronised by local aristocrats and wealthy landowners including many of the city's leading merchants – just the kind of company Harvie was keen to cultivate. He was a regular attender at the Theatre Royal, where he kept a front seat in one of the boxes – displaying 'ruffled linens' and elegant pocket handkerchiefs, perfumed by Henry Urquhart – who claimed to be one of the king's perruquiers, or hair-piece maker. The Theatre, in Queen Street, which had been designed by David Hamilton, Glasgow's most eminent architect of the time, and opened in 1805, was one of the town's most fashionable places of entertainment. This was unlike its predecessor, the smaller 'old' theatre in Dunlop Street (erected in 1782), where Harvie also had business premises. At one time he may even have attended it, as some of the performances there, in what had become a circus, were intermixed with horsemanship. But as these were also judged to be 'minor in character and degree', it is unlikely that he was a regular patron. The Theatre Royal on the other hand was thought to be one of the largest provincial theatres in Europe; built at a cost of £18,000 and with seats for 1,500 people, it boasted its ability to attract the country's leading actors.[7] In September 1822, for example, local newspapers had announced that a Mr Kean of London's Drury Lane Theatre Royal would be appearing in Glasgow, playing Shylock in Shakespeare's *The Merchant of Venice*. For one night only. Adding further to the attraction was that Mrs Vaughan – from the Theatre Royal in Covent Garden – would play Portia.

Also staged were more patriotic plays, such as *Rob Roy*, in which 'Leoni Lee' sang 'Caledonia, Land of Glory' and 'Scots Wha Hae'. Performances also included comic interludes, in which Irish songs were often sung and jokes made at the expense of the Irish. A performance of *The Cataract of the Ganges*, which involved a battle scene with 'Mr Cooke and his unrivalled stud of horses' (no doubt of great appeal to the horse-loving Harvie), was to conclude with the 'laughable Farce of HONEST THIEVES; OR, THE FAITHFUL IRISHMAN'. But Scottish comic songs were also sung, as in November 1822 when Mr Boddie sang 'We're a' Noddin', an enormously popular spinning song that was sung – not always well – throughout the city.

What would have attracted Harvie, however, was the clientele. The announcement of a subscription concert at the Theatre in January 1827 included notice that the event would be attended by the Lord Provost and magistrates, but also the Earl of Cathcart, Lord Viscount Kelburne, Sir John Maxwell of Pollock and others including the 'principal Nobility and Gentry of Glasgow and its vicinity'. It was on such occasions – when the audience would be treated to a performance by Mrs Knyvett, Mr Vaughan and Mr Bellamy, 'the First Glee Singers in Europe' – that Harvie was able to buy with due ostentation (the subscription lists were open to inspection) single tickets for the box, costing 7s, or, at £1 4s, a set of four. Despite the attractiveness of his wealth, he seems not to have been interested in any of the many daughters whose mothers presented them to him as potential marriage partners. He declined all offers.

'Lang Tam' had reason to feel pleased with himself. He had risen rapidly through the multitudinous ranks of Glasgow's men of business. He was from the Glasgow suburb of Yoker, five miles to the west of the city. According to one account he had only an elementary education and began his working life as an everyday carter, sometimes taking milk into the city. He had some success too as a horse dealer. But he also had family links with the Yoker distillery, which had been established or taken over by his brother John, who also farmed in Yoker. John's father, Thomas, had been a farmer in Balfron parish, to the north of Glasgow. It was John Harvie's eldest son John who took over the distillery and farm, however, so Thomas ('Lang Tam'), who was born later, around 1774, had had to make his own way in business. This may be the modest start referred to by his contemporaries. Nevertheless, by the early 1800s, in partnership with his nephew John (John Harvie's son) Thomas Harvie had moved directly into the retail spirits business, with cellars or warehouses in Yoker and a counting house in Glasgow.[8]

This was an astute decision, although it was almost certainly inspired by his brother's and nephew's success in distilling at Yoker and the ready availability of a product to sell. Aquavitae, or whisky, was becoming increasingly popular in Lowland Scotland, in Glasgow in particular, as a taste for *uisge beatha* displaced the former affection for rum and claret, much of which had been smuggled into the country in places where there were long stretches of largely uninhabited coastline. Migrants from the Highlands and Ireland wanted to consume the drink with which they had been familiar. The pressures associated with early industrialisation – longer unbroken periods of work, closer supervision and harsher demands on the part of employers – increased the demand for the quicker sense of release and conviviality that hard spirits offered compared to ale or beer, traditionally the alcohol of choice for the labouring classes. Whisky was drunk in prodigious quantities too at weddings and funerals and was even a medium of exchange; grocers for example offered a glass of whisky in lieu of change. Harvie understood the market and his public's palate – for which he concocted one of the city's most popular whisky blends. Previously, according to John Strang, one of the city's most reliable chroniclers, most Lowland whisky was 'only fitted for the most vulgar and fire-loving palates'.[9] Harvie dealt in both grain and malt whiskies.

From his initial base in airy Dunlop Street, where he also lived in one of the villas (in a comparatively new part of town that housed many of the leading and wealthiest citizens), and prior to his move to Westthorn, Harvie extended the business through many other quarters of the city. His carters made deliveries to the homes of well over six hundred regular customers who had accounts with him. According to the *Glasgow Directory* for 1821, and a legal record of his properties, along with a shop and cellars in Jackson Street he had shops in Clyde Street, Crown Street, Great Hamilton Street, Hope Street, London Road, Rope Work Lane and Stirling Street. With smaller premises scattered through the town, and in suburbs such as Anderston and Hutchesontown, these and other outlets meant that he was one of Glasgow's best-known drinks retailers. Hitherto, most whisky had been consumed in austere dram shops or 'tippling houses', best understood as comfortless hovels. In Glasgow as in Paris, one report suggested, the most numerous profession was that of 'retailers of spiritous liquors', or tavern keepers; in 1824 there was one tavern for every twenty families. Harvie, however, recognised that there was potential in improving the drinking environment. Thus in 'almost in every street in the city' there were signboards advertising 'Harvie's Divans', the name he used for his slightly up-market whisky shops, more like today's lounge bars. He operated these to a high standard: it was said that none of his carters or the carefully selected managers of his clean, well-kept premises were ever fined for breaching local regulations. It was this enterprise, according to Peter Mackenzie, the radical reformer, observant and well-informed Glasgow chronicler and editor of the *Loyal Reformers Gazette* (founded 1832), that was the foundation of Harvie's 'colossal' fortune.

Something of his business practice – and personality – is to be seen in a decade-long legal dispute he had with Hugh Dunbar, a change-keeper in Westmuir. In 1810 he and his nephew John had pursued Dunbar in Glasgow Sheriff Court for a sum of money Harvie claimed was due from Dunbar for a 69½ gallon hogshead of whisky valued at just over £55 that he had had delivered in June 1809. Dunbar and his wife Janet Stuart – who was unable to read or write – denied that the whisky had ever been received. Harvie was able to call on the support of James Bruce, Secretary to the Board of Excise for Scotland, who declared that excise records showed that the delivery had been made. Despite this, Harvie still lost the case, in part owing to the suspicious fact that he had invoiced Dunbar for the whisky some eighteen months after its alleged delivery. It was his normal practice to send invoices, which were paid in cash, every three months. His argument that it was Janet Stuart who had led 'the pursuer Thomas Harvie into an error' was described as being 'destitute of truth'. Rather, Dunbar claimed, he and his wife had 'trusted too much and too long to the Pursuer's affected accuracy' – and Harvie had admitted to some accounting errors.[10] Harvie, though, had stuck to his guns, expressing outrage that his character had been besmirched by being accused of extortion ('wilful or not') and other improper business practices. Dunbar had taken the case to the House of Lords in 1820, and won. It would not be the last time that Harvie's pleas would be heard by the country's highest court.

In addition to whisky, uncle and nephew also sold meal and other basic foodstuffs, presumably benefiting from the family farming venture. From around 1825 the two men ran this side of the business as the Dalbeth Mills Corn and Provisions Company. Taking advantage of his access to the grain required to manufacture whisky, the Illicit Distillery (Scotland) Act of 1822 and the subsequent Excise Act of 1823, Harvie was one of the first men in Glasgow to establish a thriving legal distillery – the Glasgow Distillery Company – which comprised two former plants, the Port Dundas Distillery and Dundashill Distillery. Here, both grain and malt whiskies were produced. Harvie bought the five-acre site from John Haig. From 1790, Port Dundas, then a new development, had been connected to the Forth and Clyde Canal via the Monkland Canal. This was a boon for the shipment of bulk goods, including whisky. Sitting alongside the elevated canal basin, opened in 1790, the distillery complex towered above the city, a highly visible monument to Harvie's pre-eminence as a successful entrepreneur (see Plate 3).

Expansion at Port Dundas was rapid. Impressive too was the range of facilities in what was a fully integrated operation: these ranged from a barn for holding grain, a seven-storey mill, a mash and yeast house, a spirit store, three bonded stores, distillery offices, excise offices, a smiths' and a wrights' shop, a cooperage, horse stables and tack, carts and wagons – and a piggery. Not surprisingly, vast quantities of coal and peat were also kept on site, much of the former being used to fuel the works' 40 hp steam engine, more powerful than any of those at Glasgow's other distilleries. The new legal environment was key to the success of such a venture. Many small illicit producers who had formerly supplied much of the whisky sold in the Scottish Lowlands were squeezed out by bulk producers like Harvie who also had the means of sending large quantities of whisky by the Forth and Clyde Canal from Port Dundas to Port Glasgow, one of a limited number of harbour towns the excise authorities approved for export purposes. Before acquiring either the distillery or Westthorn estate, and in addition to his west of Scotland clients, Harvie had established a network of customers in Ireland. Most were in Belfast and Dublin, but he sold his products in smaller towns too, such as Ballycastle, Letterkenny and Strabane. He also had a presence in England, including London, where he had a shop. Small wonder then that the *Belfast Commercial Chronicle* described him as 'the most eminent distiller of whiskey in Scotland'. To his credit, and notwithstanding the nature of his quarrel with Hugh Dunbar and his wife, Harvie was considered to be an honest trader: James Galbraith of Glasgow's Excise Office commended Harvie and his employees for the 'regularity and accuracy . . . [of] all their dealings'. But with heavy demands on his time and energy, about which we will say more in later chapters, in 1825 Harvie transferred most of his retail business to his nephew.

Harvie's motives in buying Westthorn were ones that most of his generation – and social position – would have understood. The population of the increasingly crowded manufacturing city of Glasgow had risen faster than any other major British town between 1811 and 1821 and doubled between 1811 and 1831 to over 200,000. Thus, early, what had once been an elegant city greatly admired by the English spy and traveller Defoe was on the way to acquiring the unenviable reputation for being the filthiest and unhealthiest city in the United Kingdom. Those who had the means were inclined to move away from the old, increasingly overcrowded centre.

Possession of a small estate intimated success, and Harvie was 'supposed . . . to be one of the greatest men in all Glasgow', a worthy successor to the opulent tobacco lords who had strutted the city's streets during much of the previous century. Prior to his purchase, and partly in order to gain respectability among the town's commercial elite, Harvie had in August 1815 applied successfully to become a burgess and guild brother. That he had had to pay in full for his burgess-ship rather than depend on his father or another close relative's connections may underline the fact of the modesty of his social background, as well perhaps that he was not from Glasgow.[11] At the same time he had become a matriculated member (as a Home Trader) of the Merchants' House.

Business achievement alone was not sufficient; *arrivistes* such as Harvie (he was later described as a 'mushroom laird' – a scornful reference to the rapidity of his rise from the soil of Yoker) needed the security of status and the trappings of power that only land ownership could confer. Indeed, given his modest social origins, Harvie had to try harder to be accepted by the region's landed elite whose wealth had come from mercantile pursuits; most had also been born into comfortably well-off families and, unlike Harvie, had longstanding links with the landowning classes.

Westthorn was in a fittingly prestigious location (see Plate 1). It was bounded on the north-eastern edge by Dalbeth estate, owned by James Hopkirk, grandson of Thomas Hopkirk, one of Glasgow's leading West Indian merchants and a founding partner of the Glasgow Arms Bank. James, who was one of a number of the city's tobacco merchants who had purchased mineral-bearing land during the American War of Independence, was appointed as a Justice of the Peace for Lanarkshire, and in 1809 served as chairman of the influential Chamber of Commerce – of which he was a founder member and, from 1787, a Director.[12] His wife, Christian, was the daughter of John Glassford, one of the most celebrated of the tobacco lords, who had purchased Shawfield mansion. His father too had had a hand in the tobacco trade, being a partner in Alexander Speirs and Co., one of city's largest tobacco firms. Harvie may well have been delighted to have, fortuitously, a neighbour whose diverse business interests included brewing and bottle manufacturing. Even more of an attraction was Hopkirk's public prominence. He was an instigator of the town's Tontine Hotel and the Assembly Rooms in Ingram Street. He was also one of the heritors of Barony parish, a Commissioner of Supply for Lanarkshire, a Justice of the Peace and, frequently, a commissioner at the General Assembly of the Church of Scotland.[13] Hopkirk was no friend of the lower orders, whom he was inclined to treat with contempt, so Harvie may well have derived some encouragement from his near neighbour as he too developed and made clear that he held similar attitudes to the people below.

Adjoining Westthorn on the west was Belvidere estate, originally owned by John M'Call, the son of one of Glasgow's Virginia merchants and founding partner of the Thistle Bank. He was succeeded by Robert M'Nair, a sugar refiner with premises in the city centre. When Harvie arrived, Belvidere had recently come into the hands of Mungo Nutter Campbell, soon to become provost of Glasgow – just the kind of elite company Harvie was keen to mingle with. Adding further to the delights of Westthorn is that (according to the writer of the Barony parish return for the *Old Statistical Account* in the 1790s) it had been identified as one of several 'gentlemen's houses' in the vicinity from which would be seen the spires and cathedral of Glasgow and other 'striking views' which filled the mind with 'pleasing ideas of industry, wealth, security, and happiness'.

The view in 1822 may not have been quite so idyllic. In November, a schoolmaster, John Forfar, had journeyed to the west from Edinburgh. After disembarking just outside Glasgow from the canal boat in which he had travelled part of the way, he had found himself 'enveloped in a thick and gloomy atmosphere that hovers over the ancient and venerable town of St Mungo'. The old town, it seems, was much less salubrious than it had been formerly. An army officer stationed in the barracks in the east end of Glasgow between 1819 and 1825 described it on his arrival (in October) as 'a most melancholy, dirty, smoky city'. Even so, the tallest buildings would still have been visible from Westthorn, even if they were more often than formerly shrouded in clouds of steam and smoke.

Indeed, a few years later, Hugh MacDonald, a Bridgeton-born, Chartist-supporting journalist and poet, could still record, admittedly looking south, that 'from every point [on this stretch of the Clyde's north bank] fine views are obtained of [the] richly-wooded braes of Cathkin, with the spires of Rutherglen etc., lending beauty to the middle distance'. He waxed especially lyrically about Dalbeth and Westthorn, which sloped 'gently to the river . . . clothed with fine plantations, the haunts of birds innumerable, which, as we pass, are joyously piping their mellifluous strains'.[14] We have seen already that coal mining and manufacturing industry were beginning to make their mark on the eastern outskirts of Glasgow in the 1820s, but judging from MacDonald's description of the area it would be a couple of decades before the gardens and 'fields of waving grain' were wholly obliterated by mills, printworks and foundries and their 'perfect forest of tall chimneys'.

All this mattered to a self-made, self-satisfied man like Harvie who, his critics were not slow to remark, snidely, was the first carter in the city's history to reach such heights of opulence. His supporters were more generous, asserting that a primary motive for Harvie's acquisition of Westthorn was his desire to 'obtain a residence where he might enjoy the sweets of Privacy and Seclusion on his retirement from business'.[15] And it was on the banks of the Clyde that such an aspiration could be realised, as had been recognised more than half a century earlier by the Lanark-born, Greenock schoolteacher and poet John Wilson in his 1764 panegyric on the Clyde. Just beyond the city's boundary, 'Glasgow pours her worthy merchants round / Where numerous villas crowd the fertile ground.' Over half a century later John Eadie, a preacher, wrote along similar lines in his poem 'The Clyde', in which he favourably compared the river flowing through Glasgow with the others in Scotland and indeed across the world, even the Amazon, the Danube and the Rhine. Like Wilson, Eadie waxed eloquently about the 'tribes' that lived along the banks of the Clyde, before concluding the fifth stanza with the couplet 'What villas grand and pop'lous towns / By its fair splendour show.' Eadie's reference was probably to the owners of 'houses of an expensive description' near the Broomielaw: Adelphi Street, Great Clyde Street and East Clyde Street and vicinity, that is, on both the north and south banks of the river. After the area was laid out and the houses built, their owners, 'in order to prevent any nuisances', had bought from the town council at great expense the land between their properties and the river. This had been landscaped into a gentle slope and planted with ornamental trees.

So keen was Harvie to join them, but at an even more desirable location, that he paid somewhat more for Westthorn than the upset (or the lowest acceptable) price of £19,500 set by James Sword's agents. He was familiar with the area, as he had already been supplying hogsheads and casks of whisky to innkeepers (or change-keepers) in the vicinity.

Within a short time of taking ownership of his new property, Harvie set about realising his aspirations. He was at one with others in the neighbourhood who were improving and modernising their newly acquired property. The enlargement or construction of a mansion house was central to this endeavour. The prevalence of elegant, self-contained houses 'of the English mode', wrote one contemporary in the *Glasgow Chronicle* in February 1824, was a relatively recent phenomenon, which had 'gradually extended the city far beyond its ancient boundaries', giving 'to the general aspect a sumptuousness and splendour that were formerly unknown'. According to John Bower, minister of Old Monkland parish, just to the east of Westthorn, there were 'vast' numbers of such houses, 'many of them finished in the greatest taste'. Harvie had no wish to be left behind. Robert Gray, whose Carntyne estate lay to the east of Clyde Iron Works, and who was the owner of the largest colliery in Barony parish, built Carntyne House in 1802. Harvie's nearest neighbour James Hopkirk had in 1807 replaced his house at Dalbeth with a fashionable new residence. There had been a mansion house at Westthorn since 1710, when it had been the property of James Wardrop. Thereafter the estate fell – through marriage – into the hands of James Denniston, a captain in the 50th Regiment of Foot, and subsequently to his son, Alexander Bruce Denniston. It was from Alexander that James Sword purchased Westthorn.

In keeping with his neighbours, Harvie extended and modernised the existing property at Westthorn at an initial cost of some £10,000.[16] No expense was spared on fittings and furnishings. This was an era of conspicuous consumption; material possessions that could be flaunted in the hope of impressing friends and acquaintances mattered. An inventory of Westthorn house after it was completed reveals that it contained two or more dining rooms, a drawing room, at least six bedrooms, most with dressing rooms and one with an expensive 'treble bronze chandelier', several parlours and a laundry and pantry. The principal rooms were lavishly furnished, with many yards of Brussels carpeting (even the butler's pantry was floored with 25 yards of it). There were countless mahogany chairs, some with elbows and 'red Morocco bottoms', a full-sized billiard table, sideboards and bedsteads, and rosewood tea tables. Windows were curtained in damask, along with venetian blinds. The cutlery used was mainly silver. Fittingly for an equestrian, one of the paintings in the 'new' dining room was of 'Bonaparte and four in hand'.[17] Perhaps indicative of Harvie's religious and moral leanings was 'Moses receiving the table of the law' – valued at four guineas.

There was also a pragmatic element in Harvie's decision to purchase Westthorn. As well as being a highly visible status symbol, land offered security for loans. (The terms of Harvie's purchase hints at some prudence on his part: rather than paying the full sum outright, he negotiated an agreement whereby he would pay a number of instalments, of £4,000 each, at six-monthly intervals.) The lands and mill were let and produced an annual income of over £700. A number of weavers' cottages and loom shops facing London Road produced another £136.

And like Glasgow's colonial merchants who had bought landed estates in the eighteenth century, Harvie was keen to diversify his interests. Westthorn was situated in a coal-rich district and at the time of his purchase of the estate from James Sword, boasted a going colliery. Although it was some months before Harvie and Sword's interim factor, the accountant Henry Paul, were able to agree a price for the colliery equipment (Harvie eventually offered £200 for articles he considered to be worth only £50), the presence of a substantial coal mine on the estate was clearly an inducement. There were four seams of workable coal, accessed by four pits, three of which were fitted with pumping engines. It was a substantial undertaking, so much so that in 1823 Harvie's Westthorn coal mines were the second most productive in and around Glasgow (Carntyne was the largest), that year turning out 36,749 carts of coal. This was more than each of his immediate neighbours, and a lot more than James Hopkirk's 20,820 carts at Dalbeth; Belvidere at the other side was even smaller. Testament to the scale of operations at Westthorn colliery was the presence of James Sword among the combination of Glasgow coal-masters which was formed around 1813 with the aim of maintaining high coal prices for the consumer by monitoring and restricting output from the mines of members. In 1814 Sword succeeded the leading ironmaster, Colin Dunlop, as 'preses' or chair of the organisation. When it was going well, Harvie's colliery at Westthorn added to his already substantial income. Some of the coal – his own – could be carted to his distillery at Port Dundas, so reducing production costs. Furthermore, Glasgow's burgeoning population – it had doubled in size in the fifty years since around 1770 – offered a ready market for house coals. Demand from manufacturers was increasing too, with steam-power making for the concentration of industry within and near to the city. Much of this was met by the six of Glasgow's sixteen collieries which were located in the city's east end: Barrowfield, Belvidere, Dalbeth, Dalmarnock, Westthorn and Westmuir. At the time of Harvie's purchase, it was estimated that coal sales might generate an income of £1,200 per annum.

Westthorn: the darker side

A potential disadvantage of the colliery for an estate proprietor like Harvie was the aesthetic aspect. Although the workings were some way from Westthorn mansion house – which stood in a 'garden' of around six acres – collieries were dirty, and cluttered with heaps of coal types, both large and small, and waste. At Westthorn there was a motley array of housing.[18] The colliery manager had to be accommodated in a two-storey building, as did the oversman, but dotted about in no particular pattern, and of different but always small dimensions were stubby rows of colliers' cottages, around sixty in all. As it pumped away throughout the night as well as the day, the main pit pumping engine intermittently emitted smoke, steam and rushing noises as, to a lesser degree and during daylight only, did the colliery's three steam-powered winding engines. And within a mile or so of his property, at Dalmarnock, was the city's most formidable steam engine (160 hp). This belonged to Glasgow Water Works, established by an Act of Parliament in 1806. For eighteen hours a day this vast machine pumped from the filter beds on the south side of the river some 2,300 gallons of water to supply the town's better-off inhabitants. Nearby too was the smaller engine at Dalmarnock Dye Works which powered the handkerchief press. The raw materials used to make the Turkey red dyestuffs used at Henry Monteith's factory, which included madder root, alum, bullock's blood and urine as well as sheep dung, would have compounded the noise with nauseous smells. And even though the dense clustering of industrial concerns in the neighbourhood lay in the future, Colin Dunlop's Clyde Iron Works also had a marked impact on the immediate environment. Like their counterparts at the better-known Carron works, 'hoary with soot' the 'frowning aspect' of the Clyde furnaces provided a breathtaking spectacle for those passing by for the first time.[19] 'A burning and shining light close by the Clyde, / Illumining the country around, far and wide / Ye bleeze like a beacon upon a hill tap', which provided light that 'never costs us a rap', was the local poet Alexander Rodger's response to what was one of the early wonders of Scotland's industrial revolution in a poem he composed in praise of its owner Colin Dunlop.[20] This was hardly ideal for well-heeled seekers of rural tranquillity like Thomas Harvie.

Although it was less of an aesthetic concern, another thing Harvie would have done well to be aware of was the mining community he had inherited. From 1606 coal miners in Scotland had been bound for life at the collieries they had begun to work at, or where they had been born, and so followed their fathers into the pit. This was a form of serfdom, which was not finally abolished until 1799, although this followed on from an initial Act of 1775. Ironically, one consequence of what was a restriction on the colliers' freedom to move at will, either to another colliery or to leave the industry altogether, was that the recruitment of new entrants into the industry was difficult. A corollary of this was that those workers already employed had considerable bargaining power. Despite their servile status, the first collier combinations, an early form of trade union, were formed in the 1690s. Difficult to manage and prone to take strike action, towards the end of the eighteenth century, colliers were among the best-paid workers in the country. Coal miners and their families were tight knit, the former bound together by secret oaths and a strong sense of their collective bargaining power. They also had a justifiable conceit of their understanding of underground working. These were skilled men, whom colliery owners treated harshly at their peril. By the nature of their occupation, colliers were physically strong, and not averse to the use of force, if need be. Proudly independent, they were not always intimidated by overbearing masters, or the law.[21] They did, however, value their spare time. Notoriously hard drinking was one aspect of this, understandable as a release from pit work, which was dangerous, oppressively hot, carried out in near darkness, and dirty.

Another of their pleasures, which was both widespread and harmless, was the Sunday stroll. For the colliers of Westthorn and district, and their neighbours, what handier a pathway than that on the north bank of the Clyde.

Harvie became a coal owner at a particularly fraught juncture in relations between Scottish coal masters and their workers. After emancipation had removed the 'stigma' of servitude it was easier for employers to attract boys and men into their mines. Albeit there were fluctuations in wage levels, after 1815 and the end of the war with France and Napoleon Bonaparte, when many thousands of former soldiers were demobilised, there was an end to the years of strong growth in wages coal miners had enjoyed in the decades before war broke out in 1793. By 1821 the money wages at Govan colliery, only a few miles from Westthorn, were some 25 per cent lower than they had been in 1816. Having said that, from 1821 wages at the same colliery not only rose but reached an all-time high in 1825 – a fact that caused Harvie and his fellow coal owners to embark on a ruthless campaign to break the miners' combinations that had ratcheted up wage levels.

Prior to this, colliers in Glasgow and the west of Scotland had been involved in a drawn-out battle simply to maintain their existing wage levels. To exert maximum pressure on their employers they did their best, often through intimidation which at times involved violent assaults, to deter new men brought in by the coal owners from going into the pits. Once below ground they resisted attempts by their employers to improve productivity levels by changing working practices and challenging the colliers' notions of what was an acceptable 'darg' or day's work. Older paternalistic means of settling disputes between masters and their employees were being abandoned and replaced by the dictates of the market economy.[22] Tensions grew, as did the number of disputes, and strikes, with major confrontations taking place in 1817 and 1818, without resolution.

Significantly, the leader of the Glasgow and Clydesdale Association of Operative Colliers, formed in 1816, was John Fauldhouse (or Falhouse) Wilson, a weaver who lived in Tollcross, just yards from Westthorn. Wilson was not only highly literate but also an effective organiser. By 1820 he had opened a 'Porter House' in Glasgow where his customers could read radical newspapers such as *Black Dwarf* and *The Spirit of the Union* and other publications including Thomas Paine's *Rights of Man*. On the weekend of 1 and 2 April 1820 he had been responsible for distributing in the west of Scotland the *Address to the Inhabitants of Great Britain and Ireland* calling for a general strike for the recovery of the people's rights, the starting gun for the so-called Radical Rising – the small-scale armed insurrection that centred on Glasgow and its near vicinity. Soon thereafter, as the authorities doubled down in their attempts to discover those responsible for printing the posters, Fauldhouse Wilson and others who had helped with their circulation fled the country.[23] Whether or not he had had a hand in colliery strikes that occurred in 1821 is not clear, so it may simply be a coincidence that these took place in and around Parkhead and Tollcross. By 1823, however, Wilson was back home and may well have been involved. So too, in the neighbourhood, were some of his associates from three years previous. For Thomas Harvie, this was bad news.

Even had local radicals been inclined to stir it, the pot of unrest was already simmering. And it was Harvie who had stoked the fire beneath. Around the same time as Harvie had bought Westthorn, William Craig had become the lessee of Belvidere colliery, on the adjacent estate of that name. Craig was a former royal navy surgeon who had settled in Parkhead sometime after 1814. He had learned his surgical skills as an assistant on board the *Agincourt* before becoming a fully-fledged surgeon in 1810.[24] He was in his early thirties when he took over at Belvidere. Colliery management was an unusual step for a medical practitioner to take and perhaps for this reason he was soon in difficulty. This was despite having the cushion of half-pay to support him in his business venture. The previous tacksmen, a three-man partnership of Alexander Rae, John Walker and Robert Paterson, all from Parkhead, had been forced to give up, unable to raise the capital required for steam-pumping machinery.[25] However, their successor, Craig, invested heavily in the concern, above all in steam engines. He was intent on working the main coal, in hopes of exploiting the rising market for coal in Glasgow. By March 1823, though, he had run into debt, which he proposed to pay back to his creditors by instalments while still managing the colliery.

It was and is not uncommon for mining concerns to be at risk from flooding. Belvidere, though, was especially prone in this regard; if anything interrupted the operation of the steam engine of the main pit, all of the 'dooks' where coal was cut were liable to flood. When this happened, it took 'some weeks' to pump out the water. The second pit was pumped dry by hand, an expensive labour-intensive process that barely stemmed the heavy fall of water coming through the roof. Craig proposed to overcome the problem in the first pit by replacing the current 'inadequate' steam-pumping engine with a bigger one with a 32-inch cylinder.

His creditors were content with this arrangement. Thomas Harvie, though, was less accommodating. He made it difficult for Craig and his creditor trustees to proceed, by demanding that a five-fathom-deep stone barrier which protected his coal from water flowing in from the Belvidere mine be retained. If the Belvidere men were to carry on working, there was the risk of breaking through to the Westthorn coal and then for Craig and his creditors to be sued for damages by Harvie. The alternative was to abandon the seam. In effect this meant giving up his lease of the colliery, which Craig was being pressured to do anyway. Belvidere estate's new owner, David Wardrop, recognised the potential of the coal under his grounds and was keen to take over the concern – and reap the revenues it could generate – himself.

From Harvie's perspective his efforts to stifle Craig's endeavours were justified. But it was not a stance that was likely to have endeared him to his neighbours. Craig, according to a testimonial written on his behalf by parish elders some years later, had discharged his duties as a surgeon professionally, at all times displaying 'the greatest philanthropic conduct in alleviating the distress of his fellow creatures'.[26] Not only was he well regarded in the community, but at Belvidere he had done all he could to secure the employment of his coal miners, whose livelihoods would be at risk should the water drown the mines and close the colliery. But the welfare of the collier communities in the neighbourhood of Westthorn was not one of Thomas Harvie's concerns.

Thomas Harvie, Westthorn and the river Clyde

It was with the boundary walls above ground that Harvie began to make his mark directly on his new domain. Construction work began late in April 1822. It was more or less complete by 10 June, only six weeks later.

Harvie's determination to progress so swiftly on this front requires little explanation. Much later, the reason adduced by his legal representatives was that the walls were to replace the hedges and broken-down fences which hitherto had marked the boundaries between Westthorn, Belvidere and Dalbeth.[27]

Perhaps this was true, but from the outset Harvie made no secret of his plans to more effectively enclose his property which on the south side stretched down to the river Clyde. His intentions were made public in advertisements and handbills that were published and distributed in Glasgow and its vicinity. They intimated 'that all Trespassers on the Ground, and Fishers, would be prosecuted with the utmost rigour'. Information about transgressors was to be rewarded with five guineas should those concerned be apprehended and found guilty. By arranging for gunfire salutes and other celebrations when the walls were completed, he drew attention to their existence and to his own ascendancy at Westthorn. Peter Mackenzie had little or no respect for Harvie, and his opinions therefore may well have been jaundiced. Even so, the way events associated with the walls unfolded suggests that behind Mackenzie's barbed rhetoric there was some truth. As Harvie looked down from his mansion, Mackenzie wrote, he 'could not brook the idea – he hated it, that anyone else should come near the place except himself or his chosen friends, when he was pleased to invite them to his frigid hospitalities'. In short, Mackenzie went on, he wanted to shut up the river, and bar pedestrians from walking 'as they were accustomed to do, and as their forefathers did for centuries before them', in that 'most beautiful retreat, embalmed as it still is, by the endearing name – "the Banks o' the Clyde" '. By the end of the eighteenth century, in Glasgow and the industrialising suburbs like Parkhead and Dalmarnock, walking for pleasure, to breathe cool untainted air and take exercise had become integral facets of the everyday lives of many workers.[28] The pathway at the edge of Westthorn estate, as well as others alongside, was also a well-worn pedestrian route into Glasgow for ordinary people from outlying villages as far east as Carmyle on market days; the fares for stage coach and canal travel could be afforded only by the better-off.

As we have seen, the Clyde had for decades been an object of pride for Glaswegians, and was admired by visitors who wrote poems in its praise. For some, the river and the city were synonymous. In 1783 in his 'Glasgow. A Poem', John Mayne, originally a printer's apprentice from Dumfries, paid tribute to the town's merchants' commercial nous and wealth:

Thir wylie birkies trade to a'
The Indies and America;
Whate'er can mak' ae penny twa,
  Or raise their pride,
Is wafted to the Broomielaw,
  On bony Clyde.

An unnamed 'townsman' also reflected upon the synergy of the town and its river in a panegyric, 'Glasgow', in 1824: 'On Clyde's fair banks a noble city stands', he wrote, before describing in flattering terms the town's industrial and commercial activities, not least the merchant who 'gives / His ship and cargo to the Atlantic wave'.[29] The Clyde was the artery through which the products of the 'well-packed produce of the British loom' flowed on their westward journey. Scottish poets generally had a 'perfect passion' for their native rivers and, significantly, celebrated their banks as places where people could wander, and lovers lie down and connect, rather than as routes to a particular destination, although the Clyde's north bank was used for this purpose.[30] Anne Saughton and John Wilson were a couple who had dallied along this route during the summer of 1822. Anne had given birth to an illegitimate child; Wilson was allegedly the father, although he denied this. Early in 1823 Anne and John were brought before the kirk session of Old Monkland parish in an attempt to draw out a confession of guilt on Wilson's part. Witnesses including Gilbert Barr, a sinker at Clyde colliery, had seen them like 'lad and lass', walking 'together on the bank of the Clyde'. William Durham of the same workplace had watched them 'frequently and after night on the banks of the Clyde, alone', as well as 'in the gloaming sitting together' – though he was unable to recall whether or not Wilson had his arm around Anne. That Wilson was heard to call her 'My dear' and refer to Anne as his sweetheart – but not his wife – rather undermined his protestation of innocence.

For local people as well as visitors – poets and artists of the picturesque such as J. M. Turner – the Falls of Clyde near Lanark, Corra Linn and Bonnington Linn were regarded as attractions, but the Clyde in its entirety was considered by many to be the prince of Scottish rivers. Robert Burns had put 'classic streams' such as the Doon, Lugar, Ayr, Nith and others on the map, but it was the Clyde, wrote John Black in his 1806 dramatic pastoral *The Falls of Clyde*, which was 'the most beautiful and romantic' and deserved to be better known as such.[31]

One of the river's first heralds was the Belfast-born Presbyterian, Glasgow University student James Arbuckle. His 'Glotta, A Poem', was published in 1721. In topographic fashion the poem traces the river from its origins to the city of Glasgow itself. On his imagined journey Arbuckle comments on the wonders passing by as the river wended its way to the city – mountains, other objects of natural beauty, palaces and stately homes such as that of the dukes of Hamilton, and places of interest and renown, like Bothwell Bridge. Past this point, 'Thro' flow'ry Vallies, and enaml'd Meads, / The hastening Flood at length of *Glasgow* speeds' and there – significantly – 'Its *Northern* Bank a lovely Green displays, / Whose e'ery Prospect fresh Delights convey.' These include various shades of 'blowing Flow'rs', 'wash'd in fragrant Dew', skylarks which 'o'er the Surface of the Stream . . . glide'.

The floral life that Arbuckle refers to was sufficiently rich and diverse to merit recording, a task undertaken by Thomas Hopkirk, the distinguished botanist son of Harvie's near neighbour James Hopkirk of Dalbeth. In his *Flora Glottiana* published in 1813 Hopkirk noted specifically the whereabouts of the hundreds of species he was able to identify on the banks of the Clyde. Some were unique to, or commonly found near, his own family home at Dalbeth and its near vicinity including Clyde Iron Works. Not often, but occasionally, Westthorn was singled out, with Dyers weed, or weld, being especially abundant there, as was Hawkweed, a summer-flowering plant nowadays considered to be a nuisance when growing in lawns. To see and gather these and other specimens of the floral bounty Hopkirk identified, nature lovers had to be able to walk along the river's banks. When and where they could, that is; landowners prior to and including Harvie did their best to deter passers-by. They were not hindered everywhere though: there was a much-admired, profusely stocked, bird-attracting garden at Henry Monteith's Dalmarnock Dye Works.

Enthusiasm for botany was by no means confined to the educated upper ranks. Ordinary people also took pride in identifying types of flowers, and enjoyed freely observing them, especially 'after the irksome toils of the week'.[32] Many, perhaps most, of the inhabitants of the villages in the east end of Glasgow – or their parents or grandparents – had migrated from the countryside and retained more than a vestigial affection for the natural world. Large sections of the reminiscences of the poet, hand-spinner, tambourer (a home-based embroiderer) and shoemaker's wife Janet Hamilton, from Coatbridge in Old Monkland parish – some miles to the east of Westthorn – are devoted to the joys she felt as a young woman in the 1810s and 1820s, wandering by her local river, the Luggie, and its surrounds. Intimately acquainted with her handloom weaver neighbours, she wrote eloquently too of their fondness for gardening, the sight and smells of flowers and the simple pleasure of basking in the sunshine. Later in life she bemoaned the loss of the Luggie's 'gushing waters, over which the tasselled hazel, broom, and brier bend no more, lovingly concealing the plastered nest of the thrush or blackbird, whose ringing melodies, evening and morning, stirred and thrilled the dewy air'. The 'sweet breath of the gowany and white clover lea' was 'now exchanged for the stifling and sulphurous fumes rising from smouldering heaps of hot cinders and burning slag': the waste from Langloan Iron Works. The gratifications of the countryside were appreciated by the working classes and those of similar social standing more widely than might be assumed, not least those of a radical disposition (although Janet Hamilton was no friend of the radicals). It was from their ranks that nature poets like Northamptonshire's John Clare, Paisley's Robert Tannahill and Ayrshire's Robert Burns were drawn.

There was a practical aspect to this too. Not far to the east of Westthorn, on the wooded, flower-dense bank of Kenmuir, weaver herbalists from Camlachie and Parkhead came in search of plants that they used to treat a variety of ailments.[33] Professional, formal medical provision in and around Glasgow was increasing: the Royal Infirmary had been opened in 1794. Even so, there were few qualified physicians, and traditional cures continued to be widely used on the advice of local healers. Dandelions acted as a diuretic as well as a tonic, foxglove could be helpful in the treatment of heart complaints, scrofula and mental illness, while sorrel was used as a poultice for an array of skin conditions, which were ubiquitous. It was the working classes too who made most use of a 'Physic Well', a chalybeate spring (noted for its iron salts), near the north end of Rutherglen Bridge.[34] Ordinary people were also drawn to the river at nearby Dalmarnock. During the summer months, the Clyde 'absolutely swarmed' with par – the fry of salmon – with the ford there being 'scourged' by weavers from Rutherglen and elsewhere in search of fresh, cost-free food. 'Cluggie dhu's' or mussels too were to be found, their poor-quality pearls prized by young boys in particular. On the debit side, by the early 1820s a 'great quantity of abominable and other deleterious matter' was to be seen covering the river in 'a coloured scum'. Blame was cast at some of the city's new works, the effluence from which meant that salmon were disappearing from the river, a matter of deep regret to the people of Glasgow and its neighbourhood.[35]

Access even to fish for the few salmon that were being caught was threatened by the spreading intrusion of industry on Glasgow's eastern edge, and the determination of estate proprietors like Harvie to assert their property rights by building walls and fencing. By doing so they were encroaching on the customary rights of the public. It was another manifestation of country-wide changes in attitudes to land that had been evident in the eighteenth century and became the norm in the nineteenth century. At its core was commercialisation. In the Highlands thousands of crofters and cottars were being cleared from productive land for the more lucrative rents that could be extracted from sheep farmers, while in the south, enclosure created larger, more efficient and more productive farms on land formerly inhabited by settlements of numerous small tenants and cottars. In some places popular protest resulted, but more often the reaction was resignation and the consolation that there were employment opportunities in the towns. Many mourned in song and poetry the world that was being lost, Robert Burns being the prime example. Alexander Wilson, the nature-loving radical weaver poet from Paisley who after he had emigrated to America became a renowned ornithologist, wrote a gently satirical poem on this move to privatise property in 1791, although it was probably not published until after he had left Scotland.[36] In 'The Insulted Pedlar, A Poetical Tale' the pedlar describes the former ease with which rural and small-town dwellers were able to take short cuts when travelling from place to place in the Lowland countryside. 'But now', the poem proceeds, 'wi' slabs and lime an' stane / We're vext and pested' by farmers who insisted by threats and even violent means that pedestrians take the long way round their properties. The pedlar then observes the irony that by such exclusions farmers denied themselves the benefit of the fertilising properties of the turds that he and others previously left behind when they were able to walk freely across farmland.

The utility of the verdant banks and the river itself were only some of the Clyde's virtues. Arbuckle waxed eloquently that when 'declining *Sol* turns to dusk', 'victorious Throngs of charming Maids' appeared, whose beauty was such that 'Not even *Paphos*, or th' *Arcadian* Plain' could boast they had a 'brighter Virgin Train'. The aforementioned John Wilson, in his mammoth poem 'Clyde', was struck too by the attractions of the river for the city's youth. He compared the young men who during the summer dived into or floated on the surface of the river, their strong arms and limbs like 'polished marble', to the fearless Romans who swam the Tiber once, twice or even three times before night-time. Not all swimming expeditions ended nobly, however. Late in July 1826 a sailor, James Hardy, suddenly left the two girls with whom he was walking and plunged into the river, evidently to show off his prowess as a swimmer.[37] Sadly, he was less able in this regard than he had anticipated and drowned, despite the best efforts of the recently appointed keeper of the Glasgow Humane Society – founded in 1790 to rescue citizens who had fallen into the water. The river in the vicinity of Harvie's Dyke was to claim several more lives over the course of the nineteenth century. But not that of an 'old woman' who, the *Glasgow Free Press* reported in May 1826, had for nineteen years contemplated taking her own life by throwing herself into the Clyde. She had done so, but was rescued by some nearby bathers, protesting that it had come to a poor pass that in this 'boasted land of liberty . . . a person cannot get drowning herself when she thinks proper'.

As a resort for public leisure the northern banks of the Clyde were rather like Glasgow Green, the large park that lay just outside the centre of Glasgow and bordered the Clyde. It was from here that walkers frequently began their sojourns upriver to and beyond Westthorn. The Green inspired legions of poets, such as Daniel Norris; more than 50,000 copies (of a second edition) of his 'Bonnie Walks of Glasgow Green', were printed.[38] Spread over 130 acres, the Green, not unlike the Clyde walkways, had been 'from time immemorial consecrated to the recreation and health of the community'.[39] Once a gathering and perambulating place for the city's fashionable elites, by the early nineteenth century it had lost something of its former attraction. During the 1790s it was often where radical meetings were held, as were training sessions for companies of loyalist volunteers and martial displays by visiting regiments. In the wake of Waterloo it was increasingly used for military drilling and other colourful public spectacles, although it continued to be an assembly point for radical protests and working-class marches. On 5 April 1820 – the most momentous day of the Radical War – a group of fifty or so men, armed with guns and pipes, intent on seizing weapons from Carron Iron Works, left from the Green. James Wilson, the old reformer who had led the rising in Strathaven, was executed at the edge of the Green in August 1820, in front of some 20,000 onlookers. More distasteful for Glasgow's more respectable citizens was the presence 'from morning to night' of 'idle fellows and their dogs'; dog fights were commonplace too, at the Broomielaw and to the west in Argyle Street. Distressing too were duck hunts, held further up the Clyde – a duck would be thrown into the river and set upon by a pack of ravenous dogs.

The Green, however, was still highly valued by many of the city's residents. Although obviously motivated by self-interest in petitioning against proposals to deepen and increase the flow (and height) of the Clyde as far as Rutherglen in 1825, the proprietors of properties in the

Adelphi Street area, on the south bank of the river, did take into consideration the wider community. At least they claimed their concern was for 'the welfare and beauty of the city, and its inhabitants', arguing that the Green should 'at all times be preserved' for their health and recreation. Like the Clyde walkways, the Green thereafter had periodically to be protected from encroachments, principally, it was argued, for the benefit of the working classes.

Harvie's Dyke

The two walls that marked the east and west boundaries of Harvie's Westthorn estate were no ordinary partitions. The more substantial of the two, on the western edge of his property, became known as 'Harvie's Dyke', although very occasionally there is a newspaper reference to Harvie's 'Dykes'. This western wall was a massive stone structure, symbolic of Harvie's desire to impress and to demonstrate that what lay behind it was *his* estate. But it served a practical purpose too. The Dyke stood at least 12 feet high – three times the height of most field dykes at the time – and was about 3 feet thick, some of the stones weighing half a ton and battened with iron. At the top, iron pikes protruded. It would not, according to newspaper reports, 'have disgraced any fortification in Europe'.[40] Indeed, at the river end the wall was topped with *cheveaux-de-frise* – originally an obstacle designed to block the advance of cavalry (see Plate 4). Westthorn's variant comprised sharp iron spikes in imitation of the thorns of a Scottish thistle. These were designed not to deter horsemen but rather to prevent people climbing over a wall that 'neither could be *Scaled* nor *Broken* through'. It is clear that the principal function of the walls was to stop members of the public walking on a pathway that ran along the north bank of the river Clyde at the south or river edge of Harvie's property. The Dyke, at the west end of the estate, was the more important of the two as it blocked pedestrians coming from Glasgow, on the way to villages such as Carmyle, or Clyde Iron Works which also stood close to the river. The second wall was similar, but as it dipped into the Clyde it was finished with wooden palings – again making it impossible to proceed.[41]

Completing the walls was not straightforward. Harvie's walls were not welcomed. In order to prevent younger and fitter members of the public skirting the end of the walls by walking into and round by the river, Harvie – probably in the late spring of 1822 – had collected broken bottles in Glasgow and then carted them out to Westthorn and dumped them in the water. A 'storm of indignation' resulted, and attempts were made by local villagers to pull down such parts of the walls that had been built, the more forbidding of the two in particular, the greatly detested Dyke.

To counter this, Harvie recruited watchmen. John Penman was the first, a middle-aged man taken on as early as March 1822. Another was Peter Brown, a Tollcross weaver who described his part-time job as being to prevent people who were walking that way (along the riverside path Harvie wished to close) from pulling down or destroying the Dyke. The watchmen's effectiveness was enhanced by Harvie's decision to have at least one small fort (as it was described) constructed at the top of the high bank which rose steeply from the river.

From these heady heights, shot from small cannons was periodically fired above the heads of would-be trespassers. Bulldogs were employed to frighten people off too. Again, locals were outraged. Reflecting on the events of 1823 some four decades afterwards, Adam Ferrie (of whom more later) wrote of the 'strong hatred' induced by Harvie's actions and attitude. This was particularly so among the colliers, 'that desperate class of people' who, Ferrie believed, 'would have murdered him, had they got him in a quiet place'. We saw earlier that Harvie had scant regard for those working at Belvidere. Ferrie, whose recollections cannot always be substantiated, was in this instance close to the mark.

Harvie's 'armed retainers' were able to dissuade the public from walking over the edge of his estate, or damaging his property, but it was harder for him to deal with another, more insidious danger to his well-being: a boycott by Harvie's former carter acquaintances of his Glasgow whisky shops, as a means of expressing their abhorrence of the methods he had adopted to achieve his aims. Money talks, and eventually it did.

Meanwhile, however, Harvie armed himself with pistols.

So began the lengthy, uncompromising, sometimes violent, invariably bitter contest for 'the liberty of the banks of the Clyde'.

Tensions mount

The date of 21 June 1823 was not the first occasion in recent times that Thomas Fraser had been asked to call a meeting of the east end villagers to decide what to do about Harvie's Dyke. About two weeks earlier – on 12 June – a fellow weaver, George Allan, had paid Fraser a shilling to 'proclaim a meeting of the inhabitants of Parkhead and Westmuir for the purpose of taking into consideration the cause of the footpath on the banks of the Clyde being stopped'. This had evidently been provoked by the appearance some days beforehand of a pile of stones and lime at the property of an unnamed estate proprietor near Dalmarnock, around a mile and half down-river from Westthorn (see Plate 5).

Formerly this crossing had been a ford (the 'Farme Ford'), but in 1821 a wooden bridge had been built by the Cambuslang and Muirkirk roads trustees – but it could only be used on payment of a toll. The introduction of what was called a 'pey brig', with 'bawbees and pennies . . . exacted from all and sundry who went over it by night or morning' was bad enough.[42] Adding to the growing pool of local resentment was that Dalmarnock Bridge had been constructed in such a way as to block a long-established path immediately adjacent to and alongside the river. Irritated by this new imposition, 'A Walker' wrote to the *Glasgow Chronicle* on 12 June 1823 reporting his suspicions that a wall too was about to be built. His concern was the precedent this latest incursion would create. There was 'no saying where it will stop'; indeed, he had heard hints that 'the example is to be followed by the proprietors down the river as far as Rutherglen bridge', in which case 'adieu to many a pleasant morning's walk' or a 'draught of the physic well'. Harvie was not alone in wanting to protect the privacy of his property behind high, impenetrable walls.

Consciousness raising of this kind, along with fears about what appeared to be happening at Dalmarnock Bridge, was enough to persuade the weaver George Allan to convene the 12 June meeting. Allan was someone who relished walks along the riverbanks during the summer months, as well as being recognised locally as self-taught botanist 'in a humble way', and part-time herbalist. In Parkhead the issue of access along the Clyde had been causing consternation for some time. John Williamson, the teacher there, testified later that Harvie's Dyke had been 'a subject of conversation . . . ever since the wall was built' as it was 'considered by the people in the neighbourhood as an encroachment on the public right'. A later account captured the popular mood. Public forbearance 'had . . . been completely exhausted'. The local community

> would no longer submit tamely to an aggression which was likely to strike at the foot of all their privileges, and they determined on making a bold effort to recover what they had too long allowed to be withheld from them.

It was determined therefore that the walls should be 'levelled to the ground, or at least such breaches made in it as would admit of free passage'.[43]

Hitherto what appear to have been minor, uncoordinated and sporadic attacks on Harvie's walls had been perpetrated by ordinary people – journeymen, weavers, coal miners and others from the lower ranks of society. Now, however, a more systematic campaign seemed to be under way. The evening meeting on 12 June, attended by well over fifty people, agreed that legal advice should be sought on how best to proceed. According to William Lyon, the surgeon, it was George Allan who had proposed that Harvie's walls ought to be removed by legal means – and that a committee should be elected who would consult legal experts on the issue. This comprised Allan and Lyon, as well as Robert Brown, a mason, James Macfarlane, a baker, John McCracken, a weaver, and John Marshall, a Westmuir grocer. These were individuals who were well known in the neighbourhood, and who, owing to their occupations and the frequent contact they had with local inhabitants, had their finger on the pulse of local opinion. Dr Lyon was a genial individual who commanded much respect. He, Marshall and Macfarlane were delegated to seek the views of Robert Davidson, Professor of Civil Law at the college (later the University of Glasgow), reputedly a somewhat dull if practically minded successor to the Enlightenment luminary John Millar. Also to be approached was Mr Robert Graham of Whitehill, a writer (lawyer) and supporter of liberal causes, at his offices in Miller Street in Glasgow. The three Parkhead men were to be accompanied by two representatives from Bridgeton, which lay to the west of Parkhead.

Davidson was away, but Graham's opinion was unambiguous: Harvie had no right to stop the passage along the riverbank. There were two ways for the committee to proceed. One was to prosecute Harvie through the courts and order him to remove the obstacles. Alternatively, 'the parties [could] themselves . . . remove them and leave Mr Harvie to prosecute'. This was reported at a second public meeting, held in the Methodist schoolhouse, on 19 June. George Allan had again employed Fraser to announce this, in return for a payment of one shilling and sixpence, a useful supplement for the Fraser-Christie household, which Fraser handed over to his wife.

Arguments for and against direct action went on late into the evening, but there was no agreement. At this point all the committee members stood down and had nothing more to do with the matter. Or so they said when being examined later.

It is possible that they had taken cold feet. Following the meeting on 19 June, according to John Williamson, it had been resolved to make a breach in Harvie's walls. Things were now taking a serious turn. Lyon the surgeon admitted he was aware of the purpose of the meeting on the 21st before Fraser's call. What he didn't say, however, was that on the Friday evening (20 June) he had been down at Harvie's Dyke, trying to examine the inner side of the structure from a vantage point on the outside. And only reluctantly did he admit that after the disbandment of the committee on 19 June he had taken from John Marshall what monies – 'about two pounds' – were left from what had previously been collected to fund the campaign.

The fact that to announce the meeting of 21 June Fraser the drummer had been offered even more than on the two previous occasions is suggestive that something more serious was in the offing. He was now to be paid two shillings and sixpence – half a crown. Not many years earlier the normal payment for a public pronouncement of this sort was much less – in nearby Rutherglen, on the south side of the river, the drummer was paid between one shilling and one shilling and sixpence for this kind of service.[44] Half a crown was the equivalent of more than half the daily wage of a Lanarkshire coal miner, no small amount for an ageing handloom weaver at a time when earnings in that occupation were at rock bottom. It might well have been enough to buy his silence when later questioned about the affair.

Thomas Fraser proclaimed that the third (21 June) meeting signified the marked escalation of a very local issue that had been absorbing the attention of a small group of the city of Glasgow's citizens for some time. But the principles at stake were not confined to Glasgow; there would be ramifications for the law on rights of way across Scotland. And as hinted earlier, it also brought again onto the public stage several of the individuals who had played active parts during the era of serious public discontent that had begun in the wake of the Napoleonic Wars and culminated in Scotland's Radical War.

Fraser's appeal certainly found favour. It was the optimum date and time to gather a crowd. The early summer months were when most public assemblies were held. By seven o'clock on a Saturday evening the working week was done. And for the task in hand 21 June was perfect; the longest day of the year, it would be light late into the evening. So, as he completed his almost three-hour-long promenade, a 'number of persons' accompanied the drummer. Others cheered as he arrived at Parkhead cross by the appointed hour. Within minutes a sizeable crowd had gathered. Those present promptly moved off down Dalmarnock road. At the wooden bridge they were met by a contingent from Bridgeton where, apparently, the prospect of 'the great event that was about to come off' had created much excitement, a witness recalled many years later.[45] The Bridgeton party was headed by a band playing music, while in the rear were some three hundred 'youngsters'. Others – notably weavers, spinners, iron workers, small tradesmen and a few women – joined in as the procession slowly wended its way towards the Clyde-side edge of Westthorn estate. No one individual or group, it seems, was leading the body of steady-paced determined-looking marchers. According to John Williamson, 'they [the crowd] seemed all to go as of one consent and of previous understanding'. In the vanguard, according to one eyewitness, were three hundred or so colliers, some carrying picks, jumpers, pinches, hammers and mells, and singing Robert Burns' stirring call to arms, 'Scots Wha Hae', a defiant rejection of slavery and tyranny, and a hymn to liberty, much sung at radical meetings and on marches in support of reform of the political system. Coal workers had long been used to parading in formation, as a unified body, at fairs, weddings and funerals, or during strikes. There was nothing out of the ordinary about this: processions, chanting and singing defiant songs to attract attention and entice others to join in, were part of the repertoire of community engagement and popular protest across the British Isles. Even carrying sticks, poles or implements associated with particular trades was commonplace, though more of a symbolic threat than a statement of harmful intent.

Thomas Robertson, a twenty-year-old coal miner at Clyde Iron Works who said that he had gone to the south bank of the river only to watch the proceedings, estimated the size of the gathering. And he was impressed. The numbers were 'more than he had seen all his days though he had been at an execution in Glasgow [in Jail Square, outside the new courthouse] where great crowds meet'. The direction in which the marchers were headed was 'towards the wall [built] by Mr Harvie on the boundary of his property there'.

At around the same time as the crowd was assembling at Parkhead cross, Thomas Harvie had been informed by his permanent watchman, John Penman, who lived on the estate, that something was afoot. Becoming concerned, Harvie gathered together another four of his 'servants': Peter Brown (the Tollcross weaver who had occasionally done watching duty), James Cuthill, William Stevenson and John McLure. Their orders were unambiguous: to watch the Dyke and protect it by force if necessary.

2

'A Very Unpleasant Business': The Assault on Harvie's Walls

The crowd assembling alongside the outer edge of Harvie's Dyke seemed uncertain about what to do. It was now eight o'clock. It had been a bright day, but there was a chill in the air. A gentle wind was blowing from the east. The high, forbidding, dressed-stone, iron-spike-topped wall contrasted starkly with the early summer greenery on the riverbank that fronted the neighbouring Belvidere estate. Peter Brown – one of Harvie's watchmen – thought he saw some people throwing stones and clods of earth. Others seemed reluctant to get too close, preferring instead to watch from a distance and stay out of trouble. Immediately to the west of Westthorn there was a sharp U-turn loop in the Clyde, and a narrow crossing over which it was possible to wade to reach a safe vantage point from which both of Harvie's walls were visible.

Resolution

The operation seemed to have been carefully planned in advance. This was somewhat different – though not entirely – from the kinds of popular protests that were commonplace in Scotland and elsewhere during the eighteenth century and beyond. These were generally spontaneous, or seemed to be, often commencing with market-place squabbles about the price of meal, or a threatened shortage thereof, or because burgh magistrates or soldiers had seized someone whom the community considered to be innocent of any wrong-doing. Unpopular new parish ministers too could find themselves mobbed and chased away from the manses or churches they had hoped to occupy. More often than not, women were in the vanguard of such demonstrations. Not unusually their ire was directed at individuals who had in some way caused offence or who had breached the limits of the moral economy of the labouring poor. (This is the belief that traditional rights – to fair market prices for essential commodities like meal, or unhindered access to common land to gather firewood or graze animals – should be upheld. Failure on the part of the authorities to respect these rights was not only resented but could induce violence in defence of what was a plebeian value system.) Partly this explains why burgh officials such as provosts and magistrates and customs and excise officers were commonly targeted. Mud, clods of earth, stones and sticks and occasionally dead animals were participants' weapons of choice, along with verbal insults.[1]

There had clearly been a greater degree of formality than this in the lead-up to the assault on Harvie's Dyke. And down at the Clyde on the Saturday evening of 21 June 1823 some marshalling activity was evident. Not many minutes passed before a figure with a gun appeared, who 'walked back and forth as if keeping the people back from the dyke'. Almost simultaneously, according to Peter Brown, 'a man came with a large iron pinch over his shoulder'. After laying it on the ground he was hailed by the crowd with three cheers. The pinch was an iron bar pointed at one end and wedge-shaped at the other – used by coal miners to prise or pull down rocks or coal. Other men with hammers and jumpers (small iron tools for boring rock) followed. Not long afterwards witnesses heard the sound of the jumpers being put to use. The noise intruded into the stillness of the evening and could be heard above the sound of the subdued but animated chatter of the watching crowd.

Observing all of this with growing anxiety were Harvie's watchmen, who now included two more of his employees, William Stevenson, a young checksman at Westthorn colliery (who was responsible for knowing who was in the pits at any time), and John Youl, a thirty-year-old clerk. They were located in a building which looked like 'a kind of water tower' at the top of the bank, adjoining the dyke, where the cannons had been placed (see Plate 6).

They had also been provided with firearms. The previous day, William Lyon had been fired upon from here when examining the Dyke at the river end, in preparation for its destruction: the single shot missed him by only a few inches, an action that one English newspaper account suggested had inflamed the 'Caledonian blood' of Harvie's assailants.[2]

On this evening, however, the small armoury was trained on the crowd below. The aim was to terrify them. But to no effect. Worse, Harvie's corps of defenders found themselves under threat. Stevenson and John Penman decided to leave the shelter of the bank-top stronghold to survey proceedings more easily. On so doing they caught the attention of two men with muskets, which they turned on Harvie's agents. Fearing 'they might discharge them [the guns]', Penman and Stevenson quickly retreated. Just minutes before, two armed men had been seen parading back and forth at a distance of about 12 yards from the outside of the dyke, to prevent anyone from interrupting those who were starting to take down the wall. Throughout the entire proceedings they remained 'in readiness to fire in case of being fired upon' by Harvie's watchmen.

The demolition work was now being carried out in what one near-contemporary account called 'a steady and scientific manner'.[3] Colliers bored holes in the wall into which gunpowder was to be placed. A 'tall man who had the appearance of a smith' arrived and began to hammer at the iron spikes which were fixed on top of the Dyke. Then '12 stout young men were assisted to the top of the wall, and with quarry wedges, levers, heavy hammers etc they split the stones in which the iron was fixed and pushed the forked roller into the water.' Three loud cheers erupted. The coping stones were next to fall. At this point five pounds of gunpowder that was to be used to blow a passageway through the wall came into play. It was made up into paper cartridges and inserted into one of the bored holes. It was then lit. The explosion, which could be heard some distance away, was sufficient to loosen much of the masonry. This was then pulled apart by 'several people with crowbars'. The rest of the wall was then taken apart stone by stone, amid constant cheering. One broadsheet account published soon afterwards reported that a gun or pistol was fired to celebrate 'every great tumble'.[4]

By ten o'clock the Dyke was down.

The first wall breached, the crowd then hurried along the river's edge to the second, eastern wall, a mile away. By this time, encouraged by the successful destruction of the Dyke, and confident that Harvie's men were being kept at a distance, the throng had swollen to over 2,000. David Hardie, a sheriff officer in Glasgow, was sure the number was higher – as many as 3,000. Another estimate put it at 4,000, but this is unlikely. On reaching the second wall, operations began again. By this time however, it was almost dark. Not for long though. Near the river end of the wall six-foot-high wooden palisades had been erected to block the path. Thorns and loose wood were gathered and set on fire. A 'singular scene' then resulted: 'one Party was busily employed in burning the wooden stakes' while another two men 'were . . . strenuously engaged in demolishing the wall'. With the bright light of the conflagration, 'young lads' and others were able to see what they were doing as they pulled down the stonework. Some 21 feet of stone was manhandled into a ditch. A few of the larger blocks were dragged into the river.

Even before the first wall had fallen, however, Thomas Harvie had had enough. What he feared was that the undisciplined mob would turn on and set fire to his Westthorn mansion. This, or something to that effect, he declared, they had threatened to do. It is entirely likely that his near neighbour James Hopkirk would have warned him of his own anxieties over the potential danger from the inhabitants of places like Parkhead and Tollcross, once aroused.

Consequently, around nine o'clock Harvie had hastily left Westthorn and, with his lawyer who had been hastily summoned, headed for the Clyde Street chambers of Glasgow's sheriff. There he informed David Hardie, the sheriff officer on duty that night whose residence was next door, of the 'violent outrages' that were happening at Westthorn. He demanded that steps be taken to bring them to a halt. Hardie then applied to the sheriff substitute John Dillon, who was then at home, and obtained the necessary warrant. This would enable him to read the Riot Act and order the crowd to disperse; if this warning was ignored, the military would open fire. This all took time, however, and it was not until after midnight that Harvie, now accompanied by a twenty-strong party of the 6th (Enniskillen) Regiment, was able to return to Westthorn.

The Dragoons, 1820 and its aftermath

The Enniskillen Dragoons had been raised late in 1688 to defend the northern Irish town of Inniskilling in County Fermanagh and other places – including Londonderry. The enemy was the Jacobite army of James VII and II, who was intent on regaining the crowns of England and Scotland he had effectively surrendered some months earlier.[5] During the eighteenth century the regiment was frequently posted to Scotland, to keep the peace as well as to counter Jacobite insurgencies. The Enniskillens fought on the government side at Sheriffmuir in 1715. In 1725 they were in Glasgow following a riot (the Shawfield Riot) which was sparked by Glasgow's MP Daniel Campbell's vote in favour of an increase in malt duty, thereby raising the price of ale, the everyday drink of ordinary people.

Thereafter they saw service overseas during the War of the Austrian Succession, the Seven Years War, and in the aftermath of the French Revolution. They were present at Waterloo (1815), where they led a fearsome charge, during which they 'overturned the French chasseurs like nine-pins' and may have taken as many as 3,000 prisoners.[6] In 1816 they were stationed in Bruton, Somerset, where they came to the aid of the local yeomanry in Bideford and Frome in suppressing serious disturbances over the price of potatoes. On this as in other instances, the very sight of the Enniskillens caused alarm; hitherto angry crowds usually dispersed on their appearance. In 1818 the regiment moved north to Edinburgh, before spending almost four years in Ireland. This posting culminated in February 1822 in attempts to suppress disturbances fomented by the Whiteboys – a secretive rural organisation that by intimidation and various acts of violence sought to defend the rights of small tenants.

By now renowned for their ability to quell civil disorder, late in May 1823 a body of the Enniskillens was marched from the Royal Barracks in Dublin to Belfast and then Drogheda where on 2 June they were taken by sea to Glasgow. A second and final detachment made the crossing to Portpatrick a few days later. Although they were under the command of Scots-born Lieutenant-Colonel Joseph Straton of Annfield estate in Fife, most of the men were Irish.

The regiment was brought to Glasgow to assist the magistrates, who – not for the first time – were concerned about a rise in disorderliness in and around the city. Calm had been restored after the Radical Rising of early April 1820. The circumstances in which what has also been termed the Scottish Insurrection happened are vividly described by John Strang, the Glaswegian chronicler who was not only there at the time but had even joined a middle-class volunteer force – the Sharpshooters – assembled the previous year to protect both persons and property and under the command of the militarily experienced Samuel Hunter, then the editor of the *Glasgow Herald*.

The wars with France between 1792 and 1815 had aroused palpable fears that Britain would be invaded. This period of nervous uncertainty had been followed by post-war dislocation – falling wages, unemployment, high taxes on widely used consumer goods such as tea, coffee, tobacco and shoes, and the challenge for demobilised soldiers of finding waged work. A deep 'current of dissatisfaction flowed throughout the social body'. Society, Strang wrote later, 'was disorganised and out of joint'. A 'spirit of hostility to all constituted authority' fermented in the minds of the working classes, who were 'roused to revenge their supposed oppressions and imagined wrongs'. Class 'was . . . set against class, the servant against his master, and the manufacturer against his workman'. The people were 'goaded into a fever', which ended in what Strang termed political madness – and 'judicial murder'. The 'madness' was demands for universal suffrage, annual parliaments and votes by ballot. Thomas Harvie's neighbour James Hopkirk was convinced that these calls were a sham, concealing the radicals' real motives: 'revolution and plunder'. As we saw in the previous chapter, with Hopkirk's lack of respect for those lower down the social scale and his somewhat disdainful attitude to their hardships, these suspicions had aroused his fears about what the people from the east end villages might do and about which he had warned Harvie. Prudently, Hopkirk had moved his family from the relatively isolated estate of Dalbeth into Glasgow late in 1819, as fears of insurrection mounted.[7]

In order to achieve their aims, radicals in Scotland, in association with their counterparts south of the border, had planned to set up a provisional government, in support of which they called for a national strike. It was with this that the miners' leader, Fauldhouse Wilson, had been involved. Between fifty and sixty thousand workers responded, led primarily by handloom weavers from Glasgow and Paisley. Conditions in handloom weaving, the single most common manufacturing occupation in Scotland at the turn of the nineteenth century, had long been deteriorating. From 1787, the year of their first major strike – that of the Calton weavers – they had fought to resist wage reductions and secure their livelihoods.[8] Over time, concerns over working conditions and living standards became politicised and, by 1819, as they had been during the first heady days of the French Revolution in 1792 and 1793, the weavers were in the vanguard of Scottish radicalism. In this they were joined, in smaller numbers, by cotton spinners and coal miners, along with some machine-makers and foundry workers. The industrialisation process in west-central Scotland had been especially rapid, with working people across the board becoming employees and wage earners – proletarians – rather than the journeymen they had been formerly and who might anticipate a future as a small master. The older, regulated wage-setting system was dismantled in favour of free market principles – as had happened in the coal industry. Statues regulating wages were abolished, and in 1813 trade union organisation became a criminal offence.

From 1819, in preparation for the revolt, hundreds of men in the west of Scotland were being drilled. Many of the handloom weavers had been on active service during the Napoleonic Wars and so they understood the principles of military action and formed themselves into battalions, organised on a street-wide basis, learned perhaps from what they had witnessed in Spain and France.[9] Weapons of various descriptions were manufactured and gathered. Pikes were ubiquitous, as were 'clegs', shuttlecock-like, feathered devices with a short iron spike and filled with lead; these were thrown, mainly at the cavalry. The date 5 April 1820 was the start of the radicals' march, in poor weather, to Carron Iron Works in search of armaments; others trudged from Bridgeton in Glasgow, and on

6 April from Strathaven in Lanarkshire in support of the insurgency. The raggle-taggle band of headily optimistic, poorly equipped parties of radicals, however, was easily defeated by the regular army, so bringing down the curtain on what some relieved contemporaries called 'the wet Radical Wednesday of the west'.[10] In little more than seven days the venture had been crushed. Volunteer regiments such as the Sharpshooters were also deployed – more so than anywhere else in Britain. A massive search operation was set in motion to harry, arrest and bring to trial those most actively involved. Hangings for a few and transportation for many were the result.

Historians have long debated how serious a threat to the established order the rising posed, and they continue to disagree. What is incontrovertible is that initially at least the authorities had been terrified. And not for the first time. In 1817, such was the level of unrest over post-war suffering – partly due to unemployment – especially among the ubiquitous weavers, that Glasgow's Lord Provost, Kirkman Finlay, and his circle were convinced that there was a conspiracy to overthrow the government by force. They may have had good reason for believing this to be the case; the weavers in 1819 passed resolutions at meetings that asserted their rights and their continuing opposition to the government. Consequently, such was the determination of the state nationally, and at the local city, town and county level, to gain and retain the upper hand, that, as a defining moment in Scottish history, the Radical War can be considered a close second to the defeat of the Jacobites in 1746. Despite the outward appearance of calm in places such as Glasgow, as with Culloden it was not easily forgotten.[11]

In order to ensure there was no recurrence in the city, much was hoped for from a Police Act in 1821. The first was in 1800, but its powers were largely concerned with keeping the streets clean and, increasingly, with dealing with vagrancy. Only around 1819 did the Police Commission begin to take seriously criminality – and the dangers of political radicalism. The 1821 Act allowed for more vigorous surveillance of the community, which included looking out for 'subversive tendencies' among the working classes.[12]

The importance of new measures had been emphasised in November 1820, when scenes of disorder 'highly disgraceful to this city' were reported. There was wholesale smashing of windows of the 'principal houses' in town, partly due to the popular support for Queen Caroline, whose husband King George IV had attempted to deprive her of her titles and obtain a divorce. Dragoons were called upon to restore order. Indeed, such was the 'spirit of discontent' in and around the city that in 1821 it was deemed necessary, for the 'better preserving of the place', to erect barracks to house a cavalry regiment permanently. This was in addition to the infantry barracks situated to the west of Glasgow's High Street, where some £15,000 was spent on building the new garrison on four acres of land that were feued from the Trades House.

This, however, had not been soon enough to contain yet another major disturbance. In April 1821, the annual celebrations for the king's birthday had ended in a series of clashes on Glasgow Green near the town jail. Great fires were lit with wood from the palings from nearby properties. Fighting involving the provost and his magistrates, mounted soldiers and the infantry on the one side and demonstrators on the other resulted in numerous serious injuries and an unknown number of fatalities. The actions of the mob 'were as violent and as uncontrollable . . . as have ever been experienced here', opined the *Glasgow Courier*. More 'blood had been shed celebrating the King of England in Scotland [there had been ugly scenes in Edinburgh too]', a report in *The Times* read, 'than in replacing the King of the Two Sicilies on his Throne', a reference to recent events in the south of Italy centred on King Ferdinando and the constitution.

In order to prevent further disorder on this scale, for the king's birthday in April 1823 the magistrates prohibited bonfires, the burning of tar barrels and the firing of pistols in public places, and enrolled a number of special constables to assist in the preservation of 'public peace and tranquillity'.[13] These measures were effective on this occasion, in the heart of the old town.

Policing in the villages that had grown unchecked around Westthorn, however, was minimal. The Glasgow Police Act of 1800 applied only to the Royalty of the city, not the new adjacent settlements that were part of the wider Barony. Lanark County, of which they were part, was unable to police them – until 1846 when Glasgow became an extended police authority and imposed effective law enforcement measures.

Adding to the anxiety of Glasgow's provost and magistrates in the early 1820s were the outbreaks of violence that accompanied a rash of city- and region-wide strikes by cotton mill spinners. The spinners had formed a new union in 1820, the Association of Operative Cotton Spinners. Tightly organised and bound by secret oaths, members had little compunction about using physical means to advance their cause. As at the same time in power loom weaving, workers fiercely resisted efforts on the part of masters to decide which overseers should be appointed, and which spinners to recruit to operate their new steam-powered machinery. Late in 1822 and early in 1823 it was becoming increasingly common for the spinners – and tenters in the power loom weaving trade – to be involved in vitriol (acid) throwing attacks on blacklegs, regardless of sex. Mill owners were also subject to threats and physical assaults.[14]

Charge of the Enniskillen Dragoons

The Dragoons would eventually be called into action over the spinners' dispute (in September 1823), but the regiment's first intervention in Glasgow, within days of their arrival, was at Harvie's Dyke. It was midsummer-dark when they arrived at Westthorn, having ridden at speed the two miles or so from their barracks at Port Eglinton. These were on the south side of the Clyde alongside the basin of the same name that marked the Glasgow end of the Glasgow, Paisley and Ardrossan Canal. The barracks could house several hundred soldiers, and even if this number was rarely if ever reached, their trade was a welcome windfall for shopkeepers in the vicinity. So too was the infantry barracks which had been constructed in the east end of the city in 1795. Indeed for the Westthorn disturbance the infantry were closer to hand, their east end location having been deliberately chosen as this was where political and industrial unrest could be an 'explosive' force.[15] On this occasion, though, it was the intimidating sight of horses and cavalrymen that was deemed most likely to contain the fearsome, rampaging mob which the panicking Thomas Harvie had reported to Glasgow's sheriff office.

Even in the half-light the cavalrymen were a menacing presence. Their brown and bay horses were large – no less than fifteen and a half hands in height (well over 5 feet) – and powerfully built. Their riders were dressed in short scarlet jackets and grey trousers with a distinctive white stripe. These were tucked into black leather 'Wellington' boots (so-called after the Duke of Wellington who had been responsible for their design). Fully armed, each man carried a cutting sword (or sabre), a pistol and a carbine and bayonet. The detachment was led by Robert Mansell, a cornet who normally carried the regiment's flag, or colours. Although only twenty years old, Mansell was an experienced junior officer, having joined the regiment three years earlier.[16]

If Thomas Harvie or David Hardie hoped that the appearance of the troops would have an immediate, salutary impact on the Clyde-side crowd they were disappointed. Having galloped along the main road from Glasgow, on reaching Westthorn the Dragoons found the gates locked. Their plan to ride through the estate down to the riverside and surprise the rampant crowd was stymied. Unable to open the gates, they had to call for one of Harvie's servants to get inside the Westthorn grounds. Once there, and after checking that Westthorn house was secure, Hardie and the Dragoons turned their attention to what was going on at the eastern wall below. According to Robert Mansell, what confronted them was a great fire and a massive crowd of shouting, cheering people.

The crowd, by this time fuelled with their triumph in breaking down not only Harvie's detested Dyke, but the protruding wall on his eastern boundary too, had determined to attack a third obstruction, a 'slender erection', a wooden barrier that had been erected by his neighbour James Hopkirk. It might have been even worse for the proprietors of Clyde-side estates: John West, the teenage weaver from Camlachie who was watching and listening, 'understood it to be the intention of the mob to pull down every dyke that night which ran within the water mark'.

Whether or not this was true, the effect of the sight of the Dragoons at the top of the bank was almost (but not quite) immediate. At first there was some resistance. 'Come on you Irish beggars' was one taunt. Owing to the intensity of the heat from the burning palisades, the Dragoons' horses would approach only reluctantly. But soon there was a mass exodus. The military detachment was divided into two. Some of the soldiers were ordered to dismount and, on the instructions of David Hardie, to take as many prisoners as they could. Hundreds plunged into the river and swam, waded and scrambled to the south bank from where, for a while, they continued to abuse the soldiers. Others simply fled eastwards along the north bank in the direction of Clyde Iron Works.

There were also a few signs of resistance. Shots were fired, although precisely when, how many, with what weapons and for what purpose was unclear. Andrew Chisholm, a private in the Dragoons, was sure that the firing only started after arrests began to be made. One experienced cavalryman, Thomas Cavanagh, insisted that he had been shot at with a pistol, but that the weapon had misfired. Hardie, the sheriff officer, heard guns being discharged, and while he felt these had been directed at him and the military, he conceded that he had 'heard no whizzing' of bullets. Others were unsure about the kind of weapons used – muskets or fowling pieces – but certain that they had been loaded with ammunition. Fowling pieces were much prized and used by Bridgeton's cotton spinners and calico printers who, a later witness was convinced, had fired on the watchtower at Westthorn.[17] (Some had been used by radical insurgents in April 1820.) This, however, didn't deter either Hardie or the Dragoons, who in small parties and in different directions 'secured such persons as they found about the Westthorn boundaries' or those who as daylight returned were found on the surrounding roads or concealed in hedges, long grass and ditches.

So anxious was Hardie to make arrests that those Dragoons who had dismounted 'jumped over . . . fences, sword in hand' in pursuit of fleeing demonstrators. Their first captive was Robert Thom, a Parkhead weaver. There were scuffles between the soldiers and a few of the men they were attempting to arrest. One young man 'of the name of Jordan' was badly slashed by one of the Dragoons with a sabre. A handful managed to break free. On the other hand, Robert Love, one of the Enniskillens, reported that the three prisoners he had taken 'were all skulking, seemed terrified and made no resistance'.

By the end of the night forty-three men had been seized and then held until the early hours of Sunday morning in the tightly packed porter's lodge or watchtower in the grounds of Westthorn. At around 3 a.m. the first of them were marched to Glasgow where they were incarcerated in the city's jail. They were then interrogated.

Fearful initially, the mood of the arrestees had been lifted as they made their way from Westthorn along the road into the city. The section between Tollcross and Camlachie – the neighbourhood where most of those under arrest resided – 'was thronged the whole night by people either on the lookout for their friends, or getting the news'. Older inhabitants were said to have been particularly delighted because the passageway along the river they knew from childhood had probably been re-opened. Groups of onlookers cheered the prisoners to the echo along the rest of the route. Outside the jail even the Dragoons, realising the popularity of their prisoners' cause, 'reined up their horses and . . . took off their helmets in token of their silent approbation'. In appreciation of the Dragoons' gesture, the watching crowd cheered both them and those under their guard. Never, according to Peter Mackenzie in his *Reminiscences of Glasgow and the West of Scotland*, over the period from the 1790s until after the Reform Act of 1832, 'did prisoners enter that Tolbooth in such joyous spirits'.

Two days later, the following Monday, young William O'Boyling, an engine keeper at one of Harvie's coal pits, turned up for work. He had watched the proceedings from afar on the Saturday night but in daylight he could see more clearly the devastation that had been wreaked. In the middle of the morning he wandered down to look more closely at what was left of the walls. Within ten yards or so of the remains he came across an iron jumper, which he later gave to David Hardie. Also found in the vicinity were a few other implements that had been used to bring down the walls, along with some sticks and cudgels that had been thrown aside as their owners escaped the scene – possibly fearing that these would be used in evidence against them.

It had been what *The Scotsman* described as a 'very unpleasant business'.[18] But it was far from finished.

Unity in the face of hardship

The interrogations of those apprehended began within hours of their arrival in Glasgow. Almost half of them – twenty-seven – were weavers. Eight were cotton spinners, most from Blackburn's Mill in Bridgeton, the others employed at Dunn's Mill, Calton and Orr's Mill, Barrowfield Road. Three were colliers and the other five represented individual trades. Gilbert Watson, for example, was a journeyman baker, William Welsh a joiner, and David Tait a tailor. A couple listed themselves as having dual occupations: Walter Arrol was a painter as well as a weaver; Alexander M'Phie (or McFie) too had been a weaver but was also a sinker at a local colliery. With the formerly ubiquitous handloom weaving trade in the west of Scotland in steep decline, it made sense for men to turn to alternative employment. With only a handful of exceptions the arrested men came from the village communities that lay near to Westthorn: above all Parkhead, but also Tollcross, Camlachie, Dalmarnock, Shettleston and Westmuir. The rest were from Bridgeton and Calton, other than seventeen-year-old John Gilmour, a collier, the sole captive from the Gorbals. Gilmour wasn't the youngest – that was John West, aged sixteen. The oldest, aged sixty-four, was Alexander Whyte, a mason from Parkhead.

What the authorities were most determined to discover were the ringleaders: those who had been active in demolishing the walls, and who had been armed – a heinous crime in the circumstances of the time. George Salmond, Glasgow's procurator fiscal, an implacable enemy of worker combinations and popular protest, was clear that unless the guilty parties were found and tried in the High Court (as opposed to the lesser Sheriff Court), 'the people' would soon 'get ahead of the Authorities'.[19]

What Salmond and his colleagues were confronted with, however, was a veil of silence: from outright denials of their involvement on the part of key suspects, to the sheer unwillingness by witnesses to co-operate in identifying the guilty parties. The inhabitants of the thickly crowded, cohesive east end communities involved were connected by ties of place, residence and occupation. They were bound too by family ties, and as near neighbours.

We know that before 1750 the villages in question hardly existed on what was primarily farmland. Carmyle had only been established in 1741, specifically as a muslin weaving centre. By the 1790s none of them numbered even 1,000 inhabitants; Parkhead had only 678, Shettleston 766 and Camlachie 977. Thereafter the settlements had all expanded, the numbers swollen by the influx of Irish migrants. Even so, as regards their size, Bridgeton, to the west, was the exception, with a population of around 14,000, most of whom were weavers. However, the occupational base of the villages in the 1820s remained much the same as it had been in the 1790s. As with Glasgow and the west of Scotland generally, where cotton textile production was concentrated, these were handloom weaving strongholds. By 1820 around one third of Glasgow's weavers were probably from Ireland. Most west of Scotland websters either worked on their own in the cramped upper stories of their cottages, or in small groups in loom shops, in the service of a single manufacturer. Whatever the location, they might be at the loom from dawn until late in the evening, the monotony of their work broken by songs of love and loss, but also rhythmic rousing refrains that matched the movement of the shuttle as it flew through the warp of the web and the action of the treadles that powered the loom. Uniting them was their resentment at the loss of their former independence and social standing, and feelings of despair as wage rates were slashed.[20] Only Camlachie, 'mostly inhabited by coaliers, employed in the numerous mines in the neighbourhood', was significantly different.[21]

Weavers, colliers and cotton mill operatives were in the front line of Scotland's industrial revolution, battle-hardened by the challenges of new work regimes and by life in what were in effect frontier towns. Fledgling enterprises often failed, usually in spates associated with economic downturns, throwing employees out of work without warning. Overcrowding in insanitary conditions was becoming a problem: Glasgow endured its first outbreak of typhus in 1818. In short, dislocation and destitution were never far away.

It was in part for this reason that, in the desperately difficult years following the Napoleonic Wars, Tyrone-born Mary Hutcheson had acquired the art of reading cups. Twenty-four years old and the mother of two children, she had survived by winding yarns, sewing and, during the winter months, begging on one of Glasgow's bridges; her husband, an itinerant tailor, had struggled to find regular employment. Fortune telling could pay well, with clients willing to pay from threepence to as much as half a crown for the service, which included helping people who had lost property or been defrauded in some way. Hutcheson had become, in and around Glasgow, 'pretty much known as a practitioner of the art', so much so that Ann Ross, a servant of John Macdougall, clerk and under manager of and resident at Westthorn colliery, had come to Glasgow to see her and ask if she would do readings at her employer's house.[22] There was a mystic aspect to Hutcheson's tea leaf reading sessions that included incantations and readings from the Bible – so much so that in 1818 she was accused of 'pretending to exercise or use witchcraft, sorcery, or conjuration' in order to tell fortunes as well as to cure diseases and 'procure large sums of money to such . . . persons as should think fit to give her small sums of money'.[23] Ross was one such victim, gulled by her penurious circumstances into believing that for every shilling she gave her, Hutcheson would return a pound. Hutcheson had got greedy, and after buying food for her family, and paid a nurse, she had spent £12 10s on clothes including a 'scarlet duffle'. And the rest on drink. Then she had been caught and arrested. But just as destitution – and desperation for something better when coping with the uncertainties of a society undergoing transformation – were never far distant, neither was the law, where it could be exercised. The Justice of the Peace before whom Hutcheson was brought on 6 April, when she had decided that the declaration she had made on 1 April was less than honest, was Thomas Hopkirk, the son of James Hopkirk of Dalbeth, whose estate proprietor neighbour would be Thomas Harvie.

Many of the district's residents were employed by the same firms, such as the Clyde Iron Works and Henry Monteith's dye and printworks at Dalmarnock, but also at some of the twenty-two cotton mills in the near vicinity. Clyde was the third-largest iron works in the country, turning out an average of 4,500 tons of iron each year, not far short of the bigger, better-known works, at Carron and Muirkirk. Monteith's dyeworks had been opened initially in 1785, by Charles Mackintosh and David Dale. The works were sold to Monteith, Bogle & Co. in 1802, and renamed Barrowfield Dyeworks, which mass-produced Turkey (or Dale's) Red and white-patterned bandana-type handkerchiefs. And while there were large cotton mills, most were small operations, further facilitating close relationships between employees. William Dunn, for example, employed only fifteen men, and James Oswald only thirty-two. It should be no surprise, then, that among the lists of those accused of having participated in the Harvie's Dyke riot were workers not only in the same occupation, such as handloom weavers, coal miners and other colliery employees, but also at the same place of employment. Oswald would have been especially disappointed, given his determination in the aftermath of the insurrection of 1820 not to employ anyone who had taken part in the 'treasonable confederacy'.[24]

Occupational difference was not in itself significant. Alliances were forged for various reasons, including shared values – typically a belief in natural justice and what historians have called the moral economy of the poor. Apart from combinations or early trade unions, there were in the district numerous societies that drew people with particular interests together. John Matheson, a manager at Monteith's Barrowfield dyeworks, belonged to sixteen of them, ranging from Highland societies, Bible societies and the Bridgeton Wheaten Bread Society.[25] In a letter to the *Glasgow Chronicle* of 7 February 1824 a 'Poor Man's Friend' thought that the price of bread and potatoes – staple foods for ordinary people – was higher by 25 per cent in Glasgow than elsewhere, and therefore squeezed even tighter the budgets of working-class households. The need for spiritual nourishment brought communities together too. With industrialisation and the transition from the relative regularity of rural life to the crowded disorder of mushrooming villages like those of Glasgow's east end, came a sense of nostalgia for a world that had been lost – or nearly so. Access to land and nature provided an avenue leading back to what was familiar, and to a large degree accounts for the enormous popularity among ordinary people of the poetry and song of Robert Burns, even before his death in 1796. Nostalgia, though, induced not acceptance but a determination to remain independent and to challenge land-grasping, ostentatious, oppressors, as Burns did in poems like 'The Twa Dogs' and 'The Cotter's Saturday Night'. Like Thomas Harvie.

It is impossible to weigh the influence of all of the things that might have been fuelling the fears and frustrations of the working people of the east end during the first months of 1823. On top of the factors just listed, the winter had been long and hard, and the spring was colder than usual. Even the better-off inhabitants in the neighbourhood – such as the coal-owning family the Grays of Carntyne – struggled to cope with an unusually hard frost and continuous falls of snow that lay six feet deep.[26] This bout of debilitatingly cold weather lasted from the start of January and dragged on well into February. For long periods even walking outside was impossible. Passageways were cut through the worst drifts, but night-time snowfalls closed them up again, thus interrupting supplies of basic commodities like fuel and foodstuffs. One of the benefits of living in such a colliery-rich neighbourhood was the availability – usually – of cheap coal for domestic purposes, but in these conditions, it was not easily transported even for relatively short distances.

Hardly had a thaw set in, when on the morning of Sunday 16 February, a five-storey tenement – Gibson's Land in the city's Saltmarket – had collapsed, injuring several people, causing the loss of jobs in the printing works that were housed there, and leaving many former occupants homeless. News of the fall of such a well-known building, and of the subsequent condemning of similar properties nearby, sent shock waves throughout Glasgow and even reached the London newspapers. Unease about their safety is likely to have spread to the inhabitants of Parkhead and other places where high structures – tenements, the 'Lands' in which so many of the Harvie's Dyke participants were housed – had been erected in haste at low cost and without the approval of the Dean of Guild, the city's building officer. In due course there would be benefits for the owners of stone quarries and collieries in the east end as rebuilding work commenced, but not in 1823. This year the cold weather had returned with a vengeance. 'Dreadful' was the word one west of Scotland farmer used to describe a period towards the end of May, by which time crops were ten days behind the norm.[27]

Prising open clam-tight communities

Whether or not he was aware, or concerned, 'Lang Tam' Harvie had purchased an estate that was set amid one of the west of Scotland's radical hothouses.

Parkhead and the other villages around had been deeply implicated in the Radical War. At Tollcross, radical meetings had been held in the aftermath of the notorious proceedings at Peterloo and months before the insurrection in Scotland in 1820. Those present in a crowd in which distressed weavers were predominant heard speeches condemning the divine right of kings, the much despised Corn Laws (which protected landowners at the expense of domestic consumers of grain), the waste of public money on corrupt politicians and their friends, the banks, the massacre at Manchester (Peterloo) and the recent failure of the *Glasgow Chronicle* to support unconditionally the radical movement. Not long afterwards a crowd of some 2,000 Tollcross coal miners gathered to hear a speech from Joseph Brayshaw, the radical missionary from Leeds in Yorkshire who was touring the north to establish the strength of support for militant action. Around the same time drilling was reported in both Dalmarnock and Tollcross.[28] And it was to a safe house in Barrowfield near Dalmarnock that Brayshaw – who may also have had a hand in drawing up the *Address* – had fled after the abortive rising.[29] The revolutionary

Address to the Inhabitants of Great Britain and Ireland of 1 April 1820 that Fauldhouse Wilson had helped to distribute was authored by radical weavers from Parkhead, in the house of James Armstrong.[30]

Other than fellow radicals, outsiders, expressly those representing authority, were unwelcome. Even within the communities in question, the formal organs of local government found in burghs elsewhere, were absent. This is hardly surprising. It was not clear just what constituted Glasgow's geographic entity; it was not until 1841 that the council had an accurate, up-to-date map of the city.[31] Thus, during the trade depression of 1826, in most of Glasgow precise numbers of unemployed weavers could be reported at the level of the street, with a total of seventy-four looms being idle in Bell Street, Clyde Street and Tobago Street, for instance. From the fringe villages of Parkhead, Camlachie, Shettleston, Tollcross and vicinity, however, no such returns were forthcoming; the levels of unemployment could only be guessed at. Law enforcement too was challenging, sometimes impossible in what, in effect, were opaque, closed communities.

Examples abound. In August 1823, just a few weeks after the assault on Harvie's Dyke, a landlord attempted to pursue an errant tenant to his new habitation in Vinegar Hill, near Camlachie, 'a place . . . mostly occupied by people from the sister isle [Ireland]'. Despite being supported by an officer and constables, the landlord on arriving in the village was met by a large body of inhabitants. The official party was then subject to insults, the landlord's warrant was torn up and there was a full-scale attack with stones and other missiles thrown. 'The very women were most active in the affray', it was reported in the *Glasgow Free Press* in August 1823, before the landlord and the constabulary were driven down the hill and forced to abandon their mission by taking refuge in another village. In rougher, primarily working-class communities like Camlachie the police were deemed alien, disliked as representatives of the state, albeit that of the city of Glasgow. In this case too there may have been the added dimension of nationality; the Irish immigrant communities tended to stick together. Here as elsewhere women were to the forefront when it came to the defence of neighbourhood and shared values and attitudes – resentment over the unwelcome intrusion of authority figures was one of these.[32] Women were at one with the men in their communities, with whom many lived and struggled together to make ends meet, while others met and socialised on tenement stairs, on the streets or in drinking dens.[33] These were communities small enough to ensure their inhabitants knew or at least recognised each other, and to whom, by and large they were loyal.

A further example of community cohesion in the face of outside intrusion comes from May 1824, less than a year after the Harvie's Dyke riot. William Martin, messenger at arms in Glasgow, and two other officials went out to Tollcross on behalf of Gilbert Kennedy, Collector of Taxes in Glasgow, armed with a warrant to poind (seize or impound) some of the effects of Gilbert Paterson and John Pirie. The two men, both colliers, had failed to pay Dog Tax, which had been levied since 1797–8 as one of the government's measures to raise revenue to fund the war then being waged with Revolutionary France. Showers of stones slowed Martin and his associates as they tried to enter the village. Once in Tollcross and during the poinding process the three men were abused and threatened with their lives by having their brains blown out. The warrants they had presented to the offending colliers and their wives were treated with contempt. John Pirie asserted his right to the bulldog he had, 'for his own amusement'. The tax – 8 shillings was what he owed – was something he simply couldn't afford. In such straitened circumstances the poinding was even more deeply resented: the constables, declared one of those harrying the officers, 'were a wheen scoundrels . . . that . . . had been taking away their clocks [a prized possession] and bed and bedding'. Not surprisingly, even though they had the protection of a troop of cavalrymen, Martin and his associates were harried and chased out of Tollcross and for a lengthy part of their journey back to Glasgow.[34]

Efforts a month later by the procurator fiscal to root out those who had resisted and assaulted his officials proved little more successful. Sent this time with a warrant for their apprehension was John Calder, another of Glasgow's sheriff officers, who lived in the Gorbals. Along with him was another officer of the same rank, William McKenzie, and, anticipating they would be obstructed, two 'concurrents' or unofficial bodyguards – John M'Gill and Thomas Connor. Further support was provided by Corporal Charles Scott and six of his men from the Enniskillen Dragoons.[35]

The party left Glasgow at 11 p.m. They would surprise the suspects, some of whom might be in bed. But even this formidable force was unable to carry out the fiscal's instructions in full. In order to pre-empt any alarm about their approach, around midnight Calder and Connor walked into the village unaccompanied and made for the house of a Peter Brown, a special constable who was to show them where the men sought by the fiscal lived. Names were one thing; the more difficult challenge was to find the individuals concerned in what was alien, unknown and forbidding territory. The Dragoons had dismounted, to further reduce noise. Even so, by the time Calder and his minder got to Brown's house, they found themselves under the scrutiny of several men and women on the other side of the street. Outside the house they were met by three men, one of whom was carrying two coal picks. One of them asked what the two officials wanted with Brown, before shouting, 'Damn your eyes, Calder, you damned rascal, I know you – ye'll never get out of Tollcross alive', at the same time clubbing him with the hafts of the picks. Hearing the disturbance and now fully aroused from sleep, people were 'running giving alarm through the village and raising their neighbours to assist'. Prudently, at this point Brown decided to go home, 'through fear of the inhabitants' among whom he lived; he was now a marked man. Unsurprisingly, members of the crowd refused to provide Calder with any of the information he needed, and instead repeatedly threatened to butcher the party if they did not leave. The officers were unable to serve warrants on the remaining two suspects. Nor were they easily able to arrest the collier who had assaulted Calder. After attacking him, the man in question had been surrounded by a group of women with their backs to him, 'evidently wishing to hide him'. This was Robert Kirkwood, a twenty-one-year-old collier employed by Colin Dunlop at Clyde Iron Works. Also protecting him were his two brothers. Kirkwood was one of the men accused of hindering William Martin from serving warrants the previous month and appears to have been a prominent figure in his community. Local leadership in the shape of charismatic or respected individuals had long been an integral element in popular protests in Scotland and would prove to be again in the case of Harvie's Dyke, as we shall see.

Even apparently respectable citizens could be found siding with members of the communities among whom they lived. In 1828 sheriff officers had walked out to Westmuir with a warrant for the arrest of Henry Winning, a wine seller who was alleged to have failed to repay a loan of £55 from a Mrs Gardner. In the melee that followed the officers' arrival, William Craig, the failed Belvidere colliery lessee who, like William Lyon, was a surgeon practising in Parkhead, advised Winning 'wickedly and illegally' not to allow himself to be jailed on the grounds that the warrant was illegal. Craig followed up his verbal intervention by assaulting William Dinning, one of the officers, who may have been either drunk or on the way to being so. This encouraged James Winning, Henry's father, a seventy-two-year-old retired miner, to attack Thomas Martin, who was still employed in the sheriff's office, thereby preventing his son's apprehension. George Salmond, Lanarkshire's procurator fiscal who had known Craig for some years, had good reason to believe that Craig's character was 'rather below par' and 'far from respectable'. On the other hand, as was seen in the previous chapter, among his neighbours, Craig, like his fellow physician William Lyon, was someone ordinary people (who could also be his grateful patients) looked up to and whose loss, according to three parish elders who spoke up for him, 'would be irreparable and deeply felt'.[36]

Martin had been in similar situations before, as in 1824. It was only with difficulty that Robert Kirkwood had been taken prisoner. So too were his brothers, but it is unclear how many others the warrant party were able to return with to Glasgow. Scott, the Dragoon's corporal, had become increasingly agitated as the numbers of hostile residents grew and their threats became more menacing. More than once he had urged Calder 'to retire with the prisoner already secured' as the small number of men he had with him 'were insufficient to repel any attack which might be made by the crowd'.[37] Military might had its limitations.

Incarcerated in Glasgow, alone, and charged with 'wickedly and feloniously' attacking and assaulting a sheriff officer, Kirkwood was not intimidated. He refused to give his name and remained silent under questioning.

Prising reliable information from those arrested at Harvie's Dyke, or in the weeks following, was not going to be straightforward.

3

Who, How and Why: Interrogating the Harvie's Dyke Protesters

Notwithstanding the solidarity of the east end communities in the face of what were deemed to be unwarranted intrusions, escaping the clutches of the law was more difficult in the summer of 1823 than it had been only three years earlier.

First of all, the impact of the 1821 Police Act was beginning to be felt as information was garnered on potentially subversive individuals and actions in what were now twenty-four police wards for Glasgow. Furthermore, under its terms a new Superintendent of Police was appointed. The first of these was James Hardie. Hardie, already a Lanarkshire county magistrate, was enthusiastically backed for the position by Scotland's senior law officers. These were the Lord Advocate Sir William Rae and James Wedderburn the Solicitor General. Other supporters were his fellow magistrates and Lt Col. Harry G. Smith, who had been a senior army commander during the political disturbances in Glasgow and the vicinity in the years 1819 and 1820. All commended Hardie for his zealousness and dedication, but also his intelligence, discretion and good temper. Lt Col. Smith made particular mention of Hardie's role after 1820 in dealing with mobs, a difficult assignment task during which he had shown 'the coolest determination to perform his duty'.[1] This he had done by exercising 'the most manly forbearance towards the deluded populace', by which means he not only executed the commands of his superiors (Glasgow's magistrates who after Peterloo were justifiably nervous about ordering the military to open fire when faced with large hostile crowds) but also 'avoided the unpleasant resort of the most violent measures'.[2] These were precisely the qualities required to maintain order in the troubled years following the Radical Rising. The level of consternation on the part of Scotland's conservatives – including Tory writers such as Sir Walter Scott and John Galt – about the 'subversive fervour' of the lower orders in and around Glasgow and elsewhere in Lowland Scotland was as intense in 1823 as it had been in 1819 and 1820.[3]

In addition, a fresh figure was arising in the west of Scotland's legal firmament: Archibald Alison. Until recently Alison had been practising in civil law in Edinburgh. Born in 1792, he was an ambitious Enlightenment-influenced Tory who was to become a notorious and much-feared sheriff of Lanarkshire, the scourge of trade unions and political reformers, not least the Chartists. His attitude to popular unrest had been profoundly influenced by what he saw as the catastrophe of the French Revolution. Another protégé of the Lord Advocate Sir William Rae, as recently as February 1823 he had been appointed as one of the country's three advocates general. It was a post that involved judging criminal cases and determining which should go to trial. He was renowned for his utter dedication to work and lost no time in fulfilling his new role. There was much to be done: prior to the 1790s it was not unusual for the High Court of Justiciary, or circuit court – which sat in Glasgow twice a year – to have few or even no criminal cases to deal with. In stark contrast, according to James Cleland, a Glasgow statistician, in the spring of 1820 the court had sat on six days, for twelve hours on each occasion, to deal with forty-seven cases and seventy-two panels (the accused). Over the course of that year there had been more than one thousand criminal cases, a record. Although 1820 had been exceptional, the trend was unmistakably upwards. Just as disturbing for the authorities by 1823 was that while the number of prosecutions had not risen, those that came before the court were, according to the *Glasgow Free Press* in October 1823, 'unrivalled in the deep depravity of their nature'.

Alison's most recent biographer has it that Alison's first attempt to suppress a public disturbance was in 1835.[4] This is only partly accurate. His first efforts to bring to justice and punish those behind such occurrences began ten years earlier. They began with Harvie's Dyke.

Searching for ringleaders

Held with the other arrestees in Glasgow, the handloom weaver and part-time town crier Thomas John Fraser was the first to be questioned. This was on Sunday 22 June, within hours of his being taken prisoner during the early hours of the same morning. As it was Fraser who 'by tuck of drum' had advertised the gathering at Westthorn, he surely would know who had been behind it. Fraser, however, was less than helpful. He denied that he was in any way involved in the riot or had even been in the watching crowd. What he was sure of was that, whoever had asked him to convene the meeting, it wasn't George Allan – who Fraser's interrogators suspected was the culprit. For one thing, Fraser contended, the man concerned had given him a handwritten note of what he was to announce. Allan hadn't, on either of the two previous occasions when Allan had asked Fraser to proclaim meetings about the passageway along the Clyde. He had done so verbally, in person.

All Fraser was prepared to testify to was that the individual who had approached him 'wanted his coat and had on an apron and had the appearance of a weaver'. Not satisfied with this, William Rose Robinson, the sheriff depute of Lanark who conducted the examination, returned Fraser to his cell and ordered that he be held there until the name of the guilty party was found out. Two days later Robinson re-interrogated Fraser. This time he managed to prise from him an undertaking that Fraser would 'make every exertion' to discover who had employed him and to provide Robinson with his address.

To no avail. Fraser failed to come forward with a name. Still sure that he was concealing key information, the authorities brought him in for a further bout of questioning on 8 August. This time a different approach was adopted and Fraser's wife Ann Christie was also summonsed. Probing the couple on this occasion was Hugh Kerr, sheriff substitute for Lanarkshire.

This could have been awkward for them. Judging by the questions asked of the couple, it was clear that Kerr believed, as had Rose Robinson a few weeks earlier, that it was George Allan who had initiated the protest against Harvie's intrusive walls. And little wonder. Allan was one of the eighty-eight radicals who had been accused by the crown of treason following the radical insurrection in 1820. That July, he had been in the dock of the High Court in Glasgow with James Wilson, the lifelong reform advocate from Strathaven. Wilson was found guilty and sentenced to death; to his great relief, Allan, who was less heavily implicated, was dismissed.[5]

In 1823 Fraser and his wife were steadfast in their denial that it was Allan who had commissioned Fraser. Christie agreed that the mysterious caller had been a weaver, as was Allan. Beyond that, however, her testimony seemed confused but it was also carefully contained. He was 'either bare-headed or had a night cap on and appeared just to have come off his work'. On the other hand she was prepared to acknowledge that their visitor's face was familiar, and sure that he was from Parkhead. But greatly to the frustration of her interrogators, she insisted that she neither knew his name nor where he lived.

One thing was certain: whoever Fraser's caller had been, he was a man of honour. At the time he met with Fraser he had no money on him, but offered him half a crown for his services, which he promised to pay afterwards. A week later, Ann Christie was invited by a Mrs Sym to collect a letter from the post office she managed. Inside the envelope – which, unusually, lacked a post mark – was a half-crown coin and a hand-scrawled receipt, dated 23 June, payment for 'your calling By the Drum on Saturday Last'. The paper was signed by 'your most Obedient Servant', an 'Enemy to all Encroachment'.

Truth, lies and dissembling

While the identity of Fraser's paymaster remained unknown, the interrogations on 22 and 24 June produced some important clues, even if these were often inconclusive. Much of the testimony was useless, and clearly untrue. It was as if those concerned had sworn a vow of partial silence. They went so far, but not far enough for the prosecutors. Time after time witnesses maintained that they had not been able to recognise those taking part, even though they were near neighbours. Only John Tait, a twenty-four-year-old tailor who lived at Moffat Land, Parkhead, refused to answer any questions – a brave if judicious decision as this was also exactly where one of those eventually found guilty, Alexander M'Phie, resided. Tait was interviewed on 26 June, by which time a list of those thought to have been the principal offenders had been drawn up, so almost certainly he knew that M'Phie was on it. M'Phie as we will see later, was no angel.

Not all those who were taken in the early hours of 22 June were culpable. William Rose, a weaver from Calton, claimed that he had tried to leave, but had been called a coward and subject to other 'insulting language' and so remained near the scene only to be later captured. Thomas Brown too denied any involvement, but somewhat less convincingly. A colliery labourer from Tollcross, Brown admitted hearing the drum beating but not what Fraser was calling. Sometime afterwards he had gone to a public house in Parkhead with 'another person' whose name he didn't know 'but who appeared to be a weaver'. It was an unlikely scenario: the two men 'had a little porter or rather two or three' over the course of two hours or more. After debating whether to go home or to Westthorn, Brown had opted for the latter and saw the east wall being destroyed. But, he protested, he had not joined the crowd; he had heard gunshots, but only from a distance; and had been going home on the high road to Clyde Iron Works when he was 'laid hold of and taken into custody'. William Lyon the surgeon was equally unconvincing when he tried to persuade his inquisitors that he didn't know the names of the two men from Bridgeton who had been part of the deputation that after 12 June had gone to Glasgow to seek Robert Graham's advice about how to deal with Thomas Harvie's walls.

There were those who were persuaded to admit that they had seen some of the suspects at the walls. But equally, they would affirm that the men concerned had been acting innocently. John Baird, a coal miner, was seen with a gun, but not using it. In his turn Baird, who lived in Reid's Land, Parkhead, staunchly denied his own involvement, or that he had seen anyone he knew taking down the walls. Indeed, he testified, 'he did not see a single person in the crowd which he knew'. Nor, in spite of the fact he lived in Reid's Land in Parkhead, was he sure he would be able recognise 'any of the persons who were in the crowd or employed about the dyke though they were shown him again'. A number of witnesses were sure that people from Bridgeton and Parkhead were the main actors, but they were unable to say who they were. Even in August, when re-examined and brought face to face with the main suspects who were under arrest, most witnesses continued to maintain their silence. If anything, they would concede having seen the accused at Harvie's walls, but as observers rather than participants. Thus, young John West admitted recognising both Andrew Adamson and Walter Winning. Even though the two men had been a few yards from the walls, he was adamant that neither had been 'actively involved'. All that he would allow was that both suspects had looked happy, Adamson 'laughing and carrying on as if he were pleased with what was doing', but not cheering. Nor had he heard Winning shouting or speaking to the crowd. Dugald Cameron was another suspect he recognised but he had only seen him talking to people with apparent delight at what was being achieved.

A few were prepared to describe the approximate heights and the clothing worn by some of the suspects. More than one witness saw 'a boy with a red jacket' who had been carrying a crowbar down to the river, but he was never named. Peter Brown, one of Harvie's watchmen, thought that one of the men who had brought an iron pinch to the riverbank was 5 feet 10 inches tall, 'rather stout than slender made', and wore a fustian coat. Brown's colleague, John Penman, saw 'a tall man who had the appearance of a smith'. But even Harvie's employees probably felt constrained from saying too much, fearing the consequences of speaking out when they would almost certainly suffer retribution at the hands of those they identified, or their friends and associates. An example is elderly Alexander Whyte, who had been arrested as a member of the watching crowd, even though he had been employed by Harvie as a mason for a year. He was clearly squirming as his interview proceeded. Whyte confessed that he knew a Joseph Bogle 'perfectly well by sight' and had no doubt that he had seen Bogle carrying a gun at one of the walls, but as he had been at a considerable distance at the time, 'he could not swear positively to his identity'.

After Fraser, of particular interest to the investigators were the seven members of the committee who had been elected on 12 June. Under examination none of the seven had any qualms about admitting they had been members. All were adamant, however, that they had resigned after the inconclusive discussion on 19 June over whether they should adopt the legal route in dealing with Harvie and try to prosecute him for encroaching on the public right of way, or take direct action.

A second committee had taken over on the 19th, but all those who had been members of the original one denied any involvement with the meeting that had then taken the decision to attack the walls on 21 June. It was exasperating for his inquisitors that even though John McCracken, of the original committee, had been present when twelve people had been appointed to the new group, he could only remember one name: John Duncan, a Parkhead stocking maker. This was more than anything his fellow committee members were prepared to offer, even though they had been present too, but it wasn't much.

Exhibiting admirable mutual loyalty, most – but, crucially, not all – of the members of the original committee denied seeing any of their number as the walls were demolished. They were adamant too that they had taken no active part in planning the assault, or its implementation. George Allan not only repudiated any suggestion that he had asked Fraser to call the third meeting but also tried to convince his questioners that it was simply curiosity that had taken him down to the Clyde on the evening in question. He had an alibi for his absence from the march to the walls: he had been working as a warehouseman in Glasgow on the Saturday afternoon and only returned to Parkhead after the crowd had left the sheddings at Parkhead cross. The surgeon William Lyon claimed that he had been watching from his house when the crowd gathered, but hadn't joined in, preferring instead to survey the demolition from Springbank, the estate to the east of Belvidere; he was in bed by eleven o'clock, or so he testified. Tellingly, shrewdness was one of the characteristics for which Lyon was later known, as well as 'directness of purpose, and fertility of resources'.[6] John Williamson admitted having been part of the assembly that walked down Dalmarnock Road to the Dyke, and remained as part of it as the walls were flattened. But he said he was merely a spectator. John

McCracken the baker claimed that it was only at 11.30 p.m., at the request of two of his neighbours, that he had gone down to the river near the Clyde Iron Works, 'for the purpose of seeing what was going on at Mr Harvie's property'. He did admit that he had seen 'three persons with guns which they discharged towards the south, but the military were not in sight at this time', though they came immediately afterwards. But that was as far as he was prepared to go. He maintained that he knew none of the gunmen, nor did he see anyone else in the crowd, other than his own journeyman, Gilbert Watson.

On close reading of their testimonies, the assurances of the original committee members that they had no knowledge of what was going to happen on the evening of 21 June, and that they had nothing to do with the demolition of Harvie's walls, ring hollow. Naively or otherwise, John McCracken even admitted that he had played a small part in the operation. He had 'carried down a crowbar . . . which on reaching the wall he stuck in to the green that anyone might take it'. A remarkable confession. George Allan's declaration that he had only watched the demolition effort at a distance was plainly untrue. James Scobbie was a twenty-seven-year-old Parkhead weaver who was more forthcoming than most of those present on 21 June. Probably scared into partial co-operation as he had been seen on the top of one of the walls, and having also admitted that he had assisted in 'tumbling aside' the stones thrown from both of the walls, he didn't hold back. Allan, Scobbie affirmed, was one of those who had been 'going about cheering and encouraging the persons who were demolishing the dyke'. The names of others he recognised were also drawn out by his main interrogator, Rose Robinson: Alexander M'Phie; Andrew Adamson, another Parkhead weaver whom Scobbie had seen working with a smith's hammer and a jumper preparing a hole into which gunpowder was to be placed; Walter Winning, yet another weaver from Parkhead he had spotted using a large hammer; Dugald Cameron from Camlachie, who had been sitting on top of the eastmost dyke; and John Baird, a collier, and Joseph Boyle, a weaver, both armed with guns.

There is no need to dig far into the evidence before William Lyon's protestations of innocence start to look somewhat less than convincing. There are grounds to suspect that he may even have been one of those orchestrating proceedings on 21 June. Lyon was a member of the committee that had explored the legal options for removing Harvie's obstructions. We know too that he had been on a reconnoitring mission at Harvie's Dyke on the evening prior to the riot. And while he maintained that he had simply watched as the crowd assembled, John McCracken, one of the two more co-operative committee members, testified that he and several others had met with Lyon after they had heard Fraser's drum patrol. Indeed, by this time, according to Williamson, another committee member, it was common knowledge in Parkhead that the plan that evening was to 'make a way or passage along the side of the river which had formerly been in use and which had been interrupted by the wall that Mr Harvie had built'. If this is true, Lyon would have been in no doubt about what was happening. But there is also circumstantial evidence that points to his deeper, surreptitious role in the Harvie's Dyke affair, even if during questioning he suggested that it was George Allan who had initiated the discussion about how to react to the construction of Harvie's walls. At the first, 12 June, meeting, a collection had been made, to fund the committee's activities – at this stage to consult legal authorities. Initially John Marshall, the Westmuir grocer, had acted as treasurer. But when Marshall resigned along with the rest of the committee on 19 June it was Lyon who, as he himself admitted, undertook to hold onto the £2 or so that had been raised for the campaign. It seems entirely likely that it was from this source that the half-crown payment for John Fraser's services was taken, and that this was the 'fund' which George Allan mentioned in his evidence which had been used for the five pounds of gunpowder that had blown up the Dyke. Furthermore, something that suggested the authorities knew that Lyon had been close to the heart of the business was their suspicion that he had held a de-briefing meeting in his house on the morning after the riot, which he denied. Finally, although this is unlikely to have been more than a very minor motive, he may have harboured a dislike of Harvie's involvement in the spirit trade. The evidence for this is slim, but it is the case that ten years later he wrote a paper for Glasgow's Royal Society of Physicians and Surgeons on the subject of delirium tremens, of which cases he had seen 'considerable' numbers.[7] This distressing condition he ascribed not to drinking ale or porter (although he was concerned at the 'evils and severe consequences' of inebriation, however effected), but to spiritous liquors – the basis of Harvie's fortune (see Plate 7).

But the person who not only somewhat clumsily exposed his own involvement and under duress provided the prosecution with a hefty volume of incriminating evidence against most of the individuals who actually destroyed the walls, was John Williamson. As a teacher, Williamson may have emphasised to his pupils the importance of honesty, and probably had more respect for the legal process than most of his neighbours. Under interrogation, he could well have panicked, rather than giving the guarded answers most other witnesses had offered. However, he was less accomplished in the art of evasion. Perhaps, unlike the other professional man with whom he associated, Dr Lyon, or McCracken the baker or Marshall the grocer, he was less deeply integrated into the community, and had less regard for its inhabitants and their mores.

Consciously or not, Williamson revealed how well informed he was about what was going to happen on 21 June. He knew that gunpowder was to be purchased and used. He even named his sources: George Allan, John McCracken and George Tait, a tailor in Parkhead. Furthermore, after conceding that he had been at the meeting on 19 June – but only for a 'short time' – he let slip the fact that some of those present (whose names he was unable to recall) had been asked to correspond with 'the people at Bridgeton' to 'know what they were disposed to do with regard to removing Mr Harvie's walls'.

It was Williamson who was most explicit about the identity of the shirt-sleeved man he had seen making paper cartridges with the gunpowder and setting fire to it prior the explosion: Alexander M'Phie. In a poorly judged attempt to lighten the case against M'Phie by saying he had not spent so much time at the second wall, Williamson further implicated himself by admitting that he had spoken to M'Phie 'for a considerable time' on the riverbank. Others he named included Dugald Cameron, James Scobbie and John Gilmour, the young collier who had been attempting to loosen the Dyke masonry with a hammer.

To be fair to Williamson, some of the evidence he presented did help temper the prosecution's case. He denied seeing anyone with a pistol, for example, and while 'several' people – five or six he supposed when further examined – had been carrying firearms, he said he thought these were fowling pieces rather than muskets. The former were for shooting birds while muskets had a military purpose. That weapons had been carried at all, he justified by claiming they were for self-defence, a consequence of Harvie's men shooting at William Lyon the night before. This was needlessly damning, given that most witnesses who said anything about guns swore they had been fired off simply to celebrate the wall's demise. That this happened before the military arrived was deemed important; to have been guilty of firing at the Enniskillens as they approached was a treasonable offence. Yet there were witnesses who were prepared to testify that this is exactly what did happen. But what weight to attach to their statements is open to question: Thomas Brown deponed that shots were fired after the cavalry had arrived. But Brown had been employed by Thomas Harvie.

Williamson found it hard to stay silent. Not only did he provide the names of those he had seen occupied on the walls but sometimes he offered precise details about who they were and where they lived, crucial information for the authorities as those concerned could be traced more easily. He obviously knew Parkhead well and was able to distinguish the various lands, and where they were located. So the weaver Joseph Bogle was from Harvie's Land, in Burgher Street. 'One Haddow' (David), who had worked on both walls, was the son of a change-keeper – or publican – whose premises were towards the east end of Camlachie. And if he sometimes struggled for an exact address, Williamson did his best to point out the general area where suspects could be found, as in the case of the collier John Baird, who was, he thought, from Finlayson's Land, or 'at least in a land at the west end of Parkhead'. He was stuck only with John Gilmour, who he had 'seen going about the east end of Camlachie' but didn't know where he stayed, or worked. Nor should he have; Gilmour was the from Gorbals.

Radical roots

Resulting from such intense questioning, a list of sixty-three suspects was drawn up in the two or three days following the initial arrests at and around Westthorn. They had, it was alleged:

> By beat of drum and proclamation by the common crier riotously and tumultuously, to the disturbance of the public peace, and to the alarm and terror of Thomas Harvie Esquire of Westthorn and his Servants, assembled and convocate on, or in the vicinity of the said Estate of Westthorn . . . [where the accused were] furnished and provided with crowbars, pinches, jumpers and hammers, mells and other implements with the premeditated, avowed, illegal and wicked purpose and intent on pulling down, destroying, razing and removing part of the said Thomas Harvie's stone walls situated at, or on, the Eastern and Western boundaries, and forming the March walls or fences of the said Estate of Westthorn and where the said walls terminated in the river Clyde.[8]

The defendants were accused too of engaging in assembling, exciting, encouraging, aiding and abetting in said unlawful and riotous proceedings, of using gunpowder and guarding and protecting their accomplices from the endeavours of the persons employed by Harvie to prevent the destruction and demolition of his walls.

But it was hard to pin anything substantial on most of those whom the Dragoons had arrested on 22 June. Indeed, so unsuccessful were the sheriff and his officers in prising out the evidence of direct involvement they required, all but one of the prisoners (probably Alexander M'Phie) were set free. Regardless, the investigations continued over the next few weeks.

After due consideration by sheriff Robinson of the many depositions in the case, the lengthy list was whittled down to half a dozen names. These included two men who had made themselves scarce after the demolition: Andrew Adamson and Walter Winning. Both men were in their thirties and earned their living as handloom weavers in Parkhead. Adamson had been seen making a hole in the west wall with a jumper, as well as betraying by his demeanour his obvious pleasure in the walls' demolition. Winning had been witnessed acting in a similar manner. On 8 August the six main suspects were served with arrest warrants by the sheriff substitute, along with some others who were still under suspicion.

Those who, as we have seen, had been operating behind the scenes and had almost certainly been plotting the downfall of Harvie's walls – Allan, Lyon, McCracken and others – were not among the small group who were now under the closest scrutiny. Even some who had admitted being at the scene of the disorder and having participated – but largely only as cheerleaders – were spared. For the great majority there was insufficient evidence for a successful prosecution. Particularly frustrating for the authorities was when eyewitnesses were brought face to face with the suspects. Whatever they had testified earlier in the confines of the prosecutors' offices, in person they denied having seen the accused at the walls or even, in some instances, knowing them at all.

The prosecuting authorities had also failed to land what for them may have been bigger catches. Top of the initial list of suspects was Fauldhouse Wilson, who, as we have seen, was the driving force behind the colliers' union in 1817 and very much implicated in the Radical Rising of 1820. Taking the route from involvement in trade clubs or unions to politics was not uncommon. As relatively few working people had experience of political activism, or of public-facing organisations, experienced, able individuals like Wilson were in demand and able to move seamlessly between societies.[9] He had avoided prosecution in 1820, however, and did so again in 1823, partly because little evidence about what part he played in the wall's demolition was presented. Additionally, he had become a special constable (see Plate 8).

Wilson took the decision to sign on in this capacity rather late in the day. He was not among the first tranche of recruits to this role in Glasgow. In 1817 a Secret Service Committee of Glasgow's Police Commission had taken on some 700 special constables. By 1820 there were 900. The 1821 Police Act placed greater emphasis on surveillance within the community, with the aim of identifying criminal and subversive activity and nipping it in the bud. This may well have been when Fauldhouse Wilson began to consider joining the watching wing of the police force. Informer recruits included people formerly associated with offenders, based within their communities, who would be in a position to identify potential trouble-makers and, critically, where they lived.[10] If his own testimony is to be believed, Fauldhouse Wilson was sworn in as a special constable for the county of Lanark in March 1823. He was now thirty-seven years old, living in Westmuir and working again as a weaver. How many children he had is not known, but he definitely had a 'little daughter' to support. In fact, Wilson explained his presence at the Westthorn walls on the evening of 21 June as the need to find her, as she had joined the crowd intent on pulling down the dykes. In the wake of the 1820 rebellion many employers in Glasgow had determined to rid their workforce of suspected radicals, and Wilson could well have struggled to find paid work, of which he was now desperately in need.

Wilson was not one of those arrested that night, so perhaps he was telling the truth when he said he had returned home after the large dyke was destroyed. Interviewed on 25 June, four days afterwards, he said little that would have been of use to the authorities, conceding only that he had heard that Alexander M'Phie had been responsible for drilling the hole in the wall into which gunpowder had been placed. Whether or not he was playing a dual role – as law officer and local organiser – is impossible to say. Asked by his inquisitors why he had not intervened in what was a breach of the public peace, Wilson responded – with some justification – that as the sole special constable present, this would have been in vain. Anyway, he hadn't considered it part of his duties, which were to watch and report. The case against him was dropped, leaving us in the dark as to whether his earlier radicalism had translated into active opposition to Thomas Harvie's attempts to remove people's liberty to walk along the Clyde. But if that was the case, the fact that he named M'Phie, who was one of the men eventually found guilty, marks him out as an unreliable ally.

An equally intriguing link with the 1820 rising was John or Robert Craig. Craig's was the second name on George Salmond's list of those he wished to have apprehended and examined for their part in destroying Harvie's walls.[11] In his mid forties at that time, Craig was one of the three weavers believed to have produced the text of the treasonable *Address* that was one of the signals for the rising of April 1820. Craig may even have been the lead author. After the first batch of the notice was printed, copies had been sent to Craig's house. From here Fauldhouse Wilson then arranged for them to be posted up in and around Glasgow.

This, however, was not Craig's first association with radicalism. He had been present at the Thrushgrove meeting in October 1816 – an impressively well-attended demonstration of middle- and working-class reformers demanding a 'redress of grievances'. Handloom weavers, the most distressed group of workers in the post-war era, were in the vanguard of what was then the largest ever political meeting in Scotland. This was held on the estate – Thrushgrove – of James Turner, a tobacco dealer, as Glasgow's magistrates had refused to permit the gathering to take place within the Barony. Thrushgrove was outside, to the north. Perceived to be well connected in radical circles, immediately afterwards Craig had been approached by the government spy and agent provocateur Alexander Richmond, who tried to tempt him to join a large-scale radical rising. Craig attested many years later that he had turned down Richmond's overture.

Spy or not, Craig had played a dangerous game in 1820. He was one of the district delegates to the Scottish co-ordinating committee, variously referred to as the Secret, Central or General Committee – or even the Provisional Government – that was planning the forthcoming rising along military lines. Meetings were held during the evenings and into the nights, but rarely in the same place: delegates did what they could to avoid suspicion, and arrest. In February 1820, however, twenty-seven men were seized, for fomenting 'the most wicked Conspiracy ever contrived in this Country'.[12] Craig was one of them, but possibly owing to a lack of incriminating evidence he avoided punishment. The following month he was reported to have been present during drilling sessions by the banks of the Forth and Clyde Canal, or at Merchants Park, later the city's Necropolis, under the instruction of men with military experience. He was also seen drilling a party of pikemen in Sauchiehall Road. It was reported that he had provided the pikes and other weapons and was himself armed with a sword and pistol.[13] His nephew, whose name we don't know, was believed to have been one of the party that marched to Carron Iron Works in April 1820, although he managed to escape arrest after the skirmish at Bonnymuir.

The unnamed nephew's uncle, John (or Robert) Craig, escaped too, although not from Bonnymuir, as he had taken no part in this venture. Even so, Craig was a wanted man after April 1820. A £300 reward was offered by Glasgow's Lord Provost Henry Monteith and the town's magistrates for information on those who had issued the *Address*.[14] As one of the principal ringleaders, it appears that Craig went into hiding before fleeing the country, measures taken by hundreds of others who could have been implicated in the failed revolution, or who were disappointed with the outcome.[15] According to one recent history of the events of 1820, Craig, like some other radical leaders, was never heard of again.[16]

Yet he was. As he was involved at Harvie's Dyke, like his close ally Fauldhouse Wilson, Craig had clearly returned at some point before 1823. He would have felt secure among his former political allies and much of the community in Parkhead. One of the frustrations for the authorities searching for suspects in such localities – even someone as well known as Craig – was that there was no official record of addresses and, as we have seen, even after the Glasgow Police Act of 1821, information of this kind was almost impossible to acquire in the villages to the east of the city.

Despite his participation in plans to use physical force in 1820, Craig's own testimony, given many years later, in 1834, suggests that he was a reformer rather than one of the more fervent radicals. It is possible that, like other despairing Whigs and reformers whose frustration over the failure of governments to ease the lot of the working class had caused a few of them to take up arms in 1820, he had considered whether the use of force was the best way of obtaining redress. The year 1819 had seen enormous suffering for much of the working class, above all the ubiquitous weavers, but the worst was over by 1821.

Craig's interests, however, went beyond the crisis years of 1819–20. He had no reservations about admitting his support for universal suffrage and annual parliaments. In order to achieve these, he favoured petitioning both Houses of Parliament. Certainly after 1820 (if not before), this was his favoured means of bringing about political change. Indeed, later in life Craig was renowned for his commitment to what he termed 'moral suasion'.[17]

Craig's moderatism becomes evident through witnesses' accounts of his conduct during the assault on Harvie's walls. He was on horseback, orchestrating the crowd. In this capacity he was able to draw on his experience of organising bodies of men in 1819 and 1820. More peaceably in June 1823, though, it appears that his main contribution was as a cheerleader, urging the spectators express their joy as parts of the walls came tumbling down.

But that wasn't quite all. Craig demanded self-discipline on the part of supporters of both the rising of 1820 and the fall of Harvie's Dyke: it is a trope that links both incidents. One of the striking features of the

1820 *Address* was the effort made by its authors to persuade readers of the reasonableness of their demand for freedom from despotism. We are not 'that Lawless, Sanguinary Rabble' our enemies portray us as being, it asserted. Indeed, in order to demonstrate that the fears of the 'oppressors' were unfounded, the authors of the *Address* thought it 'indispensably necessary to DECLARE inviolable, all Public and Private Property'. They also called on the Justices of the Peace and other legal authorities to punish anyone found guilty of pillaging or plundering such property.[18] This was why, when visiting the houses of farmers in search of weapons such as guns, it was not unknown for the radical intruders to insist that they were not intent on robbery, and would return what they had taken later.[19]

Of all the many individuals examined in June or over the summer of 1823, only one witness was prepared to name Craig – testament perhaps to the imperviousness of the protective shield provided by the Parkhead community. It was the youthful weaver from Camlachie, John West, who testified that he had seen Craig, whom he knew only by sight. Craig, West testified, had addressed the crowd, and 'told them they were to do nothing but what they should do . . . that they were to assist and take back what belonged to them before'. Westthorn mansion was not to be damaged even though this was an attraction for some of the hotter heads among those present. It was reported later that in order to avoid damaging those parts of the wall that were on Harvie's property, a line of chalk was drawn to show where this was.[20] Whether or not under Craig's influence, according to another source the 'general cry' was to 'injure nothing but what belonged to the public'.[21] For more cautious, prudent radicals like Craig, large-scale protest was one thing, wanton damage to property and individuals quite another, and to be avoided.

After the attack on the walls Craig seems to have slipped away, retreating once more into the anonymity of the weaver neighbourhood of Parkhead, where he returned to the loom and helped raise those of his daughters who hadn't married. He did not lose his zeal for agitating on behalf of the working classes, though. In 1826 he chaired a meeting in Glasgow of the emigration societies that called for additional government support to assist distressed weavers and their families to leave Scotland and make a better life abroad. Nine years later, now in his early sixties, he was still active, calling at a meeting in Tollcross for Parliament to be petitioned with a demand for the total abolition of the Corn Laws that ever since their introduction in 1815 had been blamed for keeping the price of bread artificially high.

Four from sixty-three: guilty men (or scapegoats)

Ultimately, Sir William Rae, the Lord Advocate, in the interest of the crown and on the advice of Archibald Alison, decided that there was sufficient evidence to indict and send for trial only four of the suspects: M'Phie, whose skills as a coal mine sinker were essential for driving holes into the walls and using explosives; the coal hewer John Baird; and the weavers Andrew Adamson and Walter Winning. All four were from Parkhead. Their 'wicked, riotous and felonious' crimes, of 'mobbing, rioting and assembling in large bodies' should be 'severely punished', to deter others from similar offences 'in all time coming'. It was particularly shocking that they and the 'mob' they had assembled had been equipped with 'implements of destruction' and discharged loaded firearms to 'deter all well-disposed persons from interrupting the . . . operations'.[22]

Despite the substantial body of incriminating evidence that had been stacked up against them, during questioning prior to the trial each of the principal suspects protested their innocence on all of the charges. All they had done, they offered by way of explanation, was follow the rest of the crowd. Alexander M'Phie admitted only to giving a 'huzza' when 'the stones were overturning'. Asked about the hole that had been driven into the Dyke, he answered that he knew nothing. He had heard that gunpowder was being bought but, he declared, he could not explain its purpose or who had bought it 'or what became of it'. Like his comrades, he denied knowing any of the people in the crowd – other than his brother. When questioned about individual suspects – John McCracken and John Williamson – he was adamant that he had seen neither man. Andrew Adamson was equally sure that he hadn't seen anyone he knew.

Their protestations fell on deaf ears.

The date for the four men's trial before the High Court of Justiciary was set for late in September 1823, the next time the biannual circuit court would sit in Glasgow. There was a typically varied diet, including murder, domestic violence, an attack on a cotton spinner and housebreaking. The venue was the rapidly expanding, status-conscious town's new jail and courthouse, situated on the western corner of Glasgow Green where it joined with the Saltmarket. Inaugurated in 1814, the imposing institution was designed in what became known as the 'Greek Revival' style by William Stark, a Dunfermline-born architect much admired by the well-known Scottish advocate Lord Cockburn as well as Sir Walter Scott.[23] While Stark did some design work at Abbotsford, his special interest was lunatic asylums; he had designed Glasgow's in 1807, with others following, in Dundee and Gloucester.[24] The eastern front of the new justiciary building boasted a Doric portico of six columns, with a sculptured pediment.[25] With fifty-eight cells instead of the thirty-two that had stretched the capacity of the old Tolbooth in the heart of Glasgow at the Trongate, the new premises were larger and grander. The same could hardly be said of the cells. Influenced by more modern theories about the most appropriate treatment of prisoners, Stark clad in iron the two cells in which those sentenced to death were held, thereby superseding the 'degrading' practice of fettering those condemned to death in chains.

The September diet began on 22 September, at 10.30 a.m. Prior to this, a party of soldiers, accompanied by the beating of a drum, had marched out to meet the two presiding judges as they neared the city, and acted as a guard of honour as they approached the courthouse. It was a solemn occasion, 'calculated to inspire awe and reverence amongst the people'.[26] The spacious circular courtroom was forbidding in its theatricality but, softening the atmosphere, around the judge's raised bench and the advocates' tables were bouquets of flowers from the city's Botanic Gardens. A short prayer was offered by the chaplain to the court, the Revd Thomas Chalmers, the charismatic evangelical minister of Tron parish. The jury was called. Fifteen was the usual number. The Lord Justice Clerk (David Boyle, Lord Boyle), presiding alongside the Hon. Lord Hermand, was driven to express his irritation at the failure to attend for jury duty of Sir Charles M'Donald Lockart of Lee and Carnwath and Sir Robert Pollock of Pollock. Their elite status notwithstanding, they were each fined 100 merks. For this reason or perhaps deliberately, the jury, as an observer from the *Caledonian Mercury* noted, was 'more from the middling ranks of the lieges than usual'. Despite the intimidating surroundings, the frank, unsophisticated testimony provided by one witness, the husband of a monoglot Gael, Margaret M'Kirdy, from Port Glasgow, who had been assaulted in the street, induced howls of hilarity. So much so that the Lord Justice Clerk threatened to have the next person seen laughing taken into custody.

It was not until the following day – a Tuesday, and cold outside – that the Harvie's Dyke case was opened. Again, the military had escorted the judges from their hotel to the court. The proceedings had begun slightly earlier than the previous day, at 10 a.m. There was then a delay as two more jurymen were reported to have absented themselves. The prisoners awaiting trial were returned to their cells. Matters resolved, Mary Little was then tried and found guilty of stealing several rolls of cloth as well as 'being by habit and repute a thief'. She was duly sentenced to fourteen years' transportation.

This hardly augured well as the men from Parkhead – the Harvie's Dyke four – were called. Since it opened in 1814 the new jail had been the site of fifteen hangings, including that of Wilson, the Strathaven radical, in August 1820.

The panels (the accused) were led from their cells along a passageway to emerge in the accused's box directly in front of the judges' bench, the highest feature of the courtroom, contrasting symbolically with the lowest, the prisoners' pen. Behind them, on rows of long wooden pew-like seats, were crowded members of the public. For the prisoners the contrast with the gloom from which they had emerged was noticeable, but less intense than it might have been in the diluted autumn light that shone softly through seven long windows at the west end of the room.

There was then another pause in the proceedings. M'Phie had failed to appear, and was declared an outlaw.[27] However, Alexander Earle Monteith, one of the men's two lawyers, pressed on, contesting the relevance of the interdict. He began by arguing that from time immemorial there had been a passage along the north bank of the Clyde. Thomas Harvie therefore had built walls on land 'not his own', but on public property. Monteith also denied that the proceedings on 21 June had been tumultuous. He proposed instead that the walls had been taken down peaceably. Notwithstanding Monteith's reputation as a successful barrister, his plea on this occasion was dismissed. The question, the judge ruled, was not whether Harvie had erected his dyke legally or not, but whether Adamson, Baird, M'Phie and Winning had been justified in demolishing it by force.

The exact order in which things happened next is not entirely clear, but it appears that at this point M'Phie arrived – or was brought in. After consultation with the lawyers defending them, the four detainees were advised to plead guilty. This they did, in the hope that they could avoid the draconian sentence of transportation (or worse) and a future furth of Scotland – the customary fate of those committing similar or even lesser crimes. Following their admission, their second lawyer, John Jardine, entered a plea of mitigation on their behalf. The panels, Jardine contended, were contrite. Poor 'unlearned men', they had been misled by legal opinion, and believed that the law authorised them to act as they did. Yes, a large crowd had formed, but there had been no malice in their actions, nor any hurt been done to any individual. He acknowledged that firearms had been used, but only as the crowd had dispersed. He concluded his speech by claiming that the prisoners were of irreproachable character; three of them were family men. M'Phie alone was a bachelor who lived with his mother. In his case, Jardine's unqualified character reference was stretching the limits of credibility.

Despite the eloquence with which Jardine made his case, the Lord Justice Clerk seems not to have been convinced. To act in a violent manner as the prisoners had was illegal. Indeed, other than riots which had involved bloodshed and other 'scenes of cruelty', he could not recollect one of 'a more serious, grave, or weighty nature'. Violent assaults of this nature were 'a direct levy of war on the King'.[28] Whoever had advised those involved had 'betrayed great ignorance of the law of Scotland'. The jury was of a similar mind and found the men guilty; after all, they had that very morning admitted their own parts in the crime.

Events then took a surprising twist. The advocate-depute, Archibald Alison, was called to move for sentence. To the astonishment of the court and the delight of the members of the public present in the gallery, he called for clemency, partly on the grounds that the guilty men had indeed acted on legal advice. This had been to the effect that they were within their rights to remove Harvie's walls. The advice was erroneous, but in seeking it they had done the right thing.[29] Whether or not this was part of Alison's reasoning is not known, but the prisoners, it was argued, were not typical criminals. True, they were weavers and coal workers, two occupations that were commonly associated with social crimes of this sort, that is in defence of popular rights in opposition to the dictates of the market and the primacy of property that were central to the processes of commercialisation and industrialisation in the first half of the nineteenth century. Two of them were slightly older than normal and, as was pointed out on their behalf, three of them had families to support. At this time in Scotland, convicted criminals were likely to be under thirty years of age, with two-fifths of crimes being carried out by teenagers.[30] Winning thought he was thirty-eight, Adamson was thirty-three, M'Phie twenty-eight and Baird twenty-four, that is an average of thirty years.

Whatever the men's personal circumstances, persuaded by Alison's intervention, the judge sentenced the prisoners to six months' incarceration. They were also ordered to keep the peace for three years, subject to a penalty of £30 if this was breached.

Without Alison's mediation, the Lord Justice Clerk made clear to the court, they would have been sentenced to transportation. On the contrary, he was now persuaded that the four men were reasonable and law-abiding, and perhaps worth saving from further criminality. Soft-pedalling even further, he ordered the city's magistrates to 'attend to the comfort of the prisoners during their period of confinement' and to take care that they be not corrupted by 'vicious' fellow prisoners.[31] This would not be easy to achieve. Both the town's new jail and the bridewell were overcrowded, resulting in no 'distinct line of demarcation as to the degrees of crime', a failing greatly deplored by Lord Boyle. Without separation of this kind, the judge regretted, no amount of religious instruction could 'prevent the growth of evil'.

The Lord Justice Clerk's consideration for the well-being of the four convicted men was welcome. But without their principal breadwinners, the wives and families of the incarcerated men struggled to make ends meet. According to one account, they were soon close to starving.[32] Consequently, a petition was drawn up and subscriptions called for to create a fund to support the absent men's distressed households. Contributions from 'the genteel part of the citizens' raised more than £100, a sum supplemented by funds garnered by a committee of 'respectable' neighbours from the Parkhead district. This was not sufficient for the entire period of the men's prison terms, but for as long as they were made, the weekly payments to their dependants offered some relief from the privations of poverty.

Physical force

At this point the names of all but one of those imprisoned for their part in the defence of the right to walk along the Clyde unhindered disappear from the historical record. The exception was Alexander (Sandy) M'Phie. He was of an angrier disposition than many of his counterparts about the hardships endured by working people. Well-known as a man who shared the values and attitudes of those from his neighbourhood and less cowed than many by the agencies of the state – above all the military and local constables – he was also prepared to meet force with violence.

Within months of his release from prison, M'Phie was one of eleven men arrested and accused of threatening and intimidating a handloom weaver in Camlachie. This was George Smith, whose three sons also worked with him – Andrew, William and Lockhart. Smith was one of the many employees of Peter Hutcheson, an influential Glasgow manufacturer who was alleged to have been intent on reducing weavers' wages across the board – although this was refuted by Hutcheson. The repeal of the unpopular Combination laws in 1824, led in Parliament by the Aberdeen MP Joseph Hume, heralded a wave of collective action on the part of many trades, including the handloom weavers. By September a combination of weavers in the west of Scotland had pressured several of

Hutcheson's workers to leave his employment.[33] For reasons not altogether clear – although perhaps fearing that Hutcheson would eventually monopolise the weaver workforce (he had already begun to recruit workers in Ireland) – the Weavers' Association had vowed to put him out of business. Smith, however, had refused to comply and had accepted four new webs, and was consequently targeted by members of the combination. Intimidation was one of the methods used to persuade him to change his mind – most notably by a mob outside his workshop parading an effigy of Smith being whipped and hanged, with a placard around his neck displaying the words 'A Traitor to the Cause' in large capital letters. After marching the effigy around the village – a warning to others of their fate should they follow Smith's lead – a riot ensued, during which the police, led by superintendent David Hardie, were driven off, until a rumour that the military were to intervene caused the crowd of around 800 people to disperse.[34] This was followed by the breaking of the windows of Smith's house and anonymous letters threatening further damage to Smith and his family and property – exposing them to 'great terror' and fear for their lives.

What concerned the authorities was not only that this incident was the first serious riot and workers' combination since the repeal of the former Combination Acts. 'Remarkable' too was the involvement of M'Phie who, following his trial the previous year, was under caution for good behaviour.

In order to crush and prevent such dangerous occurrences in future, given the 'the state of ferment among the working classes' and alarm felt by the 'well disposed', Glasgow's procurator fiscal argued for an immediate trial. Aware of the seriousness of the disturbance, the recently promoted crown advocate Archibald Alison urged that rather than being tried at the forthcoming circuit court in Glasgow, the High Court in the capital was a more appropriate venue. Mounting a case for the prosecution, however, was easier said than done. The most prominent of the rioters had 'gone out of the way', and while some of them returned to Camlachie, such was the closeness of the community that they were hard to locate. Nevertheless, a few of the suspects were arrested but freed on bail. Meanwhile Smith and his family even in the early weeks of 1825 continued to be harassed, now by the associates of the original offenders. And despite the evident distress of the Smith household, the authorities struggled to bring the offenders to trial, as the only persons who were prepared to identify them, and testify to their actions, were Smith himself and his sons.

This was not the only occasion when M'Phie narrowly avoided the clutches of the law. Late in February 1826, he along with two others, Robert Hamilton, a weaver who had recently deserted from the 79th Regiment, and Samuel McMenemy, were arrested and imprisoned in Glasgow's Tolbooth. M'Phie and McMenemy lived on the same stair in the same building in Parkhead. Indeed, confirming the foresight of the judge at the trial involving M'Phie in September 1823 and his concern about the mixing of prisoners regardless of the seriousness of their crimes, the three men's 'intimacy' had begun when they had been prisoners in Glasgow jail.

Their crime, allegedly committed on a country lane on the outskirts of the village of Camlachie on the dark, damp night of 24 February, had been to 'violently, wickedly and feloniously' assault twenty-six-year-old Benjamin Lamont. Lamont was a soldier in the 78th Regiment of Foot who had been travelling from Skene near Aberdeen to Glasgow to rejoin his regiment in Cork. Having reached Camlachie via Edinburgh, he had got lost and was seeking directions to take him to Duke Street. Not only did the assailants rob feather-capped, tartan-trewed Lamont of his money, in the form of five Bank of Aberdeen one-pound notes which he had been given by his crofter father, they also took his pocketbook and regimental passport, as well as some clothing including 'a printed cotton handkerchief with yellow and red flowers'. Lamont's assailants also shot him, as he lay on the ground. The shots – which shattered a bone and lodged in his left thigh – comprised ball, slugs and 'tile or delft ware or some other hard and lethal substance to the Prosecutors unknown'. This may have been the 'chuckie stanes' the accused had been seen picking up prior to the shooting. The soldier's wounds, which were treated initially by William Lyon, the Parkhead surgeon, proved fatal. Lockjaw (tetanus) set in and Lamont died in Glasgow's infantry barracks in the Gallowgate three weeks later. M'Phie, Hamilton and McMenemy were therefore charged with murder as well as robbery.[35]

Their trial, in the High Court in Edinburgh, was held on 19 September. The three men were known to have been hostile to soldiers – presumably owing to their role in breaking up popular disturbances; M'Phie was said have cried out 'B . . . of hell' immediately prior to the attack on Lamont.[36] Hamilton evidently had little love of army service. At the time of shooting he was living in terror of being discovered as a deserter and had even worked underground in one of Colin Dunlop's coal pits to stay out of public view. Witnesses in Camlachie on the night of the assault on Lamont, which had followed on from a wedding in Parkhead during which guns had been fired, also testified to a general feeling that there would be a 'dust' or death of some kind that night. Yet the three men escaped a custodial sentence, or hanging. Their defence was of alibi, with witnesses on their behalf all testifying that the three accused were elsewhere at the time of the assault. M'Phie it was claimed had returned from his work as a shanker between five and six o'clock and immediately gone to bed at his widowed mother's, where later he had been joined by his brother.

After a lengthy summing up by the judge, the Lord Justice Clerk, the divided jury delivered a verdict of Not Proven, notwithstanding the Lord Advocate's efforts to persuade members that the prosecution case was robust and that the panels' defence relied heavily on the testimonies of close relatives. The accused, the Lord Justice concluded, had made 'the narrowest of all possible escapes'. Good-looking young men, but not seemingly 'of spotless character', they were warned about their future conduct, advice their absence from the criminal record thereafter it appears they may well have taken.

The other way

The cause for which M'Phie and his three companions who had been prosecuted and incarcerated for their role in the attack on Harvie's Dyke, however, was not ignored. On the contrary, support for it intensified. Within days of the demolition of the walls, a broadsheet headed in large, bold letters, 'The Rights of the Citizens of Glasgow to Walk on the Banks of the Clyde, ASSERTED AND DISPUTED' had been printed and was being sold in Glasgow, in an attempt to extend the base of support. A new campaign committee was instituted. Now it was in the courts that the contest with Thomas Harvie was to be fought. Harvie responded in kind, but only after attempting by brute force and bullying to preserve what he considered to be his inalienable property rights.

Glasgow's people – from a broad spectrum of backgrounds – were not to be intimidated. The struggle over Harvie's Dyke was far from over.

It would, however, take a different form.

4

Taking on Goliath: Courtroom Contests – Glasgow and Edinburgh to the House of Lords

How challenging the battle with Thomas Harvie would be had become apparent within twenty-four hours of the assault on his walls on the evening of 21 June. A popular single-page poem sold on the streets of Glasgow a few years later recounts what happened:

> On the next night, before 'twas light,
>   The Masons were collected,
> With Stone and Lime, in a short time,
>   Again it was erected;
> There it stood like a Pyramid,
>   To be a world's wonder,
> 'Twas thought again the sons of men,
>   Could not pull it asunder.[1]

Little poetic licence was employed in this depiction of Harvie's response to the destruction of his property. As soon as the Monday following the riot, he had recruited and set to work 'as many masons . . . as could get room'. Their task was to reconstruct the Westthorn walls, only more forbiddingly than those that had been destroyed the previous Saturday.[2] There were echoes in this of Sir Robert Walpole – Britain's first prime minister – who as ranger (through his son) of London's Richmond park where he enjoyed the peace, hunted deer and entertained his mistress, had more than once had to rebuild the high walls around the park which were periodically pulled down by aggrieved parishioners who were denied entry and so lost access to gravel, water, wood and game.

If Harvie was to maintain the privacy of his Westthorn grounds by keeping people off his property, speed too was of the essence. Within hours of the last rioters being dragged out of the ditches or from the hedges where they had concealed themselves from the soldiery, local people had attempted to pass once more along the riverbank, through and over the rubble of what was left of the recently toppled walls. But to no avail. The path was blocked by the cavalry, whose numbers were reinforced in the evenings by both horsemen and foot soldiers as the pressure from would-be walkers to go past mounted.[3] At one time there may have been a thousand people on the riverbank, straining to get by, but unable to advance further. To do so would have been unwise: there was a high risk they would be shot at. A military presence had been ordered by the sheriff, Rose Robinson, who rode out to the scene several times over the next few days. His aim was to ensure that Harvie's masons were able to proceed with their rebuilding work unmolested.

Yet Harvie deemed even his rebuilt 'Pyramid' dyke to be an insufficient deterrent to would-be passers-by. As an indication of his dogged determination to close the passage and of the scant regard he had for his fellow citizens, he had cartloads of glass bottles tipped into the river, as he had done in 1822. With their 'savage' black broken-necks designed to cut the feet of children and anyone else who attempted to wade past the river end of the obstructing wall, this was what Peter Mackenzie described as a 'piece of heartless cruelty'. The top of the replacement dyke too was finished with rivetted iron stanchions and sharpened pikes, and studded with shards of broken glass.

In response, there was visceral anger over Harvie's actions among the largely working-class communities of Glasgow's east end. The impact of his renewed efforts to block the Clyde walkway, however, was much wider. Harvie's opponents now included growing numbers of people from elsewhere in the city who for generations had made use of the riverside walkway.

The struggle intensifies

Reaction to the events of midsummer 1823 was almost instantaneous. Even before the outpouring of support for Adamson, Baird, M'Phie and Winning following their trial and imprisonment late in September, an impromptu wave of hostility had been directed towards Harvie. He was subjected to verbal abuse as he passed by and lampooned in the press and in ballads which were 'publicly hawked through the streets of Glasgow, and greedily bought by all classes of the community'.[4] Even his former carter allies were said to have turned against him – 'cursing and swearing at their late favourite'.

From all quarters he was sent anonymous and intimidating letters, so many that Harvie believed a combination or plot existed 'to commit violence upon his property and person'. His suspicions were well founded.

'Sir,' wrote the writer of one letter sent to Harvie's Dunlop Street premises, 'there is twenty one of us sworne to cut your throat . . . and to brek into your house to lay holds of you.' So, he warned, 'loke to yourselv & take car of your hous in Glasgow'.[5] Some of his fellow proprietors with estates running down to the river had heard enough and had already begun to think twice about any plans they might have laid to erect walls that obstructed the footpath on the Clyde's north bank. The threatened barrier near Dalmarnock Bridge, for instance, which had precipitated the attack on Harvie's walls, was never built. Harvie, though, was not to be discouraged.

But it was not only Harvie's person and personal property that were targeted. His businesses too were under attack. His divans were shunned, former customers vanishing 'like a summer cloud'. Harvie's whiskies, once universally popular, were spurned by the city's spirit dealers, who went so far as to put up notices declaring that 'None of Tam Harvie's whisky retailed here, but only the true blue, the real Glenlivet etc.' As a result, his cash income plummeted, a matter that greatly concerned him and about which he evidently confided with his small circle of friends. The rumoured losses might have been easier to bear had he been able to sell as much coal as he had anticipated to domestic customers in Glasgow. 'Still he was check-mated . . . for the signal ran from street to street, and from almost house to house, "None of Tam Harvey's coals consumed here – let him burn his own fingers with them."'[6]

This wasn't the first time that the boycott weapon had been adopted against a Clyde-side property owner who had attempted to deny ordinary people the right to walk along the riverbank. Reliable evidence is thin on the ground, but there were some similarities in the case of Alexander Allan, some two decades earlier. Like Harvie, Allan was a successful entrepreneur – a merchant and manufacturer dealing in cotton and sugar – who around the turn of the nineteenth century had built a mansion house at Newhall, near Bridgeton, down river from Westthorn. Like Harvie, Allan was reportedly determined that 'there should be unbroken access from the grounds of his house to the bank of the river Clyde'.[7] Stymied by the existence of the public walk, he constructed a stone-walled, turf-covered tunnel through which walkers and horses and carts could pass. This concession notwithstanding, Allan's innovation (known locally as 'Allan's Pen') was so unpopular that 'the citizens found means of making the usurper regret his temerity in interfering with their right-of-way'. Reputedly, the handloom weavers he employed refused to work for him, even with the promise of additional pay. Although not directly related to this, thereafter Allan struggled financially owing to downturns in the cotton and sugar markets. Faced with these and other problems, he left Scotland for Ireland and died there in 1809.

By 1823 the boycott weapon was certainly familiar to the inhabitants of Glasgow's east end communities. Joseph Brayshaw the Yorkshire radical had been in Scotland advocating 'union societies', whose members were to refuse to purchase taxable goods. He toured the Glasgow region again in the aftermath of Peterloo, and in a speech delivered at a meeting of coal miners in Tollcross in October 1819 he had urged abstinence in order to deny the government revenue. Taxes accounted for almost half of the price paid for staple commodities; not only tea and tobacco but also other essentials such as shoes, soap and candles. Boycotting was a ploy periodically advocated by radical leaders in Scotland, some of whom were concerned by the physical and moral harm done by products such alcohol, tea and tobacco.[8] There was widespread resentment at the burden of taxation imposed on working people to fund sinecures and the pensions of state servants and other wasteful extravagance associated with a corrupt political system dominated by and serving the interests of the landed elite.

Notwithstanding the popular outrage directed against him, however, Harvie survived the temporary inconvenience of lost sales of whisky and coal; before long, his businesses had begun to recover. Indeed, he was not without his supporters. At the end of June 1823, a week after the assault on Harvie's walls, the *Glasgow Herald*, a newspaper that supported the commercial and propertied class, published a letter from 'A Friend to Justice', who argued that Harvie was within his rights to exclude the public from his lands. Those demanding to 'share with him a part of his Estate' were, the writer opined, 'guilty of a species of tyranny and oppression more reprehensible than can be traced to the mere exercise of a mistaken right'. There was 'nothing more inimical to the discovery of truth than popular clamour', which was loudest where prejudice was strongest.

But among the wider public Harvie's reputation seems never to have recovered. And retribution, when it came, was much more severe than blows to his esteem.

As far as the struggle over riverside access was concerned, of greater long-term significance was a more formal response to Harvie's actions. A new committee was formed in the summer of 1823, the composition of which differed markedly from that which had preceded the assault on Harvie's Dyke.

As we saw earlier in this book, even prior to Harvie's arrival at Westthorn, concerns had been raised about infringements 'made and making on the rights of individuals, and on the rights of the citizens at large, on the banks of the river, both above and below the town'. The reference here was to enclosures and what were called 'mounds or parallel banks' which proprietors of lands touching on the river had been constructing, apparently to protect their property when the river was swollen. Slipways and dockyards too had been built further down river. Even so, it was argued, the banks should remain open to the public and provision be made for an unobstructed pathway. This was the case made by one letter-writer to the editor of the *Glasgow Herald* in 1821. 'Owing to the natural advantages of Glasgow,' they wrote, 'it is perhaps the finest city in Europe.' It would be to the 'lasting shame and a disgrace to the present generation, should advantages, important to an extensive and increasing society, be tamely given up without a struggle'.[9] Had there been any suggestion that such a struggle would be violent or even that a demonstration be mounted in support of this end, it is highly doubtful if the letter would have been published in what was a deeply conservative newspaper.

However, one of the earliest signs of opposition to Harvie's encroachment was a letter written by 'Argus' to the editor of the *Glasgow Chronicle* in July 1822, shortly after the Westthorn walls had gone up. In this, the author drew attention to the appearance of recent incursions on the banks of the Clyde:

> It is with feelings of indignation and regret that I am forced to call the attention of our Citizens to a subject which perhaps will become of greater importance to them than they in the meantime are aware of, for it seems as if nothing is able to withstand the self-interestedness of some men. It is well known by every Citizen that the Walks on the banks of the Clyde have, from time immemorial, been kept sacred to the use of the Public, and it is only of late years that *Encroachments* have been made, which are now extending so rapidly, that, if not stopped by the exertions of the Burgesses, threaten to deprive us altogether of these Privileges.[10]

The 'privileges' concerned were not to be taken for granted. A high stone wall had been constructed on the south bank but, 'by some unknown Agency, a large Gap very soon appeared in it, through which the freest Access may now be obtained'. Credit was accorded to the magistrates of Rutherglen, who made sure on an annual basis during their 'Redding' or the riding of the burgh's sixteen-mile boundary by way of the march stones – some dating back to the sixteenth century – that there were no obstructions beyond Rutherglen Bridge. As early as 1813 Rutherglen's provost, 'on the part of the community' had ordered that £2 be added to a fund 'for keeping up the footpath between Rutherglen Bridge and Rutherglen'. Each time the riding was done, as had happened in 1815 and again in 1823, the party of inspectors, which usually included the provost and some baillies, found numerous stones missing, broken and sometimes defaced.[11] Offenders who had been found guilty of removing stones and encroaching onto burgh land were subject to 'exemplary punishment', with the highly distinctive missing stones being carved and replaced at the expense of recently elected burgesses – whose initials were also cut into the face of the stone. As many as seventy were replaced after a later riding in 1828. This concern for community rights and the attention Rutherglen town council paid to walkways along the Clyde and elsewhere in the burgh is in stark contrast to the apparent unwillingness of Glasgow's town council to intervene within their burgh boundary.

Thus, the appearance on the north bank of a '*new Proprietor*' – Thomas Harvie – who had erected high stone walls at the river's edge and blocked the passageway was for 'Argus' a matter of the gravest concern. By doing so Harvie had closed down 'one of the most delightful and sequestered Walks near to our City'. It was an act according to 'Argus' that was '*completely prohibitory*' of the ancient right of Glasgow's inhabitants to walk along the northern bank of the Clyde. He urged that 'the spirit of our Citizens . . . be roused to reclaim their right.' As the right had existed for more than forty years, and could be 'proved upon Oath', he contended, we 'may proceed with such Measures, as will cause this Wall of Division to be Razed to its Foundation'.

Despite the fervour of his language, 'Argus' called only for a public meeting and a fund to be set up, to rescue these rights from 'usurpation'.

His invocation had been ignored. But not for long.

'Argus' was a pseudonym used by Gabriel Neil, then in his mid twenties and later to become one of Glasgow's first antiquarians and a leading member of Glasgow's Archaeological Society. He was a familiar figure in the city, the partner with Francis Wood of Comedies in a small cotton spinning and power loom weaving manufacturing company in Bridgeton, a minor poet and member of Glasgow's literary coterie.[12] In 1845 he abandoned the partnership in order to devote more time to literary and historical pursuits. Although it was founded before he was born (in 1797), Neil was a supporter of the Friends of the People organisation and as a young man he became involved in protests over the plight of the working classes in the severe trade depression that had followed Britain's victory over France in 1815. With roots in what has been described as 'a restive, intensely literate religious subculture' that had influenced many of Scotland's weaver radicals in 1792, Neil possessed a fiercely evangelical, unashamedly Presbyterian religious temperament, at the core of which was a belief in liberty from oppression of all kinds.[13] He was very much a product of his time, and later in his life his 'oppressors' would include Jews and 'Papists'. Among his *bêtes noires* were the British government's apparent neglect of religion, that 'what is called emancipation was given to the popish party in Ireland', and the appointment of 'popish chaplains to jails'.[14]

Sharing the burden of letter writing was fifty-year-old James Duncan, a celebrated printer and bookseller with premises at the east end of Glasgow's Saltmarket and, in the early 1820s, a house, Hartfield, in Townhead. Very shortly thereafter (in 1824) he moved to Mosesfield, and became known by the name of this property . Nearby was Huntershill, birthplace of Thomas Muir, the reform advocate and political martyr of the early 1790s. Duncan too was deeply steeped in Glasgow's past: the family firm of which he was now head had been founded by his ancestor James Duncan in 1718, who published the first history of Glasgow, by John M'Ure, in 1736.[15] Both Duncan and Neil had been accustomed 'to Perambulate the Banks of the Clyde, and to take other short Tours in the Vicinity'. And for the next eleven months, from the summer of 1822, they wrote similar letters under a variety of pseudonyms in order to raise public awareness of Harvie's actions and the precedent these would set if not challenged. Indeed, Duncan's impact may have been greater than Neil's, being credited with having 'pummelled' Harvie with his 'many sharp and exquisite' letters. All this Harvie carefully noted and later grumbled about. What he termed 'anonymous communications' in the Glasgow newspapers and the 'insidious statements' they contained had been designed – he alleged – to 'excite the public to the destruction of the walls'.[16]

Harvie had a point. It was this consciousness raising on the part of Duncan and Neil that had provoked the public meetings in Parkhead which had culminated in the destruction of his barrier walls in June 1823.

Changing tack

Direct action had failed to change Harvie's mind. Instead, there was a resort to reason, in the form of an in-person plea to Harvie for a compromise solution before the reconstruction work on his walls was complete.

Duncan – a quiet and gentle man – arranged to visit Harvie in his 'whisky *divan*' in Dunlop Street, where he conducted much of his business. Accompanying Duncan was his agent and sympathetic lawyer friend Alexander Morrison. Duncan hoped that he could persuade Harvie – chastened perhaps by the clamour that his actions had precipitated – to allow the public to pass by Westthorn, if Harvie might be prepared to facilitate this by making a small opening in the wall. However, pompously – 'with the greatest *hauteur*' – and affecting to be insulted, Harvie conceded nothing. Indeed, despite some of his friends urging him to give way and thereby avoid even further public opprobrium, he defiantly dismissed Duncan's pleas. Westthorn was his property; if he surrendered on the point of the path, even as much as an inch, the logical consequence was that pedestrians – most of whom he considered to be lawless marauders and idlers – might even enter his dining room without permission. He would yield nothing, was prepared to take on any challenge and, if necessary, to spend £20,000 – as much as he had paid for the Westthorn estate – to maintain his dykes.

Duncan was disappointed and, unusually, angry, but undaunted. He was a crucial figure in the campaign against the walls that emerged following the midsummer evening's riot. His Saltmarket shop as well as a Mrs Anderson's tavern, the Sun, in the same street, were meeting places for Glasgow's literati. Their number included William Motherwell, editor of the recently published *Harp of Renfrewshire*. By this time Motherwell had abandoned his earlier radicalism and become a Tory; in 1819 he was appointed sheriff clerk depute in Renfrewshire.[17] Politically Motherwell stood out in what was overwhelmingly a gathering of progressives, but his affability more than compensated for any offence his political views might have caused. At the other end of the spectrum was the radical poet Alexander (Sandy) Rodger. Mainly, though, attendees were liberal-minded citizens. Described as 'choice spirits of the city', they met to discuss local matters as well as national and international politics, subjects they learned about from 'racy new books' and voracious newspaper reading. It was in the Sun – so local legend had it – that the proposal to erect a statue of William Wallace in Glasgow was first mooted, in 1818; the prospectus promoting the statue, ascribed to Motherwell, hailed Wallace's commitment to the 'cause of liberty'.[18] The Sun too was where the desirability of a legal campaign to take on Thomas Harvie was broached. Duncan and his family and close associates were the 'True sons of Nicol Jarvie', the name of the canny urban merchant who featured in Sir Walter Scott's novel *Rob Roy*. They 'knew everything about Glasgow – its ancient history, its rights and privileges in and around, and in all directions'. They were resolute in their determination to defend these.

A colourful account of the proceedings of and after June 1823 written some years later asked why 'had Tammas Harvie the assurance, the bare-faced audacity, of attempting to deprive them of the rights of their forefathers, of walking from the Green of Glasgow . . . all the way from the *Arms* Well to the mill-dams of the Duke of Hamilton at Carmyle, including Dalmarnock and Westthorn, where he had now taken up his purse-proud lordly residence?'[19] Let us show to the world, wrote 'Nicol Jarvie' (possibly Duncan) in a spirited letter to the *Glasgow Chronicle* in July 1823, 'that our civic privileges are as dear to us as our national', and that if the pleasure of walking by 'our health giving stream' are to be sacrificed 'at the altar of griping self-interest', it has not been without a struggle. Almost identical concerns at just this time were aroused even in Rutherglen where (on the south bank, where there was a pathway and a towpath) 'various dykes and fences . . . have been run across the Bank, into the River'. The town clerk, George Crawford, was instructed to seek the opinion of counsel as to the burgh's right to 'remove those interruptions, and as to the mode in which the Burgh ought to proceed to have that right ascertained'.

Similarly, in relation to unhindered passage on the north bank of the river, if neither direct action nor rational argument had moved Harvie, nor even a plea for a modest measure of generosity, the only option now seemed to be to go down the legal route – as was being considered in Rutherglen. To this end, Duncan sought the advice of his diligent lawyer ally Alexander Morrison, then in his mid thirties, who later became Dean of the Faculty of Procurators.

Along with Duncan himself and Neil, three men in particular led the way to the courts. One was George Rodgers, the manager of Henry Monteith and Company's Turkey red dyeworks at Barrowfield. Rodgers was a local man who had known and recalled fondly the walks he had taken around Westthorn since boyhood. Rodgers was joined by John Whitehead, one of the city's merchants, with business premises in Antigua Place and by the end of the decade a house in the rapidly expanding suburb of Garnethill, to the west of the old town. Described at the time of his death in 1847 as one of the city's better-known figures, 'an old reformer, strongly attached to liberal principles', he was said to have been 'always ready to bear his testimony against public abuses, or in favour of public ameliorations'. Proof of his commitment was the sizeable sums of money he left in his will for the Royal Infirmary (£200) as well as for the Old

Men's Society (£100), although the arguably more needy Aged Women's Society only benefited by £50.[20] Earlier in his life Whitehead had been a member of the 'Clique', a middle-class reforming club. In 1838 he was elected to the town council, as a Liberal. Finally, there was Adam Ferrie, who assumed the leadership of the new campaign committee.

Ferrie, born in 1777 in Irvine to prosperous and highly fecund parents, some of whose nine sons became East and West Indian traders and ship captains, had begun his working life as a muslin weaver. After learning the trade, in 1792 he became a cloth printer and manufacturer. Having moved to Glasgow in 1799, he was soon the main employer of handloom weavers in Port Glasgow, Greenock and Kilbarchan, sending much of his product to what is now Canada as well as the European continent, India, South America and the Caribbean. By 1815 his business was worth £100,000 per annum and his estate in the region of £70,000, although not for long as several associates to whom he had extended credit failed. The situation was so dire his hair turned grey before he was able to retrieve some of his wealth, which he did by focusing on his original business of calico printing. The venture was a success. Having established trading links in Quebec and Montreal, in 1824 he and one of his sons (Colin Campbell) formed a co-partnership selling a range of general merchandise in Canada.[21]

In politics Ferrie was a Whig and an admirer and associate of Major John Cartwright and Sir Francis Burdett, prominent reform leaders in England who advocated universal male suffrage, votes by ballot and annual parliaments. Ferrie has largely been overlooked by historians of Scotland's reform movement. This is despite Ferrie's claim that he was one of Glasgow's leading political activists, probably after the Peace of Amiens in 1802, and during the revival of the parliamentary reform movement north of the border following Cartwright's tour of Scotland in 1815. In September 1815 he chaired a meeting held in Glasgow's Trades Hall where the propriety of petitioning the House of Commons for 'a REFORM of the REPRESENTATION of the PEOPLE in that HOUSE' was considered and approved. Calls were made for the reform of a system in which landed influence was overwhelming, and the abolition of rotten boroughs and other corrupt practices. The meeting also drew attention to the injustice whereby the great commercial city of Glasgow, the second most populous and wealthy in the land, had no direct representation in Parliament. Towards the end of the meeting, it was proposed to thank Francis Burdett, Major Cartwright, William Maule and other members of the Hampden Club for their efforts in the cause of reform and the rights of man as established in the British Constitution.[22] Hampden Clubs were named after

John Hampden, a Puritan politician who in the 1620s and 1630s had opposed the autocratic rule of King Charles I. The members of these clubs 'knew their rights' and, knowing them, fought to maintain them. Hampden Clubs had been established during the parliamentary reform agitation of the 1810s; the first one may have been founded in London by Major Cartwright in 1812.

While this suggests that Ferrie was a respectable reformer, he was also known as a *Black-Neb*, a term dating back to the time of the French Revolution indicating someone disaffected with the government. Ferrie in his short autobiography claimed that he was often cheered on the streets, and sometimes praised as the city's Sir Francis Burdett. Self-confessedly prone to hot-headedness, he had not been entirely averse to the use of physical force. On one occasion he took part in a riot caused by some soldiers who had been throwing their weight around by insulting local girls and some 'country lads'. This was unusual. He had his red lines and in 1819 joined with the city's magistrates in maintaining order by taking on the role of head of the Gentlemen Special Constables.

From the outset of his involvement in the Harvie's Dyke affair Ferrie made clear his commitment to the use of legal means to win the case against Harvie. Tapping into the enthusiasm there was to keep open the Clyde pathway after the attack on Harvie's walls in June, he organised a meeting of representatives of the two dozen or so local committees that had been established more or less spontaneously in and around Glasgow for this purpose. These individuals were joined by members of the public who managed to squeeze into the meeting, held in the Lyceum theatre in Nelson Street. So popular was the issue that all the streets leading to the venue were 'blockaded by crowds of people anxious to obtain admission, and encourage the proceedings'.[23] Inside, and not to uniform approval, Ferrie 'spoke very severely against the very illegal way the opening of the road had been conducted' as well as the threats that were being made to take revenge on Harvie, whose stubbornness was intensifying the antagonism directed towards him. Nonetheless, Ferrie declared, provided those who supported him pledged not to harm either Harvie himself or his property, he undertook to take 'instant' legal steps to open the pathway and protect the rights of the people to use it. Ferrie's strategy was widely supported. A single-sided broadsheet published and distributed in the summer of 1823 – around the time of the Lyceum assembly – carried the headline 'Serious Outrage and Disturbance in Glasgow'. The reference was to the confrontation at Harvie's property, but also to the brisk manner in which subscriptions were being raised for the new campaign.

This, its author (Ferrie or one of his associates) asserted, was a 'more praise-worthy' approach 'than a lawless mob committing every kind of depredation'.

To advance matters a small committee was elected, chaired by Ferrie. He was joined by Rodgers, Duncan and Whitehead. John Watson too became a member, and although little is known about him other than that he was a business partner of Henry Monteith, he and his brother William were described afterwards as 'most indefatigable to the cause'.[24] In addition, also appointed to the new campaign committee were prominent local feuars – owners of small properties on land belonging to a larger owner to whom they paid an annual (feu) duty. Alexander M'Donald from Bridgeton, James Paton of Camlachie, James Reid from Parkhead, John Kinniburgh of Tollcross, and Alexander Brechin, a miller at Clydesmill, were the men concerned. Although few details have survived or can be recovered about them, what they had in common was an interest in accessing the Clyde-side path.

The campaign team was now in place. Harvie had made his position clear. Battle lines had been drawn. The legal fight for the 'liberty of the banks of the Clyde' could commence.

The campaign: first moves

Informally, what was as much a crusade as a law-abiding campaign seems to have begun just prior to Ferrie's initiative in mid July 1823. Even earlier, within days of the June demonstration, recognising that recourse to the law courts would be a costly business, James Duncan along with his friend Gabriel Neil had begun to collect money from the public with the aim of creating a fighting fund.

They began by distributing subscription papers which they issued from Duncan's shop in the Saltmarket, as well as through allies of theirs in the villages most directly affected by Harvie's blockade. This was helpful, but Duncan's masterstroke was to purchase a 'Panorama' that had recently been advertised for sale. Panoramas were large immersive paintings as much as 85 feet in diameter and 35 feet in height (although they were usually smaller than this). These were housed in tall, circular timber structures – rotundas – with a canvas attached to the inner walls covering an area from 180 degrees up to a full 360-degree panorama. Invented by the Irishman Robert Barker in Edinburgh in 1787, they rapidly gained in popularity – and continued to attract large audiences until the era of the cinema. The panoramic views, based on close observation by their artist creators, depicted anything from romantic landscapes through urban vistas (Barker's first panorama was a view of Edinburgh from Calton Hill) and exotic cities such as Constantinople and Venice, to famous battle scenes such as Bannockburn and the siege of Moscow. A form of travelling show, the panoramas would be open to the public for a series of weeks or months, on payment of a shilling.[25] Entry was from morning until dusk. The panoramic canvases were lit by natural light from above. The rotundas were topped with veils or roof lights, but otherwise enclosed, thereby fully immersing viewers and giving them the impression of being in an alternative reality. Informative and entertaining, for the lower orders they were a form of escapism from the travails of working life.

In Glasgow in 1809 there was a rotunda near the theatre in Queen Street and ten years later a further two: one in Buchanan Street and another in George Square.[26] Partly thanks to the influence of Walter Scott, the Trossachs was a favourite panorama subject in Glasgow, as was the landscape of the Clyde, along with other local subjects portrayed and popularised in paint by the Paisley-born artist John Knox. On the morning of 22 June 1823, a new panorama had opened in the George Square rotunda. It was Barker's and his collaborator Henry Burford's 'Grand Panorama of the City and Bay of Naples'. The entry fee was 6d, which included a 'descriptive book' or programme. Coincidentally, this was the day when the men seized after the destruction of Harvie's walls had been brought to Glasgow for interrogation. Could this have been the panorama that had aroused Duncan's interest in purchasing one? It certainly stirred the passions of visitors. The *Glasgow Free Press* reported 'a numerous concourse of visitors' to what was considered to be the best panorama the city's inhabitants had ever witnessed. They were excited not only by the history the painting represented, but also by its accuracy. Inspired spectators, the writer continued, 'were consumed', their souls filled with 'the vivid illusion of romance', surrounded as they were 'by the most exquisite specimens of art'.[27]

There was another panorama on display in the city, whose promoter, finding himself in financial difficulties, had put it up for auction. It depicted the battle of Waterloo in June 1815, which marked the end of Britain and her allies' long war against France. The costs involved in creating a panorama were high, and failures were not uncommon. This was the one Duncan acquired to use as a fund-raiser. He and Neil exhibited it in leased premises near to Duncan's Saltmarket bookshop. The location made sense. It was in the heart of Glasgow's old town. Despite the development of the New Town, the area to the west of the High Street, and the further westward spread of elite housing towards and beyond Blythswood, the bulk of the population lived and worked in the central part of the burgh. The district around Glasgow Cross was crowded with small mills, workshops, sheds, warehouses, retailers' shops and continuously subdivided housing accommodation.

The timing was just right too: it was Glasgow's annual Fair. By the 1820s the Fair was no longer used for dealing in livestock but had assumed the character of a popular holiday. People had time on their hands. Glasgow Green was the main locus, although there was little sporting activity. On the Green and spilling out onto the nearby Saltmarket and the Trongate were shows and stalls that featured 'dwarves, giants, Punch and Judy, prick the loop, dicing, and sellers of black jock, a mixture of sugar or treacle and spices'.[28] (See Plate 9.)

In some years there could be ugly scenes too, most commonly when locals taunted, intimidated or assaulted anyone of Irish descent who tried to approach the Fair. Also attacked were the dwelling places of the numerous Irish migrants which clustered in and around the poorer parts of the Saltmarket.

The subject of Duncan and Neil's panorama was one that resonated powerfully in the mind of an intensely patriotic Glasgow public. The battle of Waterloo (and the skirmishes that had preceded it, not least at Quatre Bras two days beforehand), in which the forces of the French Emperor Napoleon Bonaparte had been defeated by those under the command of the Duke of Wellington, had taken place less than ten years earlier. Many demobilised soldiers had returned home and were often visible within their communities – their uniforms, injuries and not infrequently their amputated limbs marked them out. Not surprisingly, Waterloo was one of the spectacles most widely exploited by the first panorama proprietors. Wellington was a national hero. His vast army had comprised a disproportionate number of recruits from Scotland. Many were from the Highlands, the source of numerous new migrants to the city. Although Highlanders tended to be concentrated in the Broomielaw and the weaving suburb of Anderston, this scarcely mattered as news of what was happening in the east end of Glasgow had travelled westwards. Like their commander, ordinary soldiers too were accorded hero status, and were awarded medals in recognition of their service. It was not uncommon for former combatants to visit panoramas depicting in vivid detail recent battles, and point to their admiring wives, children and friends the scenes with which they were familiar and the part they had played as combatants.

By slashing the price of entry to a single penny for adults and a 'bawbee' (a halfpenny) for children and announcing that all the proceeds would be used to fund the action against Harvie, Duncan and Neil's enterprise proved to be an enormous success. In July 1823, less than three weeks since the demonstration against Harvie's Dyke had taken place, with the arrest of what were deemed to be innocent protesters, and with Harvie's subsequent refusal to re-open the pathway, feelings were running high. Not so much this time against the Irish, however, but against one of their own, a Glaswegian, Thomas Harvie. Fair crowds flocked to the panorama which, 'but for the *Dyke* case, they might never have thought of doing'; other 'shows' were left trailing in its wake except when 'they alluded to the popular topic [Harvie's Dyke]'. It was, according to one account, 'exhilarating to witness the ardour and enthusiasm which pervaded all classes of the community'.[29] Tellingly, the front of the panorama was decorated by the Parkhead Botanical Society with 'choice flowers and Scotch thistles' which grew by the side of the Clyde. Writing in the vernacular, with tongue in cheek but pointedly, Duncan and Neil made sure that readers of the supportive *Glasgow Chronicle* were in no doubt about the significance of their choice of the Waterloo panorama. They began their contribution by bemoaning the fate of the 'knots o' weavers and their weans' in Camlachie who were prohibited from walking the banks of the Clyde and 'snuffen the caller air'. They then asked rhetorically who had ever seen such a 'patriotic scheme as this Panorama in the Sautmarket o' Glasgow'. This, they declared – justifiably – had attracted large numbers of entrants both well off and poor, young and old. The two men's commentary continued:

> the *sceenerie* itsel' is sae nat'ral – the stormin' o' Sebastian (red coats an' a') sae like the stormin' o' Tam's Fort o' West-thorn; an' the sortie frae Bagnone [Bayonne] jist like the sortie frae the places round us; – I declare it's just as oor wife says, 'the picture o' the thing itsel'; an' mair manfu an' sodger-like conduct wasna at the ane onie mair than at the ither.

After costs, the panorama netted £55, well over £3,000 at 2024 values, a remarkable sum that surprised and delighted Duncan and his allies.

This was but one of the campaigners' successes. Monies too were raised by simple pleas to the public to subscribe to the cause. Drums, fifes and tambourines were employed to draw their attention. On this initiative, Ferrie had led the way, issuing a placard addressed to his fellow citizens. 'You have lately been deprived of the Privilege of a footpath on the Banks of your native stream, one of the most delightful walks in the neighbourhood of this or any other city', it began. Ferrie then appealed for funds in addition to the £190 (£11,000 today) the campaigners had already raised and gave advance notice that he and other members of the campaign committee would visit businesspeople personally and invite them to contribute. The working classes, on the other hand, were reminded that as they had been accustomed celebrate the new year 'with joy and liberality amongst their friends' they might wish to direct their good cheer towards the Harvie's Dyke fund. Accordingly the committee proposed to position a 'LARGE BOX' at Glasgow Cross into which 'all may deposit their mite'. One penny, the plea ended, would be acceptable. During the first day alone some £50 (around £3,000 today) was raised. It took four men to carry the mahogany box to Duncan's shop where the proceeds were counted. That nearly half of what was deposited was in copper is further testimony of the breadth of support there was for the campaign, from widows and poor people as well as those better off. Over the course of several weeks, more than £105 'in sixpences or shillings, or copper money', was raised by this means. Larger amounts were donated by more prosperous individuals and a handful of local firms, such as Henry Monteith & Co.

The city's Literary Forum, otherwise known as the Debating Society, hosted 'two nights of vehement discussion about "Tam and his Dyke, and Broken Bottles"'. Admission was 6d. The total sum collected was £28 18s (£1,700), suggesting an attendance over the two evenings of well over 1,100 people. Concerts and 'glees' organised by Alexander Rodger and others drew even bigger crowds and produced £51. Even the town's leading painter at the time, John Knox, his reputation at an all-time high, put on an exhibition of his works, many of which were local scenes, that drew an admiring audience of town-proud citizens. Knox donated the proceeds (£31; £1,800) to the fight. Ironically, Knox's studio was in fashionable Dunlop Street, over the road from where Thomas Harvie ran his businesses. On the streets too, it seems that Glasgow was electrified by the campaign. The Gallowgate, it was reported in the *Glasgow Chronicle*, 'was as throng' as it had been for years. Bands – another major attraction – played music in the open air, despite the rain, while 'reel houses' were packed with dancers from the final Friday evening of the Fair week until late on the Saturday. When one band played 'The banks of the Clyde' and another followed with 'Scots Wha Hae' 'the people caught the enthusiasm and gave three times three huzzas'. Not surprisingly, and no doubt adding to the carnivalesque atmosphere, the howffs and alehouses did a roaring trade.

How much money was raised is not clear. Estimates ranged from £300 to £500 (that is between £17,000 and £29,000 in 2024). What is certain is that without funding on this scale, the campaigners would have struggled to engage in a legal case against Harvie. Early on they thought they had got the best of him cheaply, in Glasgow. Ferrie had raised an action before the magistrates, pleading for an interdict to stop him from completing the restoration of his walls. This was granted, and for a time the road along the river was kept open, but only until Harvie appealed against the ruling. It was at this juncture that Harvie had vowed (at the recent unsuccessful meeting with James Duncan) to defend his property rights whatever the expense. The dispute would now be resolved in a higher court. At a cost.

With the monies donated safely deposited in the bank, however, the campaigners were able to pursue Harvie. This they did by serving a Summons of Declarator on him on 11 November 1823. Harvie was outraged.

Angered by the apparent lack of respect he was convinced his recently acquired status as landed gentleman merited, he sent representatives on his behalf to meet with the feuars from the vicinity of Westthorn who had dared to adhere to the summons against him. As feuars they were bound to their superiors – in this case Harvie – on payment of an annual feu duty; accordingly, their holdings were less than secure. Harvie's agents 'represented to them and their families in colours the most terrific' of the peril they would be in by pursuing a lawsuit against 'such a wealthy individual' as Mr Harvie. Sneeringly, they conveyed Harvie's barely concealed threat that he 'was not willing that they should be deprived of their LITTLE ALL, by entering into such an action, and wished to warn them of the risk attending it'. Fearing ruin, one of the feuars withdrew his name from the list of prosecutors, although afterwards, buoyed by the support of his fellow pursuers, he returned to the fray.[30]

Building the case against Harvie's obstructions was a formidable task. The grounds of the campaigners action were relatively straightforward. They wished simply to establish that the path along the north bank of the Clyde 'from the Green of Glasgow to Carmyle, a distance of several miles' had 'remained free and unenclosed for a period of time beyond memory of man' and used and enjoyed by Glaswegians as well as the inhabitants and feuars of the adjacent towns and villages: Bridgeton, Calton, Parkhead, Tollcross, Camlachie and Carmyle. Further, they sought to show that access 'for the purposes of walking and recreation' had been free of any 'challenge, hindrance, molestation, or interruption' and, when threatened by the erection of fences or any other barrier – to keep cattle from straying for example – openings were left in them. Otherwise, they were immediately destroyed or removed so that uninterrupted passage was retained. What they had to prove was that for forty years or more prior to the spring of 1823 there had been a public footpath or foot road along the bank of the Clyde from Glasgow Green to Carmyle. Additionally, they argued that the river was still navigable as far as Carmyle, with steamboats frequently passing up and down. Along the bank were landing places at Rutherglen and near Dalmarnock as well as in the vicinity of Westthorn which had been used 'for time immemorial'. This was important: the banks of rivers, according to John Erskine's influential *Institute of the Law in Scotland*, published posthumously in 1773, were public, 'in so far as they may be subservient to the purposes of navigation' and therefore should not be obstructed.

The objectors seemed to have precedent on their side. An attempt some years earlier on the part of a David Tod, James Hamilton and other feuars to obstruct the roadway on the south bank of the river by extending their fences to it, had failed after a court ruling that the public had a right to use it, as they had done formerly.[31] In 1823 the pursuers' position was straightforward: Thomas Harvie had acted illegally in blocking the north-side path.

This was also the firm opinion of the legal team employed by Ferrie and his colleagues – who paid the three lawyers £50 each in retaining fees. One of the team of three was William Penney, a young advocate in his mid twenties, the son of a Glasgow manufacturer-merchant. He had been an apprentice in the office of Alexander Morrison, James Duncan's legal adviser. More senior was J. S. More, later a Professor of Scots Law at Edinburgh University. Best known was the third of the trio, Francis Jeffrey (see Plate 10).

By the early 1820s Jeffrey had established a formidable reputation as a defender of working-class leaders as they were pursued in the courts by the state in the troubled years after 1815. He had represented John Baird and Andrew Hardie at their trial in Stirling in July 1820. Such was the esteem in which he was held in Glasgow that in 1820 he was elected Rector of Glasgow University, where he had studied law. He was the editor of the *Edinburgh Review*, founded in 1802, a Whig-leaning journal, and had much sympathy with the distress felt by the labouring population. He understood better than many of his contemporaries the economic, political and ideological causes of the sufferings of the labouring poor. Although no radical, or even a democrat, Jeffrey recognised the very real danger of working-class revolt, revolution even, and advocated a strategy of accommodation. Whigs should work with the working classes, restrain their demands and steer them towards more conventional channels such as petitioning and legal redress.[32] With so much anger and even violence from within the working-class communities of the east end being directed towards Thomas Harvie, Jeffrey, by taking on the case against him, was putting into practice what he had been preaching in the *Review* and elsewhere.

Harvie too employed an eminent body of lawyers – 'an array of talent scarcely matched by others at the bar', according to Peter Mackenzie. Each was highly talented and marked out for success in their profession: Sir James Moncreiff (later Lord Moncreiff), Henry (Lord) Cockburn and Andrew Skene. Cockburn was to be appointed Solicitor General for Scotland in 1830 and a few years later was made a Lord of Justiciary; Skene followed him to become Solicitor General in 1834. Although on opposite sides in the Harvie's Dyke case, the respective legal representatives had much in common, not least their debt to late Enlightenment thinking. Like Jeffrey, Moncreiff had attended Glasgow University, and was an active Whig. Although from a Tory family, Cockburn too was a Whig as well as being a close friend of Jeffrey, and contributed articles – anonymously – for Jeffrey's *Edinburgh Review*. Cockburn, like Jeffrey, was elected Rector of the University of Glasgow, in 1831. Both Skene and Cockburn were members of the Bannatyne Club, a gentlemen's patriotic antiquarian manuscript publishing club, the former being a founder, along with its instigator Sir Walter Scott, in 1823.[33]

Harvie's challengers were now fighting for the liberty of the banks of the Clyde in an altogether different league.

Politics and the people

Alexander Rodger was not one of the committee of five chaired by Adam Ferrie. However, without the part Rodger played in marshalling the case against Harvie the outcome might have been very different. He provides another link in the chain that connects the struggle over Harvie's Dyke with the heady radicalism that had culminated in the risings of 1819 and 1820. A farmer's son in East Calder, Rodger was born in 1784. Having moved to Glasgow, around the age of thirteen he began work as handloom weaver in the Drygate, a crowded ghetto of mainly working people near the city's Cathedral. In 1803 he joined the loyal Glasgow Highland

Volunteer regiment, one of many formed during the ongoing struggle with France, then ruled by Napoleon and threatening to invade Britain. Following demobilisation Rodger returned to the weaving trade, this time in Bridgeton; this was his first association with the district and his familiarity with it would be crucial in the years of confrontation with Thomas Harvie. Highly literate – like many of Scotland's handloom weaving fraternity – he also wrote poetry and, now married and with several children to support, he supplemented his income by teaching music.

In the years of trade depression following the conclusion of the French wars, like many former soldiers Rodger became disillusioned as well as disaffected. He began to produce vituperative satirical verse directed against repressive, over-proud and complacent local leaders and the failings of the unreformed aristocratic system of national government, including the monarchy. The refusal of Glasgow's provost and magistrates to permit a public meeting proposed in 1816 to demand the 'redress of manifest grievances' (eventually held at Thrushgrove) induced Rodger to make a particularly bitter satirical attack, the third stanza of which runs:

> Base *Rads!* whase ignorance surpasses
> The dull stupidity of asses,
> Think ye that the privileged classes
> Care aught about ye?
> If ony mair ye daur to fash us,
> By George! We'll shoot ye![34]

He followed this by even more direct critiques of the prevailing political establishment, some of which were published in the *Black Dwarf* and other radical periodicals south of the border.[35] His hopes of having a book of his poems published in Scotland were disappointed, and instead he sent his work to the London radical printer Richard Carlile. Carlile, though, was arrested during the government crackdown on sedition in the aftermath of Peterloo. It was not until 1821 that Rodger's *Scotch Poetry* saw the light of day.

'The Wailings of Corruption' was written in 1817 following the exposure of the system of spies being used by the state to goad more gullible reformers to engage in seditious activity and to catch out and trap the unwary; Alexander Richmond was the notorious Scottish exemplar. According to Rodger, at the rotting core of the doomed system was the 'old strumpet, grown hoary in whoredom', Corruption. Personified, she bestowed her 'knights of the Spies noble order' with insignia consisting of 'a cross beamed gibbet, / From which a hemp ribbon hangs gracefully down, / With a noose at the end, where they yet may exhibit / Their chivalrous feats to amuse a whole town.' Rodger hailed the downfall of the spy network, and welcomed what he hoped would be a new order:

> For Truth must prevail over Falsehood and Error,
> In spite of the Devil, Corruption, and Spies,
> Who down to their dens shall be driven in terror,
> While man to his scale in creation will rise.

Now fully committed to the cause of political and social reform, in 1819 he began to write for the radical newspaper *The Spirit of the Union*.

This, however, led to his seizure in April 1820. His editor at *The Spirit of the Union*, Gilbert M'Leod, had already been arrested, found guilty of sedition and transported for life, for printing, in the view of one of his sympathisers, 'a silly publication', but which in court had been portrayed by the prosecution as a 'demon of mischief'.[36] Rodger, passionate in his beliefs, and whose political opinions were no secret and therefore a matter of concern for the overly alarmed authorities, was suspected of having been another of the authors of the radicals' *Address* of 1 April. Little or no evidence against him was produced, but even so Rodger was held in solitary confinement in Glasgow's bridewell for almost a fortnight. Cut off from friends, family and freedom, in pencil on the walls of his cell he wrote one of his best-known poems, the heart-rending 'Lines written in a certain bridewell, by a state prisoner, in the month of April, 1820'. In this he proclaimed his innocence of the charge of treason, declaring instead that his crime was merely 'that my views of politics / Accord not wi' some statesman's tricks'.

After his release Rodger returned to loom work, before being offered employment as a printed cloth inspector at Monteith's Barrowfield dyeworks at Dalmarnock. His patron was George Rodgers, the works manager. It is possible that the two men had met at the Sun tavern. Whatever their prior connection, what mattered was their friendship from 1821 when Rodger was first employed at Barrowfield, and the part they subsequently played together in the Harvie's Dyke affair.

We don't know what involvement if any Alexander Rodger had in the march and attack on Harvie's walls in June 1823. What is clear is that he was well known in Glasgow at the time and threw himself into the campaign to defeat Harvie in the law courts. He was warmly admired by ordinary working people in Glasgow's old town and the east end communities. At the packed concerts he organised in the summer of 1823 and beyond he performed songs and poems that both chimed with the sentiments of his listeners and galvanised them into subscribing to the campaign fund. As Robert Darnton has shown for eighteenth-century Paris, Glaswegians carried with them a small mental corpus of popular airs and songs. Bagpipes and reels played in the open or by bar-room fiddlers resonated through the town's most populous districts such as the Saltmarket. During the Radical Rising of 1819–20 'Scots Wha Hae' was commonly sung, while 'Rule Britannia', 'The Sprig of Shillelagh' and 'Hey Johnny Cope' were also part of the inclusive radical repertoire. Familiar songs such as these, re-worked, were potent aural weapons that were directed against particular persons and employers or as critical commentaries on certain events. In Glasgow in the early 1820s far and away the best-known, universally sung song was 'We're a' Noddin', the decades-old, if not centuries-old, traditional tune, the rhythm of which reflected the movement of a spinning wheel, an implement to be found in tens of thousands of working-class homes. According to one far from impressed contemporary detractor in the *Glasgow Free Press*, it 'neither admits sentiment nor pathos'. English, Irish and Scottish song books, the disapproving writer continued ironically, would be 'ransacked in vain to find its equal in the scale of degradation'. In March 1825 the song was adapted by striking female workers at Dunlop & Co.'s Broomward spinning mill to become an angry, venom-laced celebration of the shooting of John Graham, a blackleg.[37]

Similarly, Alexander Rodger adapted well-known tunes and songs to mobilise support for the campaign for the Clyde pathway. 'Come to the Banks of the Clyde', set to the tune of 'March to the Battlefield', was a celebration of the river's natural beauty in springtime. 'Roll fair Clutha' was an eight-stanza piece, sung to the tune of 'Rule Britannia'. This may have tapped into the patriotism of the time (King George IV's celebrated visit to Edinburgh had taken place the previous year), but possibly subliminally the appropriation of this tune also served to put the cause of Harvie's Dyke on a par with the enthusiasm there was for Great Britain's imperial project. Rodger's version of the song, disarmingly pastoral in its lyrics, covered similar ground to 'Come to the Banks of the Clyde', but also carried an unambiguous, uncompromising chorus, 'Roll, fair Clutha to the sea, / And be thy banks for ever free.' Freedom and liberty – globally as well as in Britain – were tropes that ran through much of Rodger's poetic output, even later in life.

The same ideals had been adopted earlier by Robert Burns, although owing to the radical and even seditious connotations of the liberty concept, Burns was more circumspect about publishing poems that could be perceived by the authorities as seditious. Cautious too about the inflammatory potential of verse that associated liberty with revolution was James Duncan. Duncan kept close to his chest until two years before his death in 1840 a copy of the potentially inflammatory 'The Tree of Liberty'. This was a paeon in praise of the Revolution in France and the part in it played by Freedom personified, and liberty. The poem was a radical call to arms that has sometimes been attributed to Burns, although a more likely author may have been Alexander Geddes, a Roman Catholic French Revolution-supporting priest who held mass in premises in the Saltmarket, not far from Duncan's printworks and shop.[38]

In these political, polemical and poetic footsteps followed Rodger. As early as 1816, in 'Bolivar' – a poem inspired by the emancipation of slaves in parts of South America – he paid tribute to the Venezuelan liberator Simón Bolivar. Other freedom fighters were feted too, including William Wallace, Robert Bruce and the Scottish reformers of the 1790s, as well as George Washington. These were 'Names which tyrants can't endure', given their resistance to oppressive regimes, whether on slave plantations or closer to home. And so close to home that he was almost on Rodger's doorstep was a local tyrant, Thomas Harvie. Deploying the rhetorical device of his verse as a verbal missile in the war against Harvie and his walls, Rodger – along with Duncan's and Neil's literary productions – played his part in the campaign to topple them (see Plate 11).

Rodger's significance for Ferrie and the campaign committee as they prepared for the forthcoming lawsuit was not simply as a fund-raiser, important as that role was. Nor indeed was it for the part he played in rousing popular feeling against Harvie, although this was of immense importance in giving voice to the working-class inhabitants of Glasgow's east end, as well as the emergent but still vote-less middle classes. Literally, his words were a 'mnemonic device and a medium', which galvanised opinion on the issue of access to and walking freely along the Clyde. But it was in the courtroom that the matter would be resolved. What Harvie's pursuers needed were credible witnesses who would provide evidence under oath, in a courtroom environment which for most would be altogether unfamiliar as well as intimidating, that for many years the pathway along the Clyde had long been free of obstructions. Rodger's was a familiar face, and he was trusted by the people in communities where, as we know, outsiders representing authority were treated with suspicion if not outright antagonism. Critically, he also knew 'every old person around' and where to find them in the muddle of cottages and crowded backlands of the unplanned villages of Parkhead, Tollcross and neighbourhood – something that Ferrie and the lawyers on their own would have found well-nigh impossible.

Courtroom confrontation

Although Harvie had been given notice of legal proceedings late in 1823, it was more than two years before the case was heard. Harvie's counsel, on his instructions, objected to the summons against him on a number of grounds. The motives of the pursuers and their legality were questioned. Ferrie and his allies were condemned as mere mischief makers, as demonstrated by their insistence on 'a supposed right and title in the public at large to walk over his [Harvie's] property for the mere purpose of amusement, and sometime of mischief and annoyance'.[39] Only the local feuars, whom Harvie had tried to silence through intimidation, had a legitimate grievance, it was proposed on his behalf. The others lived several miles away from the pathway in question; what business did men from elsewhere in Glasgow have in interfering in what was an issue for the suburbs alone? Another contested matter was the pursuers' wish that the case be heard in Glasgow rather than in Edinburgh. The former location made more sense, Ferrie, Duncan and their allies argued, as a jury in Edinburgh would have 'no knowledge of the situation of the walks', or indeed 'of the harmlessness' of the activities those involved in the campaign were anxious to pursue. Rather, such a jury would have to 'derive their information through the imperfect, and to some, unintelligible medium of plans and reports'.[40]

However, on Harvie's behalf it was maintained – not unreasonably – that such was the popular sentiment against him in Glasgow that he would not get a fair hearing. He demanded the case be heard in the Jury Court in Edinburgh, permission for which was granted in June 1825, with the hearing to be held in December. It had been delayed, as both Jeffrey and Moncreiff had been 'engaged with the assembly', that is the annual General Assembly of the Church of Scotland. This week-long convocation of the country's ministers, elders and others, described as 'one of the most curious spectacles in Scotland', dominated Edinburgh society and the newspaper press, and involved many elite figures from the worlds of law and the universities. Moncreiff's father had been a Moderator of the Assembly, and was credited with being 'the oracle of the church' before his death in 1827. His son, also on the evangelical wing of the Kirk, was deeply steeped in Assembly matters – hence his temporary withdrawal from legal employment.

The Jury Court – using a jury to determine civil cases – was a new development in Scots law. The first of these was held in January 1816. By the time the case involving Harvie was heard, both Francis Jeffrey and Henry Cockburn had become familiar with the court's proceedings and how best to sway a lay jury.

The location presented Ferrie and the other campaigners with a major logistical task, even without the prospect of additional expense. First though, the potential witnesses who had been identified had to be visited and questioned by a legal agent. Obtaining precognitions from what were necessarily older people was a time-consuming, sometimes frustrating, invariably exhausting business. Initially things went smoothly, with most of the legwork being carried out by Rodger and Alexander Morrison and, if his autobiographical account is to be believed, Adam Ferrie. Sensibly enough, what would prove to be a months-long search for witnesses began in the vicinity of Westthorn. By the end of January 1825 some thirty precognitions had been procured from residents of Bridgeton and Parkhead as well as Rutherglen, Clyde Iron Works, Tollcross, Shettleston and Camlachie. During the following months other witnesses were found and persuaded to provide evidence for the pursuers. A few more were uncovered locally but the hunt then spread west to Parkhead Toll, the Gallowgate and Duke Street and northwards to Port Dundas. The furthest flung trip in search of testimony was to Torr, in Renfrewshire, fourteen miles distant. Almost a year after the quest had begun, the campaigners had secured sixty-nine precognitions from individuals 'all of whom lived in distant parts of the Town or Villages three to six miles distant'; it was a process, according to Morrison, that had been 'attended with more than [the] usual degree of trouble and time'.[41] The difficulty of securing witnesses was compounded by the new challenge of persuading a large number of witnesses to attend the court, transporting them to Edinburgh and back, accommodating them and supervising their behaviour; several of them were very elderly and they were scattered throughout Glasgow.

After yet another delay, the court proceedings went ahead. They began on Friday 13 January 1826, an 'intensely cold' day in Glasgow when the Clyde was partly frozen over. But for which party would the day prove unlucky?

The witnesses who were to be cited to appear were taken from Glasgow to Edinburgh, the first of the pursuers' group leaving on 7 January. This was a task undertaken by Rodger. Getting such a body of individuals to their lodgings was by no means straightforward: there was concern that some of the witnesses, 'being very old men', might not be able to undertake the journey to the capital. While most of the witnesses were able to travel in two stagecoaches Rodger had commissioned (one of which was crammed full both inside and out), a second party had to be conveyed in two, more expensive, post-chaises. Expenditure mounted. In addition to Rodger's expenses, and the cost of transport, were the charges incurred for the time the witnesses were boarded – in Watson's Inn in one of the tenements of Candlemaker Row, and the Buck's Head Hotel. All this totalled just over £75. This sum did not include the payments made to the witnesses – 15 shillings each for ordinary people, but £6 to two professional men, James Bogle, a Glasgow writer (lawyer), and David Loudon, an accountant.

Just after 10 a.m., with Thomas Harvie in attendance and looking on intently, William Penney opened the case for the pursuers. His plea was forcibly put, and impressive. Penney had been called to the bar only in 1824, so this was one of his first appearances in the Jury Court. He began by emphasising the desirability of the river walk for the health of the manufacturing population in what was 'the most thickly peopled quarter of Scotland' (which Barony parish was). For people pent up in crowded mills and factories, fresh air was a boon. He then tackled the question of Harvie's right to block the passageway, drawing in summary fashion on the testimonies of the prosecution's witnesses. For forty years and more, the pathway had been open, he claimed. Farmers had used it, along with their cattle, as had children going to school, tradesmen and others on business trips to Glasgow, and coal miners and ironworkers as they went to work. The path was and had been used by churchgoers who crossed a ford to get there, Penney continued, and for weddings, funerals and christenings. All this, he argued, had happened for more than four decades prior to the appearance of Harvie's walls.

Penney then called on his witnesses, several of whom were in their seventies. William Smellie, a Parkhead weaver, was even older, being eighty-six. Born in 1740 'within gunshot of the place in dispute', Smellie's evidence was powerful. He recalled that in his teens 'many people came from Glasgow from the Old Brig', a walk he had often made himself for 'his amusement and health', going all the way to Carmyle, on the north bank. Smellie and others not only confirmed what Penney had said but also made the important point that they had rarely if ever been challenged or stopped from walking along the riverbank. Smellie testified to this effect; indeed, he had at one time been employed by the proprietor of

Westthorn but 'never got any instruction to stop any body'. Where attempts had been made to impede walkers, these were quickly dealt with. Alexander Robertson, a sixty-nine-year-old lawyer in Glasgow, recalled that James Hopkirk at Dalbeth had dug a ditch across the path; for a time a plank had been laid, but after this was removed 'the public still went along'. Colin Dunlop, another lawyer, knew of fences that had been erected but 'with stiles in them for foot passengers'. David Wardrop, a power loom manufacturer who had acquired Belvidere estate (next to Harvie's Westthorn) around 1820, had put up a fence without a stile but, Dunlop testified, 'it was immediately pulled down and walked over'.[42]

Only a few of Penney's witnesses disappointed. John Park, aged eighty-one, who had been born in Rutherglen in 1737, but who now lived in Tollcross, knew and had used the road on numerous occasions. He had fished from the riverbank and for several years had ferried passengers including weavers from Tollcross to Rutherglen in order to get their cloth stamped – approved for sale – by the stampmaster there. Under cross-questioning by Henry Cockburn, who wanted to know when Park had last walked along the path in question, he tired, saying only that this had been before the dyke was built and declaring that he had taken the oath to tell the truth and had done so. He was, he protested, 'an auld frail man, and it's no richt for the gentleman there to be fashin' me wi' owre many questions – deed it's no worth his while'. He responded in similar fashion when the judge, the Lord Chief Commissioner, William Adam of Blair-Adam, described in the *Memorials of His Time* as being farmer-like in appearance and with 'a plain, well-bred manner', insisted that he answer Cockburn. When with somewhat resigned permission on the part of the judge, Park left the court he turned round, bowed and wished those remaining a good day.

Henry Moncreiff led the case for the defender. Condensed, his arguments were threefold. First, that Harvie had been entirely within his rights to build walls that stretched down to the Clyde; this was the extent of his property – as stated in the deeds and as shown on various maps. No path, he averred, had been marked on these. As proprietor he had acted entirely legitimately. Why, he asked, if there was a public right, had no legal challenge been forthcoming, even during 1822 when the walls were being constructed? Secondly, he quibbled with the pursuers' claim that the public had a right to pass along the road in question, when in fact their appeal was for 'a right of walking for amusement', and merely 'a servitude for health or recreation'. A public road, Moncreiff submitted, could be defined, among other things, as a distinct passageway leading from one place to another, and not 'a thing which can negatively be acquired by walking for recreation'. If it had been a public road, he proposed, it would have been managed by the Justices of the Peace. The pursuers had failed to demonstrate that the road was a public one, or that it had been used without interruption for forty years or more. As the pursuers had done, he undertook to present witnesses who would testify that there was no road near Westthorn, which, he suggested, had been 'wooded down to the river'. On behalf of his client, he would dispute assertions that stiles or openings had been provided by the proprietors of riverside estates, and claim that at times the road had been impassable, most recently when a deep ditch had been dug at Dalbeth. He drew the jury's attention to the 'important fact' that no evidence had been adduced of a woman having gone along the pathway (all the witnesses had been male). This, he proposed, showed its 'incommodious condition', as 'certainly it would not have been so easy for a woman to have leapt over deep fosses', as it was for an agile boy.

Before calling his witnesses, however, Moncreiff, 'Declaiming with great Oratorical vehemency', made one further plea to the jury. This revealed the essence of Harvie's decision to fight. After asserting that the once quiet banks of the river were now frequented by hundreds of people, who resorted there not for their health, but rather for fighting or what he called blackguardism, Moncreiff painted a lurid picture of what Harvie had to tolerate. His windows were but 400 yards from the river, where naked bathers and others were to be seen loitering. He had spent a small fortune on his house and grounds, yet he is 'told they are to be covered with idlers'. It is all very well, Moncreiff concluded, for people 'to amuse themselves with the beautiful idea of recreating themselves within their own farms – but do not let them tell me that my client, Mr Harvie, is, for their convenience, to submit to every species of annoyance'.

Not surprisingly, a stream of witnesses was then called on behalf of the defence. Thomas Richardson, a Glasgow surveyor, was sure there was no path marked on plans of Barony parish he had seen; William Kyle, another surveyor, attested that there had been fences on properties stretching down to the river, but without openings. Proprietors and their employees added weight to this line of argument: Thomas Hopkirk of Dalbeth, for instance, was insistent that his father had stopped walkers as well as erecting a 'fence with large piles', as had other estate owners. George Stevenson from Cambuslang – aged fifty-five – remembered a 'strong dyke' at Easterhill, while John Ure, a Glasgow merchant, said he recalled there being a 'strong palisade' near Springbank thirty-eight years ago. Other witnesses were called to contest the pursuers' assertion that no-one had been hindered from walking along the north bank path. James Robertson, a tenant from Dalmarnock, described walkers he had seen as 'bad-looking men', who he had been instructed to turn back, which they generally did, 'except in the radical time'. When he had been the owner of Dalmarnock estate until 1804, John Buchanan, the Member of Parliament for Dumbarton, had been more selective, turning back 'idle blackguard boys' but allowing 'decent persons' to proceed. Peter Miller, a lawyer, claimed that he had been stopped by an angry James Sword, Harvie's predecessor at Westthorn, from passing through, on the grounds that he was trespassing. Alexander Stirling from Parkhead corroborated this, reporting that for fourteen years he had been employed by Sword to 'prevent passengers', albeit only on Sundays. To crown his case, Moncreiff called on witnesses from Carmyle who testified that despite their doing much business in Glasgow, they chose to go by a more direct and shorter three-mile route than the circuitous path of seven miles along the Clyde. Thereby Moncreiff hoped to cast doubt on the pursuers' argument that the riverside path was regularly used by the inhabitants of the villages close to the Clyde up to Carmyle on their way to and from Glasgow.

The defenders' proof complete, Francis Jeffrey then stood up to respond and conclude for the pursuers. Experienced in the exaggerated manner of pleading in the Jury Court, he toyed with Moncreiff's definition of a public road as a means by which places were directly connected, arguing that the riverside path did just that – connecting 'different public works and manufactories', including Clyde Iron Works and the city's Water Works, as well as leading to the high road from Glasgow to Edinburgh. And, he posited, a public road was not solely an avenue for business. The banks of the Clyde were 'a source of comfort for the workmen' of the several mills and factories in the vicinity. Footpaths, he contended, pointing to the examples of Hyde Park and Glasgow Green, could also be places for health and recreation. Point by point, Jeffrey was able to unpick much of Moncreiff's proof. Not all of the witnesses Moncreiff had cited supported his claims; indeed, a few of them 'turned out excellent Witnesses for the Public Side'.[43] One of these was William Smith, a farmer, who had been employed by James Sword to watch and prevent people passing, but, he conceded, 'he had never stopped anybody' nor had he had orders to turn back passers-by. Smith's was not the only statement that contained inconsistencies: Thomas Richardson, Moncreiff's first witness, began his testimony by claiming that he had 'often' been on the north bank of the river, but later admitted, unwittingly, he had not been there until recently.

According to Adam Ferrie, watching on, such contradictions caused some of the defence witnesses to break down under cross-questioning, not least, he alleged, as a few of the seventy Harvie managed to marshal (although not all were called) had been bribed.[44]

In his hour-long address Jeffrey also highlighted the selective nature of the defenders' evidence, as opposed to the vast body of testimony in support of the pursuers – including respectable men such as Colin Dunlop, a partner in Clyde Iron Works, and James Bogle, a Glasgow lawyer who had been brought up near Carmyle. Yet, he submitted, his clients had been 'reviled, and the community whom they represent, and the frequenters of the path', for no good purpose, and 'termed black-guards, ill-looking men, or idle and disorderly boys'.

Jeffrey held nothing back. In the final fifteen minutes of what was an 'animated, forcible' peroration he continued to undermine the evidence presented on Harvie's behalf, at the same time offering an insightful depiction of Harvie himself and his motives. Neither Harvie nor what Jeffrey called his 'coterminous proprietors' liked the 'encroachments of a public', despite its being a natural and necessary consequence of the growth of population as the number of public works multiplied in the area. Although not mentioning Harvie by name, it was clear who was in his sights when Jeffrey observed that:

> The rich merchant who has retired from business to his villa, who desires to lead a life of ease and elegance, and to exclude the vulgar from his privacy, who is fonder of trickery and embellishment, than of chaste ornament, is often more jealous than the larger and hereditary proprietor, of having his grounds inspected by profane eyes.

To this end Harvie, he alleged, acting as champion for his neighbour proprietors, and on the strength of his 'well sold Gin and Whisky', had begun to build the obstructions in question, 'although none were permitted to endure'. After defending the right of the pursuers to mount their case against Harvie even though they were residents of Glasgow and some adjacent villages but not always the communities around Westthorn, which was one of Harvie's objections, Jeffrey then reminded the jury – 'with a keen flash of his dark eye' – that there was no ambiguity about their duty. This was to 'determine whether, there was a right vested in the public' before Harvie's walls were put up. 'The poor', he declared, 'are not, and they ought not to be, intimidated by the wealth and threats of Mr Harvie.' Winding up, Jeffrey concluded, Harvie had taken on Westthorn

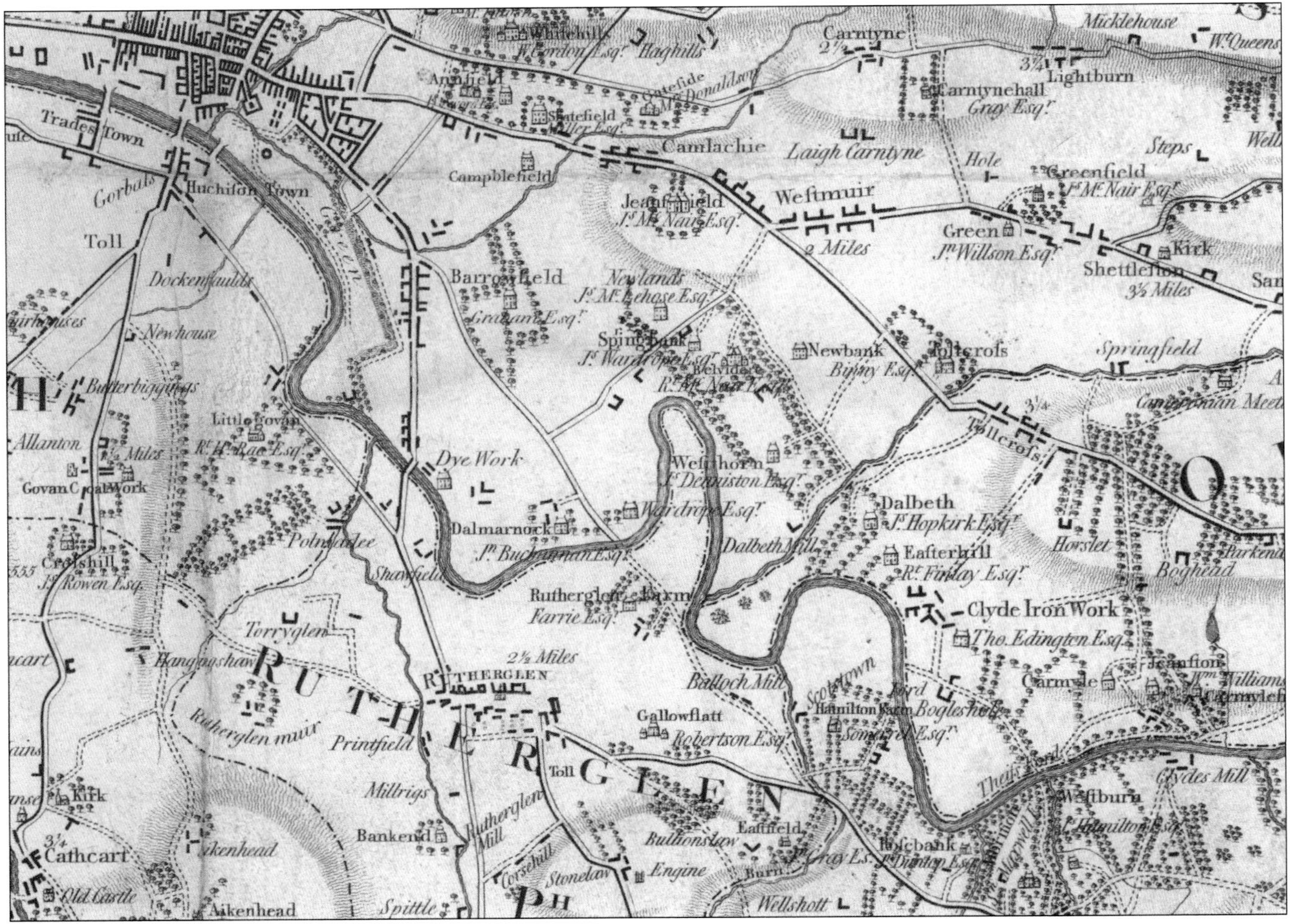

Plate 1. Thomas Richardson's map of 'The Town of Glasgow and the Country Seven Miles Round' (1795). Westthorn is in the centre of the map, as is Dalbeth Mill, which Thomas Harvie also operated along with his colliery. Nearby are the other estates and places mentioned in the text, as well as Clyde Iron Works. Parkhead was not named at this time; it emerged in the early nineteenth century south of the road junction at Westmuir, on the main Glasgow–Edinburgh road just over two miles from the city, and is marked on maps from the 1820s. By this time the area was more heavily built up, although most of the estates seen in 1795 were still there in 1823. (National Library of Scotland)

Plate 2. Handwritten script that the Parkhead drummer Thomas Fraser was asked to read out on the evening of 21 June 1823. The inhabitants of the east-end villages were 'requested to attend a public Metting at the cross of Parkhead at 7 o clock to take into consideration measures for taking away the obstruction on the banks of the Clyde'. The identity of the person who wrote the announcement was never discovered.
(National Records of Scotland)

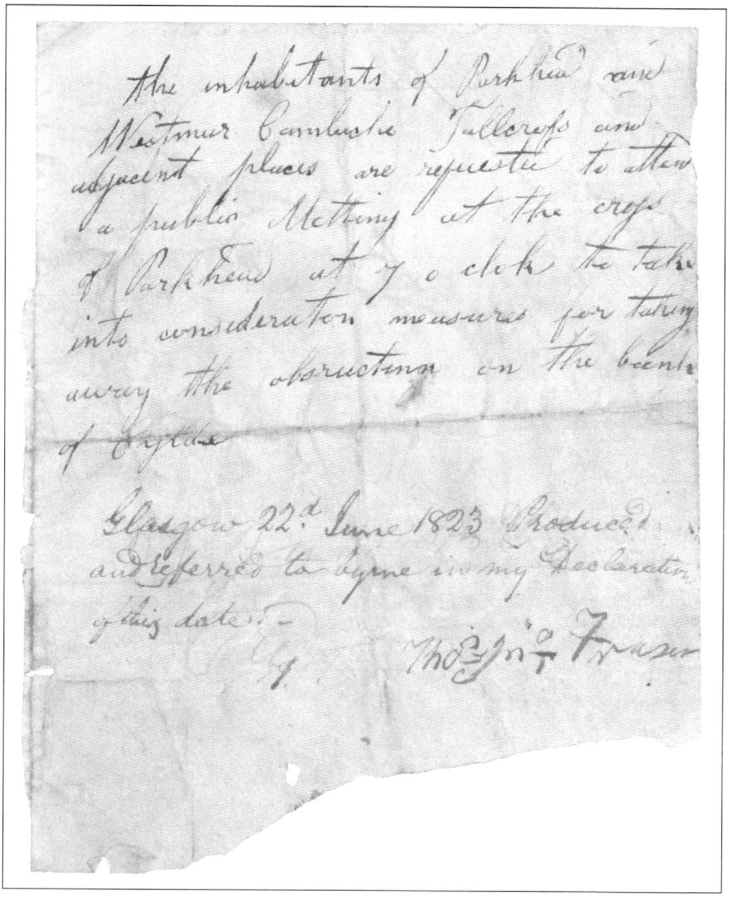

the inhabitants of Parkhead and
Westmuir Camlachie Tollcross and
adjacent places are requestid to attend
a public Metting at the cross
of Parkhead at 7 o clock to take
into consideration measures for taking
away the obsructinn on the banks
of Clyde

Glasgow 22d June 1823 Produced
and referred to by me in my Declaration
of this date —

Thos ... Fraser

Plate 3. Port Dundas, around 1825, from James Hopkirk's *Statistical Account of the Barony Parish of Glasgow* (1826). This was the location – alongside the Monkland branch of the Forth and Clyde Canal – of Thomas Harvie's two distilleries, one for malt whisky, the other for grain whisky. Operating under the name the Glasgow Distillery Company, it was probably the largest distilling business in the city at the time, when Harvie was considered to be 'one of the greatest men in all Glasgow'.
(Archives and Special Collections, University of Glasgow)

Plate 4. Harvie's Dyke. One of the two walls that Thomas Harvie erected soon after his acquisition of Westthorn estate in 1821. This was the main encroachment on the pathway along the north bank of the Clyde. It was the focus of the riot on 21 June 1823 when it was blown up and pulled down. After being rebuilt, it continued to be an obstacle to walkers for the rest of the decade – even after the House of Lords ruling in 1828 – although soon thereafter a narrow passageway was made, on the instructions of the Court of Session. (National Library of Scotland)

Plate 5. Dalmarnock Bridge, 1825, from the *Statistical Account of the Barony Parish of Glasgow* (1826). The construction of this wooden structure in 1821 was one of the factors that instigated the assault on Thomas Harvie's walls. Not only did the proprietors extract a toll from those passing over what had previously been a ford crossing – potentially wet but free – but the bridge partly restricted passage along the Clyde riverbank. There were rumours that the pathway would be blocked entirely by another proposed wall. The marchers from Parkhead Cross and Bridgeton met and assembled at the bridge on their way to Harvie's Dyke on 21 June 1823. (Archives and Special Collections, University of Glasgow)

Plate 6. Westthorn building, which Thomas Harvie turned into a watchtower from which he and his employees monitored the pathway along the Clyde at the edge of Westthorn estate. By the time of the Harvie's Dyke demonstration and riot in June 1823, the tower had been armed with canons, and from here Harvie's men fired at unwanted passers-by, as well as at the rioters on 21 June. Painted by William Simpson in the 1890s, the picture is based on a sketch made in 1836. (Glasgow Life Photo Library)

Plate 7. Dr William Lyon, pictured later in life. As a younger man, probably in his early twenties, Dr Lyon took a leading role in the agitation in Parkhead against Thomas Harvie's walls. After successfully practising for a few years in Parkhead he moved to the infirmary in Glasgow. Well known and highly respected in medical circles in the city, he was awarded an honorary degree by the University of Glasgow in 1859. He died in 1874. (Royal College of Physicians and Surgeons of Glasgow (GB250 1/12/1/27))

Plate 8. (Left) Special constable, Glasgow, 1820s. Special constables made numerous forays into the east-end villages and, easily identifiable, were often assaulted and forced to retreat before being able to serve warrants or make arrests. (Archives and Special Collections, University of Glasgow)

Plate 9. (Below) Glasgow Fair. In 1823 the period of the Fair was used by the campaigners against Harvie's Dyke as an opportunity to raise funds to cover some of the legal costs they were soon to incur. The side shows and other entertainments attracted crowds of people to the Fair, who were persuaded to contribute to the collection box set out at Glasgow Cross by Adam Ferrie. (Archives and Special Collections, University of Strathclyde Library)

Plate 10. (Above) *Francis Jeffrey, Lord Jeffrey, 1773–1850* by Colvin Smith. Painted around 1825, this shows Jeffrey as he would have looked when he represented the campaigners legal fight against Thomas Harvie in the Jury Court in Edinburgh in 1826. (Scottish National Portrait Gallery)

Plate 11. (Above right) Alexander Rodger (1784–1846), otherwise known as Sandy Rodger, was a self-taught weaver, a volunteer soldier who spent much of his life in Bridgeton (then a suburb of Glasgow), a cloth inspector and manager of a pawnbroker's shop. He was also a musician and prolific poet. Politically a radical, he campaigned fearlessly (and with hardly a pause) against Harvie's encroachments. A poet–activist he was well known throughout Glasgow and mourned long after his death.

Plate 12. (Right) Gabriel Neil (1797–1862), a Glasgow antiquarian, was one of the most active members of the city's Archaeological Society and a Harvie's Dyke activist. Described as 'a good authority on all that related to Glasgow in former times', Neil was a close friend and ally of the publisher, printer and bookseller James Duncan. Neil too sold books. Both men were amongst the first objectors to Thomas Harvie's attempts to block the pathway along the Clyde at Westthorn. Neil brought an evangelical dimension to the campaign, re-purposing radical tracts and verse from 1816. Later in life he lived at Edgefauld, Springburn; he was buried in the Gorbals burial ground. (Glasgow Life Photo Library)

Plate 13. Lord Brougham, 1st Baron and Vaux, *c.*1825. Edinburgh born, in 1778, Brougham was a leading Whig politician, reformer and lawyer. He had Glasgow connections, including being rector of the university from 1824 until 1826. Known for his oratorical skills, Brougham was recruited by Thomas Harvie to advocate his case in the House of Lords. Brougham accepted the commission but apparently had little sympathy for Harvie's stance, and evidently spoke without much enthusiasm. (National Portrait Gallery)

Plate 14. The front of one of the bronze commemorative medals awarded to the five men who spearheaded the campaign against Harvie's Dyke. Powerfully symbolic, in the centre of the medallion is the figure of Justice, protecting old Father Clyde with a sword. Beneath her feet lies the defeated figure of Rapacity or Selfishness (Thomas Harvie) while, above, a herald holds a banner on which is inscribed the motto 'Defend Your Rights'. On the reverse side were the names of the campaign committee and the thanks of the 'Citizens of Glasgow', for 'Successfully Defending their Right to a Path on the Banks of the Clyde 1829'. Despite their immense significance at the time, two of the surviving medals now lie more-or-less forgotten in Glasgow Museums Resource centre at Nitshill. (CSG CIC Glasgow Museums and Libraries Collections)

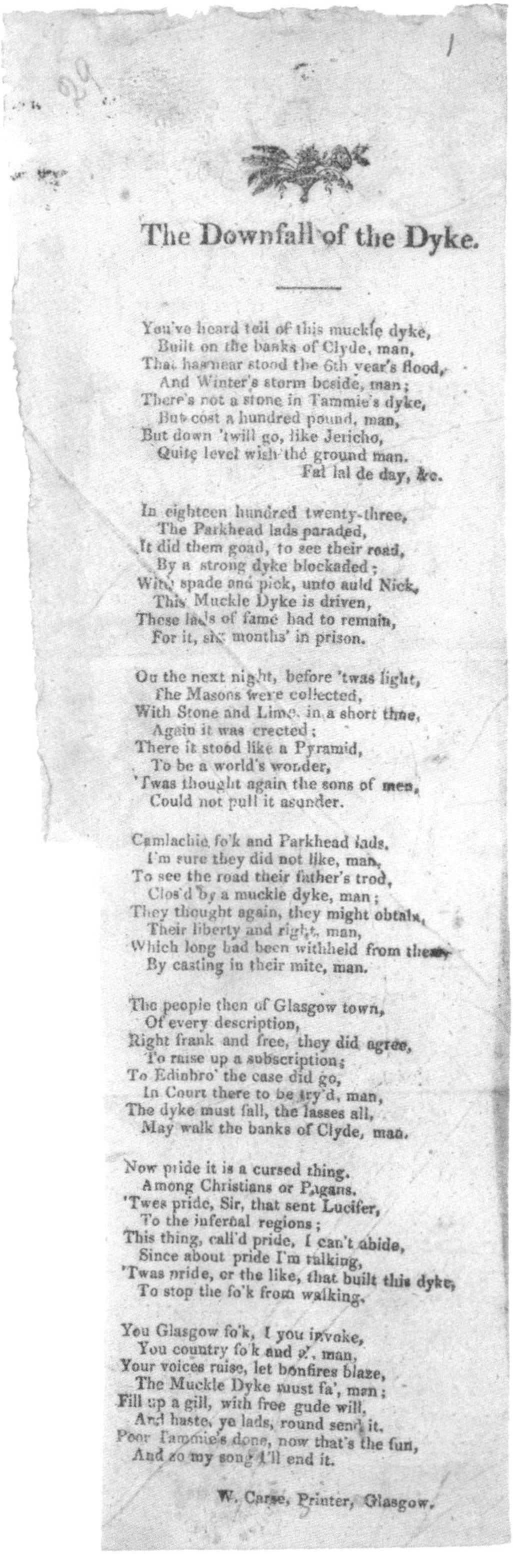
The Downfall of the Dyke.

You've heard tell of this muckle dyke,
Built on the banks of Clyde, man,
That has near stood the 6th year's flood,
And Winter's storm beside, man;
There's not a stone in Tammie's dyke,
But cost a hundred pound, man,
But down 'twill go, like Jericho,
Quite level wi' the ground man.
Fal lal de day, &c.

In eighteen hundred twenty-three,
The Parkhead lads paraded,
It did them good, to see their road,
By a strong dyke blockaded;
With spade and pick, unto auld Nick,
This Muckle Dyke is driven,
These lads of fame had to remain,
For it, six months' in prison.

On the next night, before 'twas light,
The Masons were collected,
With Stone and Lime, in a short time,
Again it was erected;
There it stood like a Pyramid,
To be a world's wonder,
'Twas thought again the sons of men,
Could not pull it asunder.

Camlachie fo'k and Parkhead lads,
I'm sure they did not like, man,
To see the road their father's trod,
Clos'd by a muckle dyke, man;
They thought again, they might obtain,
Their liberty and right, man,
Which long had been withheld from them
By casting in their mite, man.

The people then of Glasgow town,
Of every description,
Right frank and free, they did agree,
To raise up a subscription;
To Edinbro' the case did go,
In Court there to be try'd, man,
The dyke must fall, the lasses all,
May walk the banks of Clyde, man.

Now pride it is a cursed thing,
Among Christians or Pagans,
'Twas pride, Sir, that sent Lucifer,
To the infernal regions;
This thing, call'd pride, I can't abide,
Since about pride I'm talking,
'Twas pride, or the like, that built this dyke,
To stop the fo'k from walking.

You Glasgow fo'k, I you invoke,
You country fo'k and a', man,
Your voices raise, let bonfires blaze,
The Muckle Dyke must fa', man;
Fill up a gill, with free gude will,
And haste, ye lads, round send it,
Poor Tammie's done, now that's the fun,
And so my song I'll end it.

W. Carse, Printer, Glasgow.

Plate 15. 'The Downfall of the Dyke', a poem composed and published in broadsheet form *c.*1828, soon after the House of Lords had ruled that Harvie had had no right to block the passageway along the Clyde. This was one of several popular poems and songs that were written in support of the campaign, many written by Sandy Rodger. The creator of 'The Downfall of the Dyke' is unknown, but the poem neatly summarises the progress of the campaign against Harvie from its outset in 1823. (National Library of Scotland) estate 'with his eyes open' and 'though it might suit mighty well, to talk of his establishment; and though the neighbourhood of the poor, may, to some delicate sensitivities be disagreeable, their privileges are neither to be despised nor trampled on'.[45]

At this point – after 10 p.m., by which time the hearing had lasted twelve hours – the Lord Chief Commissioner summed up, assessed some of the evidence about which on the defenders' side he had some doubts, and reminded the jury of the issue they had to decide upon: had there been a public footpath or road along the north bank of the Clyde from Glasgow to Carmyle for at least forty years? In accordance with Jury Court procedure, the jury had to be unanimous in their verdict – a principle that had aroused much opposition in legal circles.

The twelve jurymen then retired. Their deliberations took only a few minutes. On their return to the hushed courtroom the foreman – nominated to speak for the jury – announced their decision. Unanimously, they found in favour of the pursuers. Applause broke out in the crowded courtroom. Some of the more venerable witnesses for the pursuers shed tears. Looking on in silence was Thomas Harvie, in attendance throughout but now coming to terms with the fact that he had been defeated.

News of the people's victory reached Glasgow the following day, Saturday. Triumphant celebrations were held in James Duncan's premises in the Saltmarket, which were 'crowded almost to suffocation'. Two of the city's most popular street criers, 'Hawkie' and 'Jemmy Blue', distinguished by the Kilmarnock cowl – a nightcap – he wore, were recruited to announce the good tidings. John Muir, the campaigners' preferred printer, who had produced the broadsheets reporting the executions of the radical leaders John Baird and Andrew Hardie in Stirling in September 1820, turned out thousands of broadsheets as fast as was humanly possible.[46] Advertised by hawkers and the like as 'a true, and particular account of the great and glorious victory over Tam Harvie and his big dyke' and costing a halfpenny each, they were purchased in 'extraordinary' numbers across Glasgow. In the evening bonfires of the kind most commonly seen on the streets on the occasion of the king's birthday were set alight. Two locations stood out. One was at the wooden bridge near to the jail where Alexander M'Phie and his co-defendants had been tried, sentenced and imprisoned just over two years earlier. The other was positioned at the notorious Allan's Pen, near Rutherglen Bridge, traditionally the starting point for the walk from Glasgow Green towards Harvie's Dyke. Described as a 'pyramid of coals', it was reputedly one of the 'most tremendous' bonfires ever seen in Glasgow. Some celebrants even marched out to

Westthorn and the westmost wall – the Dyke – where they gathered and then set ablaze some gorse bushes and fired off rockets.

Their joyfulness, however, was short-lived. Within days, Harvie lodged an appeal against the Jury Court's ruling. He had other legal options, and the finance to fund them. By such means, he believed, he would win his case and see off his less well-heeled opponents. Could money tip the scales of justice in his favour?

5

'Poor Tammie's Done, Now That's the Fun / And So My Song I'll End It'

Hearts sank as the news broke that Harvie was determined to carry on the fight. The 'stiff-necked defender' (Peter Mackenzie's term) did so first by appealing to the Outer House of the Court of Session, which dealt with civil cases. When the judges 'would hear no more of his reclaiming petitions', he turned to the Inner House, where appeals were heard. Despite 'every quibble, trick and legal manoeuvre' Harvie lost again. The same happened in the Admiralty Court – which ruled on maritime matters – to which Harvie appealed on the grounds that as the Clyde had long been a navigable river this was where the dispute should have been heard initially. Yet again he was ordered to pay expenses to the party led nominally by George Rodgers.

Ferrie was the chief fund-raiser – although by this time his Glasgow business was in difficulty, with payments on bills due being suspended. The attention he had paid to the dispute with Harvie may well have contributed to this. In May 1826 he sailed to Canada, to pursue new commercial opportunities there, but he returned to Scotland in December.

Prior to this, however, possibly drawing on his own diminishing resources, but more likely supplemented by subscriptions from fellow merchants, bankers and other better-off supporters (who knew little or nothing of his financial problems), Ferrie managed to keep the campaign alive. He appealed too to the general public who were invited to donate smaller sums in the mahogany collection box that was once more stationed once a week at Glasgow Cross. Such was the fervour of the city's public and the firmness of their resolve to stand up to Harvie that even depositors contributing small sums were applauded 'with the Cheers and hearty Congratulations of the surrounding Crowd'.[1] Complementing such donations was another exhibition of paintings by John Knox. The appeal this time was wider, to the taste and 'national feeling' of Glaswegians, who were invited to assist in contributing to a legal battle that would determine not only their rights, but also, for many, their health, and pleasure.[2]

For the same purpose and at the same time Gabriel Neil, with Walter Duncan of the Bible Warehouse in the Saltmarket, published *The Book of the Chronicles of the Isles, Comprising a Curious and Interesting Record of the Times from the year 1745 to 1826, arranged into Chapters and Verses*.[3] This was a compendium of plays, pamphlets and poems by a variety of authors previously published in 1816. Messianic in tone, the volume appears to have been compiled in the hope that the radical zeal of the previous decade could be re-ignited in the interests of this new phase in the campaign against Harvie's encroachments.

Some of the contents were fervently idealistic and gave voice to those radicals who after 1815 were challenging the new orthodoxy of political economy, with its 'laws' that decreed that any interventions in the market economy were futile. Thus the author of the play 'Equality, A Political Romance: Without Either Kings, Ghosts or Enchanted Castles' mused on how to restore the Garden of Eden. A land of equity called Lithconia was proffered as a solution, a place without towns and where labour would be the only currency (barter, it was claimed, led eventually to money transactions); each house would be identical, two stories high with nine bedrooms and a kitchen and hall. This was an American publication, but such schemes were very much in the ascendant in Scotland in the mid 1820s, when Neil's book was published. Indeed, in the autumn of 1826 the Owenite-inspired community at Orbiston near Motherwell was established. Although this was a short-lived venture, around the same time a Co-operative Bazaar was opened in the east end of Glasgow, where workers were able to sell goods or services according to the time spent making or delivering these. Profits for capitalists were thereby eliminated, with any surplus proceeds going to employ out-of-work members and, in future, build houses and asylums for the aged and infirm.

In the *Chronicles* too was the poem 'Albion's Lament For the Loss of Liberty; Addressed to the Friends of Reform'. This was a condemnation of political jobbery, 'lordly tyrants', commercialism, the suffering of 'poor mechanics', and 'Caledonia's woes'. One antidote proposed was religion, to soothe the 'gnawing pain' of the hungry. Also called into action were Scotia, Ossian, Britannia and 'Independence' – in search of the 'happy hour / When tyranny shall cease, / When kindred man is bound to man / With ties of mutual peace.' Tyranny's nemesis liberty was a conspicuous element in the language of radicalism in Scotland dating back to the Declaration of Arbroath in 1320 and a resonant aspect of the rhetoric of the radicals of 1819–20. It was equally applicable to the struggle over Harvie's Dyke.

Although Harvie is never mentioned by name, it can hardly have been coincidental that fictional figures who featured in Neil's *Chronicles* collection were proxies for attitudes he was condemned for holding. Thus, the central character in the play 'Gotham in Alarm: A Farce, in Three Acts' is Lord Fungus, whose opening lines included the boast that even as a young man he had foresight 'that I would be great and dignified'. When playing with his 'compeers of the green' he was 'ever the ruler – and even after, when in menial guise I furbished knives and watered horses . . . the dawnings of my present greatness were apparent'. Even more telling, Fungus would afterwards keep his distance, 'stand aloof, strut, and look big, and awe them into silence . . . and keep down the noses of the ragged sooty knaves, at rough oppression's grindstone'.[4]

'The Public Meeting, Or Lord Shallow at his Last Gasp', is set in a 'Populous City' and features, in caricature, Lord Shallow, 'A Ruler', whose greatest fear is the mob, information about which comes from 'Scout', a spy. The play opens as Shallow awakes from a dream, petrified by a crowd of the 'guilty gatherings of a thin skin'd rank consumptive rabble – the sweepings of a host of idle looms'. The core of the play is a public meeting of the distressed working classes (probably the Thrushgrove gathering of October 1816), much feared by Shallow ('starving men are dangerous neighbours'), but at which – as in reality – the anticipated rioting or disturbances failed to materialise. Yet it was reported to Shallow, at the end of the meeting, an 'emboldened' speaker had 'told the people of your Lordship, and how you did try to cheat them of their rights – to keep them from expressing their just sense of the deep-seated misery which hung around their country'.[5] Thomas Harvie was not Lord Shallow, and 1826 was not 1816, but he was representative of the class of men radicals had as little time for as they had a decade earlier.

How important Gabriel Neil was for the campaign is hard to judge (see Plate 12). What can be said is that his evangelicalism may have bolstered the moral basis on which the campaign was fought. Ideals of morality and social justice were as evident in what Neil published in order to boost the campaign after 1823 as they had been in the fiery post-war political climate less than ten years beforehand when his *Chronicles of the Isles* first appeared. Neil was prophet-like in his belief in the importance of Christian religious adherence, and its application in everyday life, later writing to the editor of the *Glasgow Constitutional* that 'we are in the midst of enemies and snares . . . the Philistines are upon us'. Although the hold of the established Church of Scotland over urban society had weakened from the later eighteenth century, if anything religious fervour grew more intense. There was a Relief Church in Tollcross, and although nothing is known of its congregation it is likely that as in other dissenting churches in Glasgow in the early nineteenth century, weavers, spinners and calico printers were among its adherents. The Covenanting tradition had long informed forms of popular protest in eighteenth-century Scotland and continued to kindle and inflame radical unrest into the nineteenth century, including Chartism, which in Scotland had a palpable religious and ethical dimension. This was more so in those communities – again where weaving predominated – where the depth of social suffering was deepest. Here calls for temporal and spiritual salvation were most marked, although there were those such as William Aiton, a lawyer and agriculturalist and from 1816 until 1822 a sheriff substitute in Lanarkshire, who condemned the decline of interest in religious doctrine and the rise of its corollary, the engagement in politics, of the lower orders and their encouragement by Whigs as the greatest and most dangerous error of the times.[6]

Thomas Harvie: troubles and torments

By dint of hard work on the part of Ferrie, Neil, Duncan, Rodger and others, public opinion was galvanised behind the campaign to restore open access to the banks of the Clyde. Harvie on the other hand was becoming increasingly isolated. Even those friends who had backed him thus far, 'now saw . . . little short of a malevolent hostility in his intentions in troubling the Public so much'; they despaired of his imperviousness to the fact that the Jury Court had ruled against him in January.[7] But even a dramatic downturn in whisky sales that same year, 1826, caused by a glutted market, which meant heavy losses for distillers such as Harvie, and failure for smaller firms, was not enough to divert him.

Closer to home too, at Westthorn, he was embroiled in another dispute, this time with his coal miners. Westthorn colliery was but one of around eighty in the west of Scotland where combinations – early trade unions – had appeared following the repeal in 1824 of the repressive Combination Acts of 1799 and 1800. By 1825 there existed a united body, the Glasgow and Clydesdale Association of Operative Colliers, members being bound by oaths and secret masonic-style hand grips. In the summer the colliers at Hamilton Farm colliery – a few miles to the south-east of Westthorn – went on strike. Their aims were higher wages and a reduction in the darg – the amount of coal each miner was expected to put out each day. The men's action was a success. The Hamilton colliery lessee, Colin Dunlop of Clyde Iron Works (which were within sight of Westthorn), was forced to concede as colliers at his other pits also withdrew their labour and forced Dunlop to shut down his furnaces. Subsequently the Colliers' Association grew in both strength and confidence across the Lanarkshire coalfield as well as in Fife and the Lothians. Backed by the Association, the colliers restricted output, so that by the end of the year stocks of coal at many pits were reduced to a level which meant that winter demand would not be met. Initially Dunlop acceded to the colliers' demands, for which they rewarded him with a gold medal, a cup and a snuff box, purportedly worth one hundred guineas. The situation, however, was untenable. Dunlop was losing £2 on each ton of iron produced from his furnaces.[8] Several colliery owners including the Duke of Hamilton, as well as their lessees, resisted and refused to employ striking miners. But the decisive battle was fought at Clyde Iron Works and at the mines in the near vicinity in the spring and early summer of 1826.[9] One of these was Westthorn. Thomas Harvie therefore was in the thick of the dispute.

By this time Dunlop had had enough and took the lead in confronting the Association. Taking advantage of the economic downturn of 1826 and the consequent availability of higher numbers of unemployed labourers, tradesmen and handloom weavers, Dunlop dismissed and ordered to be cleared from their houses those colliers in the combination who were insisting on higher wages. Early in April 1826 a 'melancholy gloom' afflicted Tollcross. Within days of Dunlop's orders one of Glasgow's Messengers at Arms and his assistants turned out the 'discarded' colliers and their families from their homes. Their windows were then boarded up to prevent damage being done. Within days the displaced miners had been replaced, but only by men who were prepared to abjure combinations and output restrictions. This was something many were willing to do; the alternative was prolonged unemployment and acute hunger. Something in the region of 500 willing recruits turned up on 17 April, from many parts of central Scotland, having trudged to the Clyde Works during Sunday 16 April and overnight. Dunlop was to select new recruits at 4.30 a.m. on the Monday morning. To protect those desperately seeking work, more than seventy armed guards surrounded the works, to defend both personnel and plant from attacks by 'skulking' bands of 'sulky looking men'.[10] Other masters followed Dunlop in taking on the Association. One of these was Harvie. He very quickly announced a reduction in the cutting rate of 9d a cart. Those who accepted the new rate were 'assailed with mud and stones' by the 'combined' colliers who lined the road from Glasgow that led to Westthorn.

The struggle, though, was by no means over, with sporadic disputes continuing well into 1827. This included Westthorn. Determined to break the grip of the colliers' combination and resist demands for an increase of their daily wage from two to three shillings, Harvie dismissed fifteen of the most troublesome men. Within days there were newspaper reports that he had been 'proceeding with proper energy' in introducing free labour into his pits. Soon the fifty or more new recruits ('unassociated' colliers, and stout labourers) were reported to have succeeded in putting out coal 'beyond expectation'. They were paid two shillings a day, that is a quarter of what the Association colliers had been able to earn at the peak of their influence – a devastating outcome for members. As most of the new recruits lived in Glasgow and had on occasion been attacked by colliers dismissed by Harvie, they had to be escorted to and from the colliery by special constables, watched in surly resentment by those they had replaced as they walked past. The union men who were now out of work had to depend on charity, their wives' earnings, for example, as tambourers (hand-working embroiderers), or search for work either at other pits or as limestone quarriers. After some weeks of struggle, a small party of them, on the lookout for such employment, found release in a violent drinking bout.[11] This had resulted in an apparently random assault in John Muir's change house in Riddrie. Fired up with whisky and other alcohol, a group of striking Westthorn colliers had attacked with a hoe, a spade and even a breakfast knife two apparently innocent labourers, James Haggarty and Thomas Macue.[12]

Although the new men may have been obliged to Harvie for employing them, there was no sign of the gratitude shown by their counterparts at the Clyde Iron Works' pits. When embarking on his recruitment drive in 1826, Colin Dunlop offered his recently employed colliers a basic two shillings and sixpence a day until they were skilled enough to make more from piece work. This was more than at Westthorn. In addition, as a humanitarian gesture Dunlop had given each of the colliers who had come ready to work for him, but were surplus to his needs, a token one shilling and sixpence. Labourers and weavers were given one shilling each, with which to buy some breakfast. Such magnanimity was not part of Harvie's personality. Miners' living conditions were notoriously poor in most of Scotland's colliery communities, but so bad was the quality of the housing accommodation Harvie provided for his colliers that some years later, even after improvements had been made, his rows of one- and two-room cottages were still described as 'barely habitable'.[13]

Resentment about his hostile attitude to those he employed as well as the collier and weaver inhabitants of nearby villages continued to fester.

It may well have been around this time that Harvie had proposed a perverse solution to the Westthorn walls issue. He was adamant that the large dyke should remain, without any opening. On the other hand, he was prepared to remove some of the coping stones that overhung the river and erect a stair or flight of steps in the west side of the dyke 'so as to let people ascend to the top of the wall'. But to what end? On the other side, there were to be no steps; accordingly, everyone who attempted to pass by was in danger of falling into the river.

It certainly did not help to restore any lingering public sympathy there may have been for him that in September 1826 one of Harvie's carters, William Wilson, ran over and killed a child playing innocently on the kerbside in Glasgow's Graham Square, off the Gallowgate. This was one of the busiest thoroughfares in the town. The accident was witnessed by a great many horrified people. Wilson had been drunk – on liquor bought and drunk in one of Harvie's shops, where he made deliveries. When the fatality occurred he had been driving two carts together too fast in an area from which carts were normally prohibited.[14] Harvie was not held responsible despite Wilson being one of his employees, but the incident itself and the subsequent court case in December 1827 meant that Harvie remained an unpopular figure in the eyes of the public.

There was, however, some welcome relief for him. The outcome of the court proceedings – again held in the Jury Court – was successful. The child's father, a 'very respectable journeyman painter', lost his plea for damages of £1,000. Ironically, on this occasion, pleading Harvie's defence, was his tormentor of the previous year, Francis Jeffrey.

Perhaps buoyed by this, Harvie ploughed on with his appeal against the several court rulings that had followed his initial defeat in January 1826. In December 1827, following a further bid on Harvie's part to overturn the Jury Court's decision, the Court of Session denied him his wish for a new trial. The Lord Ordinary and the jury found too that Harvie had no right to close up the path. Furthermore, he was ordered 'forthwith' to remove any obstructions or impediments, although he was permitted to enclose ground belonging to him alongside the river, provided he incorporate into any fences or walls 'wickets or proper openings for allowing free navigation'.[15] Again Harvie demurred, protesting that Rodgers and his fellow pursuers should define the extent and limits of the path, which should be 'least injurious to the defender's right of property'.

Still determined to win the principle of his right to protect the full extent of his property, Harvie then turned to an even higher court – the highest in the land, the House of Lords, in London. Surely, he thought, with his financial heft, here he would defeat his contemptible pursuers whom he had condemned as representing a 'motley assemblage', a party of 'low weaver bodies'.

The indignation of the Glasgow public at Harvie's ploy was soon combined with despair. On Harvie's part no expense was to be spared as he transferred his hopes from what he termed 'a parcel of *doited* old Scotch judges' to the British house of peers.

To the Lords

To promote his appeal in the Lords he employed the three men who had represented him in the Jury Court, James Moncreiff, Henry Cockburn and Andrew Skene. This time the retaining fees he paid were of a different order: a rumoured 500 guineas went to Moncreiff, who would travel to London to plead on his behalf. The others were to remain in Edinburgh and build Harvie's case from there. In London, only the best representatives would do. For a further 200 guineas he recruited Henry Brougham.

Brougham was one of Britain's best-known reformers (see Plate 13). Edinburgh-born (in 1778) and educated, he was one of the founders of the *Edinburgh Review*, in 1802. Two years later he moved to England, was called to the bar in 1808 and in 1810 became an MP. At this point in his career, on some issues he was on the radical wing of the Whig party, and he was a leading proponent of the abolition of slavery. As her Attorney General he provided legal advice to Princess – later Queen – Caroline in her defence against the charge of adultery brought by her husband King George IV in his divorce action against her. All things considered, Brougham's support for Harvie seems incongruous. True, he was hostile to trade unions, and nervous about the potential for disorder and even rebellion on the part of the working classes. He was appalled by the prospect of universal suffrage. Yet he was an avid supporter of state-supported education, and of mechanics institutes as a means of improving the lot of working people.[16] For present purposes what is likely to have been significant is that in 1825 he had been appointed Rector of Glasgow University. He was well known among the city's leading citizens. Harvie, then in his ascendancy, could count himself as one of these and might have met Brougham. In any case, Brougham was recognised as a fine court rhetorician and captivating speaker who had performed brilliantly in the House of Lords in 1820 in defence of Queen Caroline. It was little wonder that Harvie employed him.

Harvie's pursuers did their best to match their adversary's exertions. In this Ferrie took the lead. Not only did he re-ignite the fund-raising methods among the Glasgow public used previously, but by doing some of the legal legwork himself he kept a lid on the near crippling expense of the Lords process. This involved attending consultations with counsel in Edinburgh, gathering the proofs and travelling to London at least twice in the winter and early spring of 1828 to further the campaigners' cause. Representing the campaigners were James Kaye of Snaigow, 'a most able and promising man' who died relatively young. Joining him was the 'eminent' English barrister M. G. Adams. Their plea was that the Jury Court judgment should be upheld, on the grounds that the evidence presented had proved that the path had been open for forty years.

After some months of preparation by both parties, on 29 April, in the Lords, Moncreiff in a 'brilliant' speech opened the case for Harvie. The man both he and his opponents sought to persuade was the Lord Chancellor, John Copley, 1st Baron Lyndhurst.

Not only did this occupy the Tuesday; Moncreiff resumed his speech the following day. At this stage Brougham entered the fray. The crux of the two men's argument was that the Jury Court ruling had been flawed as the judge had underplayed the evidence from witnesses that there had been interruptions to the free passage along the footpath. There had been uninterrupted possession of the part of the path concerned they conceded, but only for twenty-seven or at most thirty-two years and not the requisite forty years. Moncreiff pulled out all the stops. Brougham, on the other hand, appeared uncharacteristically subdued, owing, he admitted afterwards, to his doubts about the justice of Harvie's case, 'a bad cause in every respect'.[17] (Henry Cockburn too appears to have had doubts about the justice of his client's defence, later inscribing his printed copy of the *Proceedings* of the case with his initials and the comment, 'I wish the Scotch had oftener made such a struggle of shutting up walks.'[18]) Initially it seemed that Moncreiff had won the day. Ferrie, who had been watching the pleadings, returned to Glasgow, convinced that the Chancellor had been sympathetic to Moncreiff as he made the case on Harvie's behalf. Harvie's representatives in London also reported along these lines to Harvie back in Glasgow who, it was observed, 'strutted in afresh, booted and spurred, to the old Tontine coffee room', gloating and crowing about the turn events were taking.

On 6 May there was a further hearing, after which the Lord Chancellor announced that he would defer judgment, given the prominence of the case. Indeed, he declared, 'it was the most important case ever before him since he sat on the Woolsack'.[19] This was on 8 July, when he returned with his verdict. During what was described as an eloquent speech, the

Chancellor declared that the decision had fixed the law as to the rights of the public 'all over England, Ireland and Scotland, for all time, as to the prescriptive rights to roads'. All that was required from now on, whether the land in question belonged to a peer, prince 'or even the King himself', was proof that the privilege of using it had lasted for forty years. All the powers in the land, he concluded, could not legally take that right away. In the present case it was probable that the pathway in question was 'the principal road of what is now the great City of Glasgow' – something of an exaggeration, but it hardly mattered. Accordingly, he moved 'that the judgment of the Court of Session be affirmed' and awarded £100 of costs to the defenders – substantially less than the actual expenses they had incurred.

The news, which took two days to reach Glasgow, 'occasioned great and almost universal rejoicing'. The judgment, in the opinion of the editor of the *Glasgow Free Press*, had given a 'death blow to the system of interruption and exclusion' which had 'so much been acted upon nearly all the banks of our favourite healthy streams'. The citizens of Glasgow have been triumphant, announced a broadsheet headed 'Downfall of Harvie's Dyke', published on 10 July, with the welcome tidings from London. 'HUZZA! – HUZZA! – HUZZA!!!', The Liberty of the Banks of the Clyde for ever!', it concluded.

Once more, however, such celebrations were short lived. The broadsheet's assertion that 'the dyke must shortly come down' was, even at this late stage in the dispute, far from assured.

No surrender

Following the House of Lords decision, Ferrie, Rodgers and their allies returned to the Court of Session to obtain a new order for Harvie to remove the walls that were blocking the Clyde-side pathway.[20] He was given eight days in which to act. At the same time – 22 January 1829 – William Kyle, one of Glasgow's most experienced land surveyors who was familiar with the Clyde-side estates, was asked by the court to produce a report 'with a view to the arrangement of the future exercise of the said right of road, in the manner least prejudicial to the defender [Harvie], and consistent with the just rights of the parties'. Accordingly, Kyle recommended and laid out a plan for a six-foot-wide walkway, on the model of the path further down the river, from Glasgow to Govan.[21] Even at this juncture, Harvie continued his resistance, refusing to take down what Peter Mackenzie called his 'insolent wall'. Indeed, still resentful about his humiliating defeat in the law courts, rather than dealing directly with Kyle he employed his agent, the lawyer Alexander Barlas, to negotiate on his behalf. John Whitehead represented the campaign committee, along with their longstanding legal agent, Alexander Morrison. Encouraged by the Westthorn campaigners' apparent success, across the river in Rutherglen the town council agreed unanimously to order the town clerk to write to a Major Walker, a Mr John White (of the Shawfield Chemical Works founded in 1820, and owner of Shawfield Estate) and a 'Mr Barles' who had evidently been following Harvie's example, 'requiring them to clear a passage along the left bank of the river'.[22]

On Harvie's behalf, Kyle's proposal was vigorously objected to at the next hearing of the court. This was despite the fact that in May Harvie had verbally approved what Kyle was proposing. Indeed, in what was a rare intervention in person, he had turned up early in the morning of 27 May 1829 to watch as William Kyle's assistants staked out the line of the proposed pathway. Evidently, he had not been pleased with what he had seen. The path to Govan, it was argued, lay in a straight line along the bank of a navigable part of the river, which was 'thickly studded with villas and manufacturing establishments'. This path therefore was in 'universal use . . . as a daily and necessary medium, of communication'. By contrast, the pathway past Westthorn had been a 'mere track, at most two or three feet wide'. If this acknowledgement that there had been a path of some kind could be read as an unwitting concession on Harvie's part, the rest of his protest against Kyle's proposals was largely a regurgitation of arguments that had been heard and dismissed before. The Glasgow to Carmyle path was 'absolutely useless for any purpose of public convenience'. Rather, it was 'little more than a resort for dissolute idlers'. Without the check that might have been provided by the regular passage of respectable individuals, Harvie had had to request the services of a special constable to protect his property and 'restrain the licentiousness that would otherwise prevail, and not infrequently to preserve the public peace'. Harvie's delaying tactics had repercussions in Rutherglen. The optimism with which the council had acted in March in ordering the three proprietors to clear a passageway on the south bank was now – only a fortnight later – rapidly receding. The right of way they assumed to have been established seemed less certain, to the extent that the council resolved to delay further proceedings in the meantime.

Over the river, by November some progress had been made, though on Harvie's part it was both grudging and minimal. 'If there was to be a footpath towards his dyke at Westthorn, it should be the narrowest possible one', recalled a contemporary witness critical of Harvie's stance, some three decades later.[23] Still, a pathway was laid out, which Harvie proposed to fence on both sides. A doorway had been opened in the western wall (Harvie's Dyke). Just over 7 feet high, it was marginally under 3 feet wide, with a round cast iron pillar in the middle to prevent cattle passing through. At the wall at the eastern edge of Westthorn another opening had been made, albeit tighter than the other – less than 2 feet wide at its narrowest.[24] Even so, there was a way through. The pursuers – Ferrie, Rodgers and the campaign committee – had to undertake to keep the path in good repair at their own expense, without encroaching in any way on Harvie's property.[25] They also failed in their bid to insist that Harvie should pay for drains in places identified as being soft and wet. Nor were they able to persuade the court that Harvie should shoulder the expense of Kyle's reports. In the grand scheme of things, these were minor setbacks.

By the end of 1829 the campaigners had largely succeeded in achieving what they had set out to do, almost seven years earlier. The liberty of the banks of the Clyde had been secured. Yes, Harvie's Dyke still stood. Indeed, the eastern boundary of what would be the post-1832 Reform Act parliamentary constituency of Glasgow was formally identified as the point where the river Clyde was joined by Harvie's Dyke. Marked on a map that gave expression to a new democratic age, 'Mr Harvie's Dyke' remained a formidable structure. No longer, however, was it an impassable obstruction.

Joy at the end of a long road

The committee of men who had led the legal campaign were feted throughout Glasgow. Such was the depth of gratitude felt by the public for the five campaign committee members that a call was made for them to be rewarded with medals. Yet another public meeting was called, this time 'for Promoting the Subscription to procure Medals, Commemorative of the Triumph of the Citizens of Glasgow in Establishing Their Right to a Path on the Banks of the Clyde'.[26]

At what was a joyous meeting an eclectic assortment of poems were read, along with extracts from *Blackwood's Magazine* and the Bible. A palpable heady millenarian current ran through the proceedings that celebrated what those present judged to be an immensely significant victory of right over might, of freedom over oppression.

Scottish poets featured prominently. Allan Cunningham and Thomas Campbell were the most prestigious, but pertinent works from lesser poets were also included and read aloud by performers intent on celebrating in the most noble terms the recent victory by the Clyde. The rising poet of Glasgow – and the Clyde – Dugald Moore was one of these. A private soldier's son, born in Stockwell Street in Glasgow, he had only recently made his debut as a published poet with *The African: a tale, and other poems* (1829). The first stanza of his 'Columbus on First Beholding America', mirrors the feelings of joy and relief of the beneficiaries of the Clyde walkway campaigners following their success in the House of Lords:

> God of my sires! O'er ocean's brim
> Yon beauteous land appears at last;
> Raise, comrades! Raise your holiest hymn,
> For now our toils and past:
> See o'er the bosom of the deep,
> She gaily lifts her summer charms,
> As if at last she long'd to leap
> From dark oblivion's arms.

The outcome was celebrated too in allegorical poems such as James Sheridan Knowles's 'Triumph of Malachi, King of Meath, By Whom the Danes under Turgesius were Expelled Ireland', published the previous year in the *Edinburgh Literary Journal*. Knowles, Cork-born and better known as a dramatist and actor, came to Glasgow in 1816 where he wrote plays – the one that established his reputation, 'Virginius', a tragedy, was first performed at the Theatre Royal in Glasgow. He also wrote poetry and, largely to make some money, in 1823–4 edited the liberal *Free Press*.[27] The 'Triumph of Malachi' opens with a call to arms for Erin's cause, 'the one the tyrant fears, / The freeman dares to die in!', and ends in triumph:

> Then fled the Dane, while Erin's son,
> New-burst from bonds inglorious,
> Stood free the gory plain upon
> That saw his arms victorious.

Sandy Rodger, very much the driving force behind the gathering, offered yet another song to acclaim the people's triumph. The message of 'Come, Fill a Bumper' was unambiguous. Friends and neighbours were invited to drink 'to the *right* we has struggled for sairly', and fairly won. Rodger demanded that his fellow citizens pledge to 'prize what we've purchased so dearly', that 'Now may we tread with glee Clyde's lovely margin free, / High as the dyke was – 'tis tumbled right rarely.' Restored as a right of way, the banks of the Clyde were now full of life, and cheeriness, 'Throng'd with each class that loves liberty dearly' – the enduring trope that had united Harvie's opponents. Befitting the occasion, the song concluded with a toast to the 'brave honest hearts of our Committee', which Rodger urged those present to honour. What would we have done without them, he asked: they stood strong, fought hard and sought to stem 'tyranny's tide'.

Another message, a moral one, was simple but profound: with pride comes a fall, an idea starkly put in a poem – 'Napoleon's Grave' – which described Napoleon Bonaparte's rise to glory through 'conquest and crime', before turning to his tragic demise. 'Such a name thrown away, / Such a glory to be wasted', declared the poet, who ended the poem acclaiming Freedom's revenge before noting the ordinariness of Napoleon's resting place, not by the Seine as he wished but in the Valley of the Willows (now the Valley of the Tomb, or Vallée du Tombeau) on St Helena, where he was exiled and lived alone for the last years of his life. Above his grave, before his remains were repatriated in 1840 and later buried in Les Invalides in Paris:

> Towers no high crested column
> His ashes above . . .
> There's nought but the willow stems o'er his tomb wave,
> And pale wild-flowers alone deck his low captive grave!

This, the assumption (or hope) was, would be the fate that lay before Thomas Harvie.

The Concluding Address at what was in effect a thanksgiving gathering was even more direct, even if Harvie was not referred to by name. The last lines are telling, in praise of the campaigners who had 'won from Selfishness its close-hugg'd spoil' and whose memory should be secured for all time:

> 'Tis not the value of the wretched coin
> That avarice takes from Poverty, that makes
> The miser and the cut-purse seem the same,
> But 'tis that Right, hath over Might, for once,
> Stride with the dignity of conscious worth;
> And, therefore, on the deathless Medals' shield

Stamp the proud record, and the emblems meet,
Which shall, when even the generations die
That centuries may see rise from their sons, –
Tell distant ages, as they raise their stones
Which show where cities had their dwelling place –
That these held men – had Civic Hampdens[28] too,
Who 'Knew their rights, and knowing durst maintain!'

Enough money was subscribed for at least one 'massive' gold medal, which was later presented to Adam Ferrie, but perhaps due to financial constraints, bronze versions were cast too. Ferrie was delighted, and frequently wore his medal at public functions in Canada, where he permanently emigrated to in 1829, shortly after attending several dinners held in his honour in Glasgow, at which he was also presented with various pieces of silver plate. The medals' designer was William Warren, professor of drawing and superintendent in Scotland of the British School of Engraving in John Street, Glasgow. The medals were struck by the highly esteemed engraver and medallist Thomas Wells Ingram, formerly of the Soho Mint in Birmingham, established in 1788 by Matthew Boulton, James Watt's business partner (see Plate 14).

Powerfully symbolic, on one side of the medallions was the figure of Justice, protecting with a sword old Father Clyde. Beneath her feet lies the defeated figure of Rapacity, or Selfishness (that is, Thomas Harvie), while above, a herald holds a banner on which is inscribed the motto, 'Defend Your Rights'. In the background are trees representing the walkway by Westthorn and the base of a monument suggestive of Glasgow – possibly the base of Admiral Nelson's monument that dominated the Green. On the reverse side were recorded the names of the campaign committee: Adam Ferrie, George Rodgers (whose name was misspelt as Roger), James Duncan, John Watson and John Whitehead. The five men named were thanked by the 'Citizens of Glasgow', for 'Successfully Defending their Right to a Path on the Banks of the Clyde 1829'.

Deemed worthy of recognition too was Alexander Rodger, the campaign poet and song writer as well as one-time organiser, although he was not one of the medal awardees. Indeed, there were those who credited him with being 'a principal, if not the chief instrument . . . of ultimately establishing the right of the public to a footpath on the banks of the Clyde'.[29] Tirelessly, 'in the face of many difficulties and reproaches', he gathered evidence (and witnesses), promoted subscriptions, 'got up concerts and exhibitions, and did all he could think of to raise funds to carry on the law-suit'. Yet for reasons unknown – perhaps as he hadn't been a formal member of the campaign committee, or due to his class background, or his fearless and outspoken radicalism – there was no medal for Rodger. During the campaign period Rodger had worked hand in hand with middle-class reformers. It is an open question, then, whether despite this and his adoption of peaceful campaigning methods, his known association with the radical cause – as in 1820 – may have been hard to discount even by the liberal-minded, reform-backing members of Glasgow's middle classes who had led the campaign in its later, legal, stages. It was some years afterwards that former radicals or those assumed to have been radicals were deemed acceptable by their former persecutors. Towards the end of the 1830s, and even more so after the defeat of Chartism during the following decade, radicalism was less the fearsome threat it had appeared earlier in the century, particularly in 1819 and 1820.

Indeed, in 1836 some two hundred of his fellow citizens did present Rodger with a box of silver sovereigns, but whether or not this was related to his role in the Harvie's Dyke struggle is not clear. What is certain is that throughout most of his adult his life Rodger stuck by his deeply held principles, uncompromisingly expressed. His 'The True Rights of the People', written in 1839, was a toast to 'Freedom, the goddess whom Britons adore', whose name was being sullied by the country's lords who starved and oppressed the 'groaning' people. 'True Rights' was included in a penny publication, *The Altar of Liberty, Or, Songs for the People*. These angrier productions were written in the wake of what Rodger and other working-class radicals felt was the betrayal of the Reform Act of 1832; their hopes, based on Whig promises about the extent to which the franchise would widen, had been dashed.

Although his role in the Harvie's Dyke affair seems never to have been formally celebrated, Rodger's contribution to the cultural life of the city was recognised at a 'great festival' held in the Trades Hall in his honour in 1843. He was sixty years old and would die within three years. Many – around four hundred – 'of the most honoured citizens of Glasgow came forward to testify their respect for the genius and virtues of their humble, but gifted townsman', as did others from further afield.[30] In the chair was the imposing figure of Professor John Wilson, 'Christopher North', advocate, poet and essayist, above all for the Tory-leaning *Blackwood's Magazine*. In 1820 he had been appointed Professor of Moral Philosophy at the University of Edinburgh. Wilson was a giant of the Scottish literary scene who had befriended many of the greatest writers of the age, including William Wordsworth, Samuel Taylor Coleridge and Sir Walter Scott.

It was greatly to Rodger's credit that while from a young age he had been 'a staunch and active Radical', Wilson was able to pay tribute to Rodger's poetic achievements, toasting him as 'the Bard of the West'.[31] Fifteen years later, his fellow poet Robert Burns would receive almost identical praise, but from Sir Archibald Alison, then the sheriff of Lanarkshire (and an ally of Wilson). And half a century after his death in 1846, Glasgow's east end poet and political activist was still remembered fondly. In 1897 his poetry and songs, including those he had composed during the 1820s when the struggle with Harvie was ongoing, were published in a new edition of his works, edited by a member of Bridgeton Burns Club – reflecting local pride in a local man. Rodger is Glasgow's best-known largely self-taught or autodidactic poet of the radical era.

Occasionally, even individuals who had actively participated in the initial attempt to remove the Westthorn walls by force found their place in the city's chronicles. Around the middle of the century, Hugh MacDonald, then gathering material for his *Rambles Round Glasgow*, came across 'poor George Allan', whom he described as 'one of the Harvie's Dyke heroes'. Although he was too young to have had any first-hand knowledge of what had gone on at Harvie's Dyke, MacDonald was well informed. Born in 1817 in Bridgeton, where he lived for the rest of his life, MacDonald had been employed as a block printer at Monteith & Co.'s Barrowfield works and, as a fervent Chartist, would have been familiar with Glasgow's east end radical traditions.[32] Allan was living at Kenmuir near Carmyle, a tenant of what was described locally as the 'narrow house'. Allan, as we saw in Chapter 1, had been a prominent radical in 1820 and was responsible for calling at least two of the meetings that were held in Parkhead in June 1823 to discuss what to do about Harvie's encroachments. He had played a prominent part as the walls were demolished and for a time was the prosecuting authorities' prime suspect.

Some three decades later, evidently still working at the loom, Allan was to be found on summer Sundays on the banks of the Clyde, regaling passers-by with his knowledge of botany and plant lore, and singing songs extolling nature's virtues. In one song he wrote, set to a Gaelic air, class difference was a theme, but transcending this was something altogether more meaningful: 'We grudge not the worldling his pomp, power, and pleasure', Allan sang. The next line ran 'Tho' nameless and poor, down life's rough course we steer', before the song's final flourish: 'Far frae the haunts of men', joyously, 'we flower-lovers go.'[33]

Allan's fellow committee members from Parkhead, on the other hand, had been forgotten, their association with the Harvie's Dyke protest eclipsed by other concerns. William Lyon was remembered not for his role in planning the 21 June demonstration but as a well-regarded surgeon who, after establishing his reputation as an able physician, eventually left Parkhead for the city. In 1844 he was appointed to the Infirmary in Glasgow, where he presented papers and wrote on aspects of medical practice, including the pressing matter of fever control. Such was his eminence that in 1859 he was awarded an honorary degree by the University of Glasgow.

Peter Mackenzie hoped that the names of the four men who were tried and sentenced in September 1823 for their participation in the Harvie's Dyke riot 'may yet be rung on the banks of the Clyde with those of the other men who pioneered the way for the victory before the jury'.[34] He would have been disappointed. Only locally, and even then sporadically, have the names of the Harvie's Dyke quartet been remembered. History has been more generous with the names of their successors, those who fought the legal battle.

Thomas Harvie: the fall

For Harvie, the defeat in the House of Lords was little short of disastrous. He had gambled everything on success and lost. One estimate was that his expenses for this action alone amounted to £3,000, a sum inflated by his being 'fleeced and cheated by all hands'.[35] This was in addition to all the costs he had incurred since 1823, in rebuilding the walls, defending them, and battling with George Rodgers and his allies in the Scottish courts.

As one acid-laced contemporary report put it, 'His purse strings were at an end.' Unable to pay his opponents' costs, he had no alternative but to declare himself bankrupt. He was ruined. His business empire and the Westthorn estate were built upon less secure financial grounds than many supposed; they were mortgaged to the hilt. Even before the final judgment of the House of Lords, he was struggling financially. His debts amounted to £60,000. At first it was thought that he might survive, as several of his creditors were wealthy corn merchants. This was in March 1829. Yet on 21 April 1832, following a ruling by the Court of Session's Lord Fullarton granting a sequestration order, *The Scotsman* included the Glasgow Distillery Company in a list of sequestrations. Harvie was named as a partner in the firm and as an individual. His creditors were to meet in the Black Bull Inn a few days later. The dismal situation was not improved when, as the sequestration proceedings got under way, it became apparent that Harvie's collieries (he had one at Easterhouse as well as the Westthorn pits) were 'a loosing concern'. The colliers were refusing to work unless they were paid in advance, and while the main steam engine at Westthorn had to be kept going to prevent flooding underground, no coal was being worked, other than what was sold to cover the operating costs. The result was that many colliers deserted what less than a decade earlier had been one of Glasgow's most productive collieries.

By 1835, of between eighty and a hundred colliers' dwelling houses on Harvie's lands, only around fifteen were occupied; many of the rest were almost derelict. Numerous other small houses on the estate were also unlet. Without protection the estate was at risk from vandalism, or perhaps from acts of revenge; sometime before 1835 the lead from the roof of the lodge from which small cannon fire had been directed at the rioters in June 1823 had been stolen. Equally, on Sunday fast days the banks had had to be watched, presumably for the intrusions of revellers.[36]

In 1834 the two distilleries at Port Dundas belonging to Harvie's company were advertised for sale, at an upset price of £17,000. Harvie's whisky shops were 'displenished' and shut down. Advertised at the same time was a second lot: Westthorn estate and mansion house. Bids were to commence at £21,871, with the sale being held in Edinburgh's Parliament House.[37] The fine furniture with which he had filled Westthorn house was rouped (auctioned) and sold off. The house had been let in 1830 to John Struthers, auctioneer. He was succeeded by George Wilson from Dalmarnock. Eventually, in 1836, Westthorn was sold to James Farie of Farme, in Rutherglen, a successful coalmaster whose Farme colliery lay directly across the Clyde from Westthorn.

His reputation sullied, Harvie became an object of both fun and vilification. He was the subject of at least one popular song, one line of which ran, 'every stone in Tamie's dyke would cost a hunder pounds'. Commentators at the time and years later portrayed his life as a stark morality tale. His ordinary background and good fortune in business were the starting points. 'Self-conceit – the odour of riches paid to him, elevated him beyond his natural latitude; and he looked on the very race from which he sprung with sovereign contempt.' His 'doggedness, or haughtiness', according to the same critic writing for the *Glasgow Gazette*, or just headstrong determination, caused him to 'knock his own head against his own thick wall. It overthrew and demolished him. He fell under the ruins he himself had literally created.'[38] He became virtually a non-person, vanishing from the city's Post Office directories, in which in the 1820s he had appeared as the owner of several city centre properties, primarily business premises, but also the townhouse he owned in Dunlop Street. After his sequestration he was left with only one shop – which he may have rented – a provision store in College Street.

No-one, it seemed, had much pity for him. Aged sixty-five, Harvie died suddenly on 7 May 1839, having 'dropped down in an apoplectic fit' while in his College Street store. All he left was an estate worth £67 8s 4d (£67.40, £8,572 today). This was the sum garnered at the roup of his few belongings including pieces of household furniture and clothing that he owned at the time of his death. After the grandeur of Westthorn he spent his final months, possibly longer, living with Margaret McOwat in what were probably rented premises in Duke Street, which was very close to his business premises. What part she played in the relationship is hard to say, other than that she was very young – in her early to mid teens – in comparison to Harvie. Most likely she was a carer or housekeeper, who may late on have become Harvie's wife (although there is no formal record of this, and in another account he was said to have died 'a Bankrupt Batchelor'). Yet Margaret is described as his relict, which normally means a widow. Margaret is almost certainly the person referred to in the Parish of Glasgow's burial record in 1843 as a servant, nineteen years old.[39] She had succumbed to 'fever' early on during an outbreak in July. By autumn typhus was ravaging the poorest parts of the city, to which the illness was largely confined.

Harvie was hardly a pauper, but neither was he able to live in anywhere near the style to which he had become accustomed in his heyday. His passing was barely remarked, other than in a brief factual note in the *Glasgow Chronicle* that was thereafter printed in other papers.[40] Nor was anyone inclined to pen the kind of glowing obituary accorded to the other business leaders of the period, who had established Glasgow as the Second City of the Empire. Fleeting, unflattering references were all that he merited, as in John M'Dowall's *People's History of Glasgow* (1899): 'purse-proud' and 'ignorant', Harvie had died 'a ruined and broken man'.

Conclusion: Memory, Legacy and the Historians

While the Harvie's Dyke struggle has largely been relegated to the fringes of Scotland's people's history, it was not always thus. For many decades this momentous event was remembered with pride, particularly in the city of Glasgow, for which it had a special meaning. But the episode had a wider significance too. The opposition mounted against Harvie's infringements has been credited by Harvey Taylor in his *A Claim on the Countryside: A History of the British Outdoor Movement* with being the first effectively organised campaign in Britain to defend the right of way as a public amenity. It was not until 1824 that rights of access aroused similar action in England, in Yorkshire, two years after the first stirrings of discontent over Harvie's blockading of the Clyde passageway. Historians in Scotland have also failed to recognise the significance of the Harvie's Dyke campaign as a precursor of the better-known and formally constituted Association for the Protection of Public Rights of Roadway in and around Edinburgh (established in 1845) – later the Scottish Rights of Way Society.[1] But this is not the only aspect of the Harvie's Dyke protest that historians in Scotland have overlooked. The direct links between some of the personnel involved in the riot and subsequent campaign over the Westthorn walls and those in reform circles, dating back to the 1790s as well as the Radical Rising of 1820, have not been noticed, let alone explored. Consequently, an opportunity to enrich our understanding of Scottish popular politics in the period has been missed.

Little wonder then that a recent authoritative assessment by Gordon Pentland of what is known about radicalism in Scotland up to 1832 concluded that the 1820s have been 'something of a blind spot' for historians.[2] Only by investigating events, personalities, structures, groups and the rapidly shifting contexts in which politics were practised, he argued, can we begin to achieve an accurate description of the developing political culture of Scotland across these years. In a similar vein, those writing about the rising of 1820 have been urged to undertake deeper archival research to better understand the radicals' political philosophies – and just what it was that motivated them.[3] The *Address to the Inhabitants of*

Great Britain and Ireland that was distributed throughout the west of Scotland on 1 April is not only ambiguous because it can be read both as a challenge to the status quo and as a loyalist declaration, but also only takes us so far. This book has set out to peel back the layers of testimony relating to the Harvie's Dyke riot in 1823 and the subsequent campaign against Thomas Harvie, and peer behind the curtain of neglect created by the long passage of subsequent time. This Conclusion takes stock of the evidence so far presented and employs it to challenge or at least to substantially modify long-held understandings of the Scottish radical tradition during the crucial years before the Great Reform Act of 1832.[4]

Harvie's Dyke remembered

In 1851 Robert Reid or 'Senex', then in his late seventies and one of Glasgow's most knowledgeable antiquarians, concluded when writing about the Clyde pathway near Dalmarnock that he needed to say little about 'the famous case of Harvie's Dyke' as it 'must still be fresh in the recollection of most . . . readers'. It certainly was for one of Bridgeton's older residents who as a boy had been an awestruck eyewitness as the walls were being pulled down. Writing in 1864 – and having lived through the period of the parliamentary reform movement up to 1832, Chartist demonstrations in 1839 and 1848, and the agitation against the Corn Laws that were repealed in 1846 – he declared that he had never participated 'as actor or spectator, in anything as truly magnificent as that great opening of the Banks of the Clyde'.[5]

The struggle and its resolution were considered to be highly newsworthy. From the midsummer demonstration at Westthorn in 1823 that resulted in the demolition of Harvie's walls until the House of Lords ruling in 1828, the case was reported and avidly read about not only in the Glasgow press and broadsheets, but also in newspapers in Scotland, England and Ireland. In 1855 a contributor to the *Christian News*, while frowning at the sight of a nunnery close to Westthorn ('anything but a pleasant feature in a Scottish landscape'), hailed 'Harvie's Dyke' as being 'famous in the history of popular rights . . . [with Thomas Harvie's actions] being an attempt to circumscribe the liberties of the citizens of Glasgow'. At a time when landed power was still in the ascendant and landowners old and new throughout the country were vigorously asserting their property rights, the people's victory was a momentous, lasting achievement. David had taken on Goliath and won, or so it seemed.

Evidence of the longevity of the warmth of the public's memory of the affair in Glasgow is not limited to Senex's memoir. Late in 1849, Adam Ferrie, aged seventy-six and now settled in Montreal in Canada, paid a visit to his native city. As a supporter of democratic reform and other liberal causes in Scotland, since leaving he had established a reputation as a prominent campaigner for the abolition of slavery and an outspoken advocate for improving conditions at sea for the many thousands of migrants who braved the Atlantic crossing to Canada. Among these were paupers from Ireland, at the outset of their journeys in dire circumstances owing to the devastating potato famine of the later 1840s. Ferrie was a distinguished member of the Legislative Council of Canada – a royal appointment. Partly for this reason and hailed as 'one of the old veterans of 1793' (the year when eighteenth-century radicalism in Scotland, stirred by the French Revolution and Thomas Paine's *Rights of Man*, was at its height), Ferrie was treated to a grand dinner in his honour in Glasgow's Trades Hall.

The dinner was attended by many leading figures – local politicians, city officials such as the influential buildings and streets engineer and architect John Carrick, as well as businessmen and landowners – but it was Ferrie's role in leading the fight against 'Mr Thomas Harvie of stone dyke notoriety' that was the main focus of the speeches. The chairman, Baillie John Mitchell, opened the list of toasts with one for 'The Immortal Memory of the Removal of Harvie's Dyke, by legal means'. Thereafter, a respectful silence followed a toast to the memories of Ferrie's four colleagues, now all deceased. The gathering, however, was not simply an occasion for looking back. Present were members of Renfrew town council, currently in the throes of a courtroom struggle with the Campbells of Blythswood, who were intent on closing up a footpath that had run from the burgh of Renfrew to the confluence of the rivers Cart and Clyde. Accordingly, the opportunity was taken to acknowledge the inspiration Ferrie had provided, above all his fortitude in carrying on the campaign during the six years from 1823 until 1829, and his ability to raise monies from the public.[6]

Unfortunately, his last effort in this regard was less satisfactory. A fund, designed in principle as a means in future 'of preventing those of aristocratic principles, from attempting to rob the people of their just rights', had been established in the final months prior to his departure from Greenock for Canada. Ferrie was the fund's treasurer. The expectation was that with interest the £384 deposited would grow. However, with Ferrie overseas and the trustees appointed to manage it dead, by the time of his return to Scotland in 1849, no-one was sure of the whereabouts of the fighting fund. To all intents and purposes it was – and is – lost.

Ferrie's reputation remained untarnished. He and his wife were the only passengers mentioned by name in the west of Scotland press when they left from Greenock in April 1850 on the maiden voyage of the steamer *City of Glasgow* en route for New York, an event reported to have been watched by 100,000 people. He was also remembered on less notable occasions. On a spring afternoon in May 1852, someone signing themself 'D. B.' decided to row from Glasgow Bridge to Dalmarnock, to explore and report on the condition of the upper reaches of the Clyde. Within ninety minutes and assisted by the flowing tide, D. B. and companion had travelled almost four miles and reached the city's Water Works, the furthest point on their journey. There they stopped and spotted on the opposite bank 'the celebrated dyke' and what was described as a Martello tower at Westthorn. Resting on their oars and after noting how clear the shallow water was, they drank 'a bumper to the health of Mr Adam Ferrie, late of this city, and his numerous friends in Canada'.[7] Not dissimilarly, seven years later, a journalist from the *Glasgow Gazette* in 1859 offered thanks 'to all the good men and true, who combated [the] . . . case and brought it to such a triumphant conclusion for the PUBLIC', thousands and tens of thousands of whom now benefited from having access to the pathway.

Yet the details of the Harvie's Dyke incident wore thinner over time. Even in 1858, it was felt that for younger readers of the *Glasgow Sentinel* it would help if the story of Harvie's Dyke was told anew, as a key component of the city's civic consciousness and to act as an inspiration to others. By the later decades of the nineteenth century new generations of Glaswegians had to be prodded to recall what they had been told of the affair by their grandparents and mothers and fathers, or picked up in conversation with older people, or simply read in passing. Only a handful of them would have been familiar with the *Narrative of the Proceedings in the Case Rodgers and others, v Harvie, For the Recovery of the Liberty of the Banks of the Clyde*. This had been published in 1829 by Hugh Cameron, in the Gallowgate, and John Smith, whose office was near the Post Office in Nelson Street. The duo's bold aim was to present a 'concise history' of the Harvie's Dyke affair, with the intention that it should 'serve as a MEMORIAL of past proceedings, and a faithful RECORD' of the recovery of the 'privilege which the citizens of Glasgow, and the inhabitants of the surrounding villages thought worth contending for: and which, after a severe struggle, they succeeded in wrenching from the grasp of an encroacher'.

By the twentieth century, the Harvie's Dyke affair, no matter how much a 'cause célèbre' it had been previously, had all but faded from public memory. Even so, there was still a place at the Scottish Exhibition of National History, Art and Industry held in Glasgow in 1911 for the display of the medal presented to James Duncan in 1829. Despite their immense importance at the time they were struck, two of the medals that have survived now lie more or less forgotten in Glasgow Museums Resource Centre at Nitshill. But at least they have been kept. Otherwise, the Harvie's Dyke affair became the province of antiquarians and local historians, as in John Ord's *Story of the Burgh of Calton*, published in 1912. In 1933 James Cowan, a journalist with a keen interest in and an eye for Glasgow's past, wrote an article for the *Glasgow Evening Citizen* recounting his walk along the north bank of the Clyde. Coming across what remained of the 'old dyke' at Westthorn, he remarked that the contest over this was 'much more familiar to the last generation than it is to ours'. Now, almost a century after Cowan's musing, even less is known about the encounter.

Legacy secured?

The public memory of the campaign over Harvie's Dyke remained vivid until the middle of the nineteenth century. What though of its legacy, its impact? In the courts, the Harvie's Dyke case – normally referred to in the footnotes of legal texts as *Rodgers* v *Harvie* or *Harvie* v *Rodgers* – was for many years deemed an important milestone. Key principles were either established or reinforced by the decision. The definition of a right of way was clarified: it was a 'right of passage' on a more or less defined route, from one terminus to another, and not simply a right for the public to stroll or wander about. (This remains the basis of the definition of a public right of way today, of which there are some 7,000 in Scotland.) To be designated a right of passage, paths must have been used for this purpose for a specified number of years, provided there had been 'undisturbed and peaceable use and possession'. Gates could be used to enclose cattle, but not to interfere with the 'convenience of the public'. But the House of Lords ruling on the *Harvie* v *Rodgers* case had established that once a line of footpath had been defined and determined, a proprietor was entitled only to put in swing or wicket gates, and that these should be 'easily opened' by those using them.[8]

Although Glasgow's magistrates had been notable by their silence on the Clyde passageway issue in the early 1820s, by the 1880s the city's authorities were taking their obligations to the community in this regard more seriously. In 1887 the town clerk, James D. Marwick, and J. Lang, the clerk of police, were asked to report to the Clyde Navigation Trust about a footpath on the south bank of the Clyde which ran eastwards from Oatlands to Rutherglen Bridge and beyond. The path had subsided by some 12 feet where it ran over the underground workings of Govan colliery, one of Scotland's largest coal-mining enterprises. Furthermore, William Dixon, the proprietor, had reduced the width of the path by erecting a 7-foot-high fence. This had the effect of endangering passers-by during stormy weather or when the river was in flood, as they could no longer walk on the higher ground which had been fenced off. Marwick and Lang – almost certainly with the Westthorn case in mind (Marwick was a historian of Glasgow) – were in no doubt what should happen. As the path was mainly used 'for the purposes of business and recreation', especially by workpeople who necessarily used it night and day, in all seasons, whatever the state of the weather, it was essential that it was well maintained and passable. The path, they were convinced, had been an 'undisputed right of way . . . enjoyed by the inhabitants of Glasgow for time immemorial'. However, as this usage had recently been altered 'to the disadvantage of the public', it was the responsibility of Dixon's trustees (William Dixon had died in 1859) to remedy the current situation and remove the fence 'to a suitable distance from the river'.[9] What other steps they took was a matter for the trustees, provided they preserved the public right of way.

As this instance shows, despite early optimism, the legacy of 1829 was not altogether secure. The gains made by the Harvie's Dyke campaigners had continuously to be defended. Ironically it was Adam Ferrie who, early on, was confronted by the fact that it was one thing to establish the right of passage principle, and quite another to enforce it. During his visit to Scotland in the winter of 1849–50, he had walked out to the scene of what he considered to be his greatest achievement – Westthorn. He had been disappointed, however, to find that the Lords' judgement and the ruling of the Court of Session had been 'set at defiance by some of the proprietors of the lands on this route . . . most particularly one of them immediately above the Waterworks'.[10] This was perilously close to Westthorn.

Worse was to follow. Six years later, in many parts of Scotland what were described as encroachments upon the poor man's liberties were becoming numerous. Near Rutherglen and at another location nearby, palisades were blocking the walkway along the river. These may have been the obstacles that persuaded Ferrie, on another trip to Scotland in 1855, to write to Glasgow's Lord Provost, urging him to have them removed.

Concerns about violations such as these multiplied, with the *Glasgow Sentinel* declaring in May 1858 that 'the inestimable privilege achieved by the heroes of Harvie's Dyke is in serious danger of violation'. The old spirit, the paper's editor regretted, 'is not now amongst us'. The people of Glasgow and its suburbs were in the 1820s 'not . . . quite so patient or submissive' as nowadays. Consequently, with most violent protest being nipped in the bud by the authorities and rarely engaged in by workers, who were now intent on demonstrating their preparedness to promote their interests by constitutional means, it was proposed that the appropriate vehicle by which to object to the new obstacles was a Footpath Protection Society – of the kind extant in Edinburgh and that had just been formed in Paisley.[11] Certainly something had to be done according to 'M.D. & Prof' in a letter to the *Glasgow Herald* in 1864. The path along the Clyde was not only narrow, with high wooden palisades blocking 'every glimpse of rural nature', it was also spread with 'coarse engine ashes, that make the feet sore to tread upon'. The campaigners' legacy of 1829, a boon to the 'poor sons of toil' and a 'sacred trust' to be handed down through posterity, had been besmirched. The 'boasted right to the banks of the Clyde has been reduced to something no longer worth having'. So important was the matter that Glasgow's citizens were urged by the letter writers to bestir themselves again. At the next town council elections 'no man should be elected who did not pledge himself into the recent encroachments upon the banks of the Clyde, and to spare neither trouble nor expense to make them inviolate'.[12]

But it was not only the freedom to walk along the Clyde that was under threat. By mid century from across Scotland came reports of similar problems of access. Near Glasgow a path to Cathkin Braes had been shut off, while rights of way at Little Govan, Polmadie and Shawfield were also under threat. In the vicinity of Duntocher, Lord Blantyre had closed an old public pathway. Near Oban the 'laird of Dunolly' had 'against all law', closed a portion of the seashore. In 1847 Lord James Hay's closure of a path alongside the river Don was reported – and resisted. Like Harvie two decades beforehand, Hay had recoiled at the sight of working people strolling along within sight of his drawing-room windows. There were well-founded rumours that the 6th Duke of Atholl was planning to close access to Glen Tilt, having in 1847 attempted to turn back a party of Edinburgh University botany students. Before long, this case, like that of Harvie's Dyke, led to a prolonged lawsuit, with another following when Duncan McPherson, the new owner of the Glen Doll estate in the southern Cairngorms, closed Jock's Road, a well-worn route to Braemar. In the north and west, landowners whether established or the nouveau riche – often successful industrialists and other businessmen from the Lowlands and England – sought to extend and reorganise their estates with the aim of maximising their income. Like Thomas Harvie in the 1820s, they were keen too to enjoy exclusive rights to their properties. The ideal was to limit access to their own family members and friends, others they wished to impress, and those prepared to pay for the right to hunt, shoot and fish. As regards those properties that abounded with woodland, Christopher Smout has wryly written that, increasingly, 'only owners and their guests were welcome'.[13] By the 1880s Scotland's landed class appeared to be on a collective mission to block popular rights of way, remove rights to fishing, restrict the freedom to climb mountains on paths that had existed for more than forty years, and deny the public the liberty to explore forests, let alone shoot a rabbit for the pot. Described as an 'onslaught' that should be resisted, appeals were made for funds so that 'not an inch' of ancient right was allowed to lapse. Readers of newspapers such as the *Glasgow Weekly Herald* – one of many Scottish radical or liberal newspapers to feature and promote rights of way cases – were reminded of the legacy of the Harvie's Dyke success. The campaign was hailed as a 'glorious example' that should rouse the public from its apparent torpor over land rights – an issue that in the north and west of the country instigated the Highland Land War which broke out in 1881.

In the east end of Glasgow the call to arms was particularly pertinent. The right to walk freely on ancient pathways, it was argued by the *Weekly Herald*, was in a sense 'a matter of life and death to our humbler citizens, who are in growing danger of suffocation from want of pure air in the city and free spaces in the country'. In the early 1880s the earls of Blantyre and Home had initiated Court of Session proceedings to exclude anglers fishing on the Clyde where it flowed past their properties, and to stop walkers from using the riverside path beyond Carmyle. The two aristocrats' actions were followed less than ten years later by the deeds of a Mr Hamilton, owner of a nearby estate that incorporated Kenmuir Wood. This Hamilton had cut down, much to the dismay of the residents of Carmyle and other places nearby, who had been accustomed to walking there and enjoying the pleasures some of the woodland offered. Having removed some of the wood, Hamilton had then put in a stake-and-wire fence on a path that ran parallel to the Clyde, which walkers could use only in single file, if that. Echoing what had happened down river at Westthorn almost seventy years previously, a public meeting was called in June 1891 by a local Vigilance Committee. The assembly was attended by a thousand people from Baillieston, Cambuslang, Carmyle, Shettleston and Tollcross. Passionate speeches were made by speakers from the temporary platform erected beside the river. One regretted the 'lukewarmness' of the public that had led to roads between Baillieston and Carmyle being shut up by landowners, while others condemned Hamilton's 'robbery' and urged that 'no effort should be spared' in maintaining 'what had been handed down by their forefathers'. As at Westthorn in 1823, there were those who insisted that nothing was to be destroyed, although as a Mr M'Culloch from Glasgow neatly put it, where the inalienable rights of the people were concerned, 'justice was not violence'. Sufficiently aroused, around half of those attending the meeting then marched, led by a Boys' Brigade pipe band, to the river near to what remained of Kenmuir Wood. Watched by a small police force, parties of what were described as 'young working men' then proceeded to cut the fence wires and remove the wooden stobs to which they were attached. They did so accompanied by cries of 'Gi'e them Harvie's Dyke' from an older, unnamed but angry man who demanded a cannon by means of which 'he proposed to remove all traces of landlordism from the landscape', including a 'handsome mansion standing in its own grounds half a mile off'. The man concerned may have been drunk, but the sentiments he expressed were inspired by the story of Harvie's Dyke that had been told and circulated by a local baillie in the weeks prior to the Carmyle meeting.[14] Clearly, the legacy of the protest of 1823 lived on. After a little less than two hours, not a vestige of the fence was left, following which those present left and returned to their respective villages.

Historians and Harvie's Dyke

The importance of the Harvie's Dyke affair in Glasgow's history, the extent to which it loomed large in the public's memory for several decades and continued to inspire similar protests for much of the rest of the nineteenth century, is beyond doubt. Yet the medals struck in 1829 pale into insignificance when set against the efforts devoted to securing the memory of the leaders of the 1820 Radical Rising. In 1832 a monument was erected for two of the three men executed for their alleged roles as ringleaders in the revolt, John Baird and Andrew Hardie. The other victim of execution, James Wilson, was not to be forgotten; a monument – a decorated obelisk – in his honour was erected in Strathaven, on the site of his former home, in 1846. The following year, 1847, the remains of Baird and Hardie were exhumed from where they had been buried in Stirling and reinterred in Glasgow's

Sighthill cemetery, the site marked by a grander commemorative monument, 'an abiding *lieu de mémoire* of Glasgow's and Scotland's past'.[15] Another monument was erected in Paisley in 1867. Relics too played their part in maintaining the memory of 1820, as for example a scrubbing brush inscribed by Andrew Hardie when he had languished in prison in Edinburgh Castle. This is held by Glasgow Museums. Flags and banners, weapons and the handkerchief dropped by James Wilson at his execution assisted in arousing emotions in the promotion of the radicals within 'a narrative of continuing struggle' dating back to the 1790s; martyrs to their cause, Baird, Hardie and Wilson are often claimed to have been an inspiration for the reformers of 1832 who demanded an extension of the franchise, the Chartists who sought political rights for the working classes, the Labour Party and, with less justification, even the SNP.[16] Various events commemorating 1820 were held in the twentieth century, primarily at the behest of the socialist movement in Scotland (the Independent Labour Party spearheaded the centenary celebrations in 1920) and Scottish nationalists.[17] The rising is remembered in September every year by bodies such as the 1820 Society. In 2020, the 200th anniversary, a slew of books appeared, indicative of the level of academic interest there is in the subject and the desire of their authors to sustain it as a momentous landmark in Scotland's history. Among the wider public, there is less enthusiasm, although this is not to disregard the sincerity of those who continue to commemorate the event.

Why then have the Harvie's Dyke campaigners been left by history's wayside? The attack on Harvie's walls was in an urban context equally if not more notable an episode in Scottish history than when in 1724 – a century earlier – over a thousand aggrieved tenants and cotters in Galloway had pulled down the stone dykes that landowners had erected around their great cattle parks: the Galloway Levellers. Why do we know more about riots in Scotland that were single, one-off events with short afterlives such as the Porteous Riot (1734), the Tron Riots (1811–12), the handloom weavers' strikes of 1787 and 1812, which failed to halt the demise of that once-dominant trade, or even the food riots of the east coast of Scotland in 1847, which marked the end of this type of popular protest in Scotland? By contrast, the Harvie's Dyke action was, in the short run, successful and, in the long run, in spite of setbacks, enduring.

Part of the explanation may lie in the fact that, other than short periods in prison, none of those involved in the struggle for the liberty of the banks of the Clyde had lost much besides time, effort and, in some cases, money. No-one had been beheaded or transported – the usual prerequisites for martyrdom.

More convincing in explaining why historians have overlooked the Harvie's Dyke affair is how Scotland's working-class and radical history has been told and understood. This is a problem that partly originates in the original source material, rather than with any failing on the part of historians. The unwitting culprit, in this regard, is Peter Mackenzie.

Mackenzie was a lawyer, journalist and parliamentary reformer. Born in Dumbarton in 1799, he was twenty-one at the time of the Radical War and lived for the rest of his life in Glasgow. In 1831 he founded and edited *The Loyal Reformers' Gazette* – a lively weekly paper from which he published a selection of articles in his two-volume *Reminiscences of Glasgow and the West of Scotland*, published in 1865. Although not always entirely reliable, he was present at and a credible witness to the happenings he wrote about until 1864, when he gave up the *Gazette*. Both his newspapers (the name of the *Gazette* was changed periodically) and the *Reminiscences* have provided invaluable evidence for historians of Glasgow and Scottish politics (as well as social history) for the period from the end of the Napoleonic Wars – when he moved to Glasgow – until just before the Second Great Reform Act of 1867 (1868 in Scotland). His coverage of 1819–20 is lengthy – over one hundred pages – and is an essential primary source for what happened in 1820.

However, in the second of his volumes of *Reminiscences* Mackenzie devoted a hefty thirty pages to 'Tam Harvie and the Dyke', and a further three to what he called 'The Poor Prisoners of West-thorn', Andrew Adamson, John Baird, Alexander M'Phie and Walter Winning. Just why this material has been disregarded is at first sight inexplicable. Mackenzie, however, was not helpful. He made no reference to any radical involvement in the campaign against Harvie. 'Sandy' Rodger the poet-activist is mentioned, but only as a fund-raiser. Adam Ferrie appears, but simply as the leading campaign organiser. No mention was made of his politics and commitment to reform. Altogether absent are the other former radicals who were concerned with Harvie's Dyke. It is possible that Mackenzie was unaware of the parts played by John Craig and the other more prominent radicals from 1820, but this seems unlikely given his intimate knowledge of Glasgow and its people.

Yet he took pains to distinguish the events of 1819 and 1820 from what he called 'the banks of Clyde case'. In his opening paragraph on the issue, he confessed to 'fatiguing our readers too much about *politics*'. Instead, he depicted the Harvie's Dyke confrontation as a kind of morality tale – which to an extent it was. There were too many men in the city, Mackenzie asserted, who were 'upstarts of no genuine reputation, only known for their successful audacity'. He deplored those of his fellow citizens who 'bow like menials to the man of reputed wealth, though his character be as black as the knave of clubs'. In Mackenzie's sights was Thomas Harvie. But Mackenzie's conception of politics was narrow. His interests lay in constitutional parliamentary reform. His was a narrative of reform agitation that ran from the 1790s, through the Thrushgrove gathering of 1816 to its apotheosis in the Whig-backed popular agitation of 1830–2.[18] He was inclined to depict 1820 as a kind of folly, the executed leaders as dupes led astray by government spies and agents provocateurs – which he believed he had exposed in a book published in 1833.[19] Consequently he failed to appreciate that the Harvie's Dyke protest and campaign could also be political – an instance where ordinary people from many walks of life united in their opposition to the actions of an aggressive, high-profile city businessman and landowner who had shown a flagrant disregard for what were perceived to be rights established by custom. The attack on Harvie's walls owed much to a phenomenon deriving from the previous century, namely what has become known as the concept of the moral economy – which can be interpreted as encompassing popularly held rights enjoyed 'beyond memory of man'. The demonstration at Westthorn and the legal crusade that followed were mirrored in other parts of urban Europe in the 1820s – in cities such as Hydra, Madrid and Palermo – with retributive actions being directed against those specific individuals perceived to have violated the trust of the population at large.[20] The riot which had initiated the campaign in Glasgow was similarly a reflection of the potential of urban communities to obtain satisfactory responses to specific demands, based on a belief in the principles of justice and honour – which Glasgow's municipal authorities had failed to uphold. At this stage in the march of industrialisation in Scotland struggles over custom were as just as prevalent as disputes over wages and working conditions.[21] Protests about customary rights were also acts of rebellion, in opposition to top-down social innovation that in this instance had curtailed the east end of Glasgow's communities' right to walk and play on a tract of land they had long considered their own.

But the preconceptions of historians too, consciously or otherwise, have made it difficult for them to incorporate the Harvie's Dyke affair into their narratives. Traditionally, working-class movements in the nineteenth century have been explained as having two strands which, combined, culminated in the early twentieth century as the Scottish (Council of the) Labour Party. Thus, the revolutionary year 1792 begat 1820 which – eventually – begat the first majority Labour government led by Clement Attlee in 1945. This was the approach adopted by the socialist journalist and

Labour politician Thomas Johnston in his seminal *History of the Working Classes in Scotland* (first published in 1920), in which the nineteenth century is covered in two chapters, 'The Unions' and 'The Communist Seeds of Salvation'. (Johnston said not a word about the Harvie's Dyke affair.[22]) Essentially the argument of Johnston and his successor historians is that organised labour, effectively the trade unions, was in the first half of the nineteenth century focused on workplace issues associated with early industrialisation. In this account key events included the general strike of the handloom weavers in 1812, and attempts by the cotton spinners to organise collectively, culminating in a major strike in 1837 and the subsequent transportation of the leaders in 1838. Thereafter, building on the moderatism and search for self-improvement that characterised artisanal culture in Scotland, the unions strove for respectability, adopted a more conciliatory attitude to employers and the capitalist system, and operated within the bounds of the law. The other contributory strand consisted of demands for political reform, represented by Thomas Muir and the 'martyrs' of the 1790s, the Radical Rising of 1820, the Chartists and the early socialists. In this light 1820 can be understood as an early instance of a merger of the two strands, with the radicals' demand for constitutional reform – manhood suffrage and annual parliaments – bound with, it has been asserted recently, the world's first general strike.[23]

Whatever motivated the relatively small number of ill-equipped insurgents in their skirmishes with the military at Bonnymuir and Strathaven early in April 1820, the assumption often made is that, with the defeats and the subsequent executions of three of the alleged ringleaders and banishment to Australia of many more, radicalism in Scotland went into hibernation. Or turned towards trade unionism. Demands for political reform were now led by the Whigs and more moderate reformers, essentially the middle classes. Under ceaseless pressure from cost-cutting employers, despairing workers had little choice but to narrow their focus and concentrate on the bread-and-butter issues of wages and living standards, and the control of work processes.[24]

In this view, it would be more than a decade before the radical movement revived, warmed back to life as campaigning over the Reform Bill got under way. One author has gone as far as to suggest that for ten years after the rising it was only a handful of old weaver agitators no-one listened to who carried on what remained of militant political endeavour, the assumption being (as with Mackenzie) that this was the only way that radicalism was expressed.[25] After 1820, this line of argument proceeds, the working classes were represented by 'reformist elements', mostly drawn from the nascent middle class.[26] This is broadly the interpretation favoured by Irene Maver, Glasgow's pre-eminent historian, who although describing the city's radicals as 'demoralised' in the wake of the failure of 1820, has identified a continuing strand of 'pugnacious local activism' in the city. The implication, however, is that this manifested itself mainly after 1830 and was linked with electoral politics.[27] The root of the problem here is that too often the Radical Rising is studied in isolation. The sources its investigators use rarely stray beyond 1820. Narratives conclude sharply with the executions of the three radical leaders, perhaps with a coda on the other arrestees who were transported to Australia in December. Then, usually without explanation, attention turns to the parliamentary reform agitation of 1831, for which, without any hard evidence, the radicals of 1820 are credited. Whether by accident or design, the consequence of all of this has been a failure to notice other manifestations of radicalism during the subsequent decade.[28] It is little wonder then that Harvie's Dyke has been largely overlooked or that the radical actors concerned have slipped below most historians' radar screens.

For all that, there is some merit in the proposition that 1820 was a salutary moment for working-class radicalism in Scotland. If the Harvie's Dyke campaign is at all representative of popular movements after 1820, there was clearly a recognition of the futility if not the dire consequences for those found guilty of bearing arms. Even though a massive crowd had marched to Harvie's Dyke in June 1823, physical force was in the main employed prudently. The violence of the demonstrators was never wanton, other than the actions of a handful of hotheads. Gunpowder, metal tools and brute force were used only for the very specific purpose of pulling down Harvie's intruding walls.

Compared to 1819 and 1820 the temper of the times had changed. No longer were the labouring poor suffering to the degree they had endured in the years immediately following the Napoleonic Wars, which had culminated in the militancy of 1819 and 1820. Then, subversive voices were not only heard but listened to. Radical orators promising that the property and possessions of the better-off would be seized and divided equally by the poor, had attracted would-be insurgents, unflatteringly described as being lean, pale, unwashed, unshaved and uncombed, 'thinly-clad, and out at knees and elbows'. They marched unevenly in small numbers to the sound of fifes, carrying with them 'many "a banner with a strange device"' – caps of liberty or a bundle of willow rods denoting unity and strength. In the background, arms were being requisitioned, stolen or manufactured in countless home settings and made ready for the planned rising. This frenzy of activity, though, was short-lived, its ringleaders shunned by what may have been a silent, loyal, law-abiding majority in those communities where they had risen to prominence.[29] It may well have been partly in recognition of this widespread unease among the population at large, with insurrectionary threats to secure political and related ends, that even in the radical *Address* of April 1820, and during the attack on Harvie's walls, violence was repudiated and private property respected. If so, Ferrie's call to take on Harvie without resort to physical force may not have had as much influence on the course of events as might be assumed. Indeed, moderation and a distaste for physical force may well have been longer-established features of Scotland's working-class reformers than is suggested in more excitable accounts of the insurrection of 1820; undoubtedly such traits would later account for the restraint and appeal to reason of Scotland's Chartists.[30]

In any case, certainly by 1823 emphasis was being placed on legal and constitutional ways of marshalling dissatisfaction with the perceived shortcomings of the state. There were exceptions. Perhaps driven by despair, some groups of workers continued to resort to violent means in order to defend their livelihoods when their occupations were under threat. In and around Glasgow, this meant mainly the struggling handloom weavers. Ameliorative government intervention was notable by its absence. Of the Harvie's Dyke demonstrators the prime example is Alexander M'Phie, the handloom weaver who had been obliged to find alternative work as a colliery sinker. We saw in Chapter 3 that in 1824 M'Phie was implicated in attempts to intimidate the fellow weaver George Smith and his sons, who had continued to work for an employer the Weavers' Association wished to bring to heel. M'Phie was said to have been party to the manufacture of murder-threatening effigies, stone throwing and chanting to further the Association's ends. There were tensions in cotton spinning too, which also led to ferocious assaults on strike- and custom-breaking workers. More sinister than threats using effigies was the use of vitriol (sulphuric acid) as a means of avenging a perceived wrong or punishing workers who broke ranks and continued to work, perhaps at a lower rate of pay. It was 'the deepest shame for the character of a certain class of our working population', wrote a correspondent to the *Glasgow Free Press* at the end of 1823, that the 'diabolical system of throwing vitriol upon the objects of their revenge is again revived in all its atrocity'.

It may well have been that the fervour with which the proposed assault on Harvie's Dyke was met in the cluster of villages centred on Parkhead on midsummer's eve in 1823 owed something to the handloom weavers' plight. There are historians who see 1820 as essentially a weavers' revolt; in this view 1823 can reasonably be interpreted as a continuation of their protestations against the loss of their craft status, a catastrophic fall in their earnings and the unresponsiveness of government to their plight. The villages that formed the nucleus of the protest over Thomas Harvie's walls were heavily dependent on the weaving trade and the employment it generated. The inhabitants of places like Parkhead were in the eye of the storm when it came to wage reductions and worsening working conditions. But in the specific circumstances of the time, in which pressure mounted against Harvie's encroachments on the Clyde pathway, this doesn't explain why colliers were in the vanguard of the evening procession to the offending Dyke. There was another reason for this.

We noted earlier that industrial relations in the coal industry in the Parkhead and Tollcross area were fraught in the early 1820s. They would become more so, including at Westthorn. Harvie was hardly the colliers' favourite employer. Colliery owners and managers in central Scotland had been attempting since the previous century to reorganise underground operations and break down customs regarding the darg (the amount of coal expected to be cut by each collier). They wanted too to curtail the ability of combinations, which had long frustrated their desire to recruit workers as they wished and at the rate of pay they chose. Tensions over these issues may have been running especially high at Westthorn in 1823 and might well explain the local colliers' antipathy towards Thomas Harvie. But it is unlikely that earnings were the problem. In 1823 such data on wage levels as is available suggests that miners' wages in or near Lanarkshire were on a rising trajectory from 1821 and peaked in 1825.[31] Indeed, the handloom weavers' dire circumstances notwithstanding, for many sections of the working class, the first years of the 1820s were relatively prosperous, contrasting sharply with the privations of the previous decade. But Harvie's Dyke was not in itself an economic issue; it was, as we have seen, a matter of customary right.

There were other issues that aroused the people's passions in the aftermath of 1820. Indeed, the defeat of the insurrection and the harshness of the punishments handed down to those deemed guilty of leading it, bred resentment among the working classes that manifested as small-scale but angry disturbances in the months and years immediately following. The most spectacular instance of popular disenchantment was the nationwide outpouring of sympathy with and support for Caroline, the estranged wife of the Prince Regent, son of the recently deceased King George III.

Determined that she should not become his queen, George IV instigated a Bill of Pains and Penalties against her, alleging, in lurid detail, adulterous behaviour. Among the protesters against the Regent's actions, which were judged to be unconstitutional, were parliamentary reformers and radicals, who used the occasion to heighten popular discontent and demand reform of the existing system.[32]

What the agitation over Caroline indicates is that working people were not only interested in direct reforms of the political system, notwithstanding the deep-seated dissatisfaction there was with it and the near-universal support there was for more radical change than was favoured by more moderate reformers and the Whigs. The focus of so many historians on 1820 itself has detracted from the significance of the wider discontent of which the rising was part. As Alexander Richmond, the weavers' advocate in 1812 and 1813, observed, working-class anger was directed towards the symptoms of a system of political economy that had effected 'almost a total revolution' which, far from promoting greater comfort and happiness, had caused society to go backwards. Reform, it has been argued, was pursued through 'countless local campaigns', its language adopted by other causes.[33] In a recent perceptive analysis of the uprising of 1820 it has been contended that the participants, whether as strikers or pike-carrying marchers, had no 'singular vision' of what they wanted, beyond 'making the current system work better on their behalf'.[34] It makes sense then, that it would be in particular neighbourhoods that unique, place-specific economic and social pressures were felt most acutely, and where those who felt especially strongly about a certain question would meet, discuss and organise to address it. Abstract principles including the defence of long-established rights were embodied in specific local individuals and issues, filtered through local priorities.

These were precisely the circumstances in which the Harvie's Dyke protest arose. Arguably it was the most momentous of the local disorders just referred to. And it was, in part, a continuation of the radical critique of the emergent economic, social and political order that pre-dated 1819–20. The most obvious indication of this was the involvement in 1823 of some of the men involved in the rising of 1820, namely George Allan, John Craig, Alexander Rodger and John Fauldhouse Wilson. We know too that Rodger's and possibly Fauldhouse's association with radical politics pre-dated 1820. Adam Ferrie had been an avid parliamentary reformer long before this, as were some of his allies from the Harvie's Dyke campaign. Significant too, and further emphasising continuity after 1820, are the communities of Parkhead and Tollcross and their surrounds, weaving and coal-mining strongholds where many radicals and their supporters resided. These were 'control rooms' from which the rising of 1820 was directed, and were still operational in 1823. In short, the Harvie's Dyke dispute demonstrates that if radicalism was slumbering after April 1820, it was only doing so lightly. Radicalism in Glasgow in 1820 had suffered a devastating blow, at least its militant wing had. But neither the working classes nor their allies further up the social scale had lost heart entirely. Injustice could still rankle and provoke a powerful response.

Beyond and between class

In making sense of Scottish society in the early nineteenth century, it would be foolish to ignore class formation – the making of a Scottish working class or, more accurately, the working classes. Neil Davidson has argued that 1820 marked a qualitative shift in the emergence of working-class consciousness. Yet at precisely the same time – the 1820s and 1830s – contrary forces were at work which served to weaken nascent bonds. Those forces included self-improvement among artisans and other skilled workers, concerted action on the part of employers to break the hold of certain groups of workers over production processes, and a determined effort on the part of the middle classes and evangelicals to improve the manners, habits and attitudes of working people.[35] Too much can be made of class division, of a supposed gulf between the working classes and the middle classes, the former retreating from political activity after 1820 and the latter taking over with a more moderate approach to political campaigning. The Harvie's Dyke campaign can be seen in this light: the failure of the violent assault on Harvie's walls involving largely the working classes, followed by the success of the campaign led by members of the middle classes in the courts. However, this construction of events is altogether too crude.

For one thing, opposition to Harvie's walls came from both working people and the small informal association of liberal-minded men, interested in books, ideas and current affairs, who met in James Duncan's shop in Glasgow's Saltmarket – the principal meeting place for the city's self-styled literati, who can also be defined as bourgeois commoners, to use the term coined by Edward Thompson. It was in environments like this that the near-universal support there was in nineteenth-century Scotland for political and social reform was born, the maternity suites of hegemonic Liberalism.

Looking back to the Harvie's Dyke riot from the vantage point of 1859, one observant writer described how the 'stumped *orators* from Glasgow' (who were also described as 'clever fellows') had come out to 'inflame' the weavers and colliers of the east end. They had an easy task. 'It was not necessary to say much to them about their supposed *rights*, for these they [the inhabitants of the east end villages] understood perfectly'; they too and their 'mothers and grandsires before them' had long walked along the banks of the Clyde 'without molestation' and had no intention of doing otherwise.[36]

There was anger – outrage even – among the working-class communities in the east end about Harvie's incursions. But even at this early stage the initial assault on the walls was led if not instigated by individuals who can be considered middle class – albeit the lower ranks thereof, the far end of the bourgeois commoner category. This included self-employed men who ran small businesses: the grocer John Marshall who chaired two of the Parkhead meetings, and the baker John McCracken. Prominent too were the two articulate professionals, the teacher John Williamson, and William Lyon the surgeon. And there were other respected, probably charismatic, men within their community – the artisans John Duncan, a stocking maker, and George Allan, a radical weaver who was also valued for his intimate knowledge of natural remedies for everyday ailments. Furthermore, this small Parkhead leadership cohort was prudent enough to seek legal advice prior to the demonstration of 21 June, which, they had been convinced, legitimised their actions. They may not have been entirely comfortable with the ferocity of some sections of the crowd when evening turned to night, but in spite of their later protestations, they had a hand in fomenting it; they had raised the temperature of popular opinion by holding open meetings to discuss their objections to Harvie's walls. It would have been difficult to hold the enraged communities back. With Harvie showing no sign that he would give way, public forbearance 'had now been completely exhausted' and would 'no longer submit tamely to an aggression which was likely to strike at the foot of all of their privileges'.[37] Ignored as they were, riot was the only means they had of securing the rights they were in danger of losing.

Despite the turbulence of the night of 21 June 1823, for the vast majority of the inhabitants of the communities concerned, their interests coincided. This is captured in verse in the broadsheet poem 'The Downfall of the Dyke' published in the aftermath of the House of Lords ruling (see Plate 15). The fourth stanza opens by acknowledging the role of the east end communities:

Camlachie folk and Parkhead lads,
  I'm sure they did not like, man,
To see the road their fathers trod,
  Clos'd by a muckle dyke, man.

The fifth stanza, however, then describes how:

> The people then of Glasgow town,
> Of every description,
> Right frank and free, they did agree
> To raise up a subscription;
> To Edinbro' the case did go,
> In Court there to be try'd, man,
> The dyke must fall, the lasses all,
> May walk the banks of Clyde, man.

The triumphant campaign led by Ferrie and his allies owed not a little to the whole-hearted support they were able to garner from artisans and other ordinary people from Glasgow's east end, who provided vital testimony in the Court of Session concerning the former usage of the Clyde pathway. This, we know, was marshalled by Alexander Rodger. The collaboration between the classes this indicates is symbolised by the friendship between Rodger and the nominal head of the campaign committee, George Rodgers of Barrowfield – who employed Rodger as a cloth inspector for at least ten years from 1821.

Further blurring the dividing line between the classes was the identification by the Glasgow-based committee of those concerned in the subsequent legal campaign as 'the people'. The people, the campaign literature implied, and as the first two lines of the stanza quoted above suggest, were deemed to be united by their exclusion from privilege and their detestation of the high-handed manner in which Thomas Harvie had acted. Opposition was directed less at estate ownership or employers *per se*, but rather at one who abused his position and had failed to fulfil his reciprocal role in what were customarily assumed to be paternalistic relationships. In the circumstances of the time, when both capitalists and the labouring classes were vulnerable to the vicissitudes of the trade cycle, there was little in the way of a safety net. The Poor Laws were failing to meet the needs of industrial, urban society.[38] In this milieu, Harvie's near neighbour and fellow coalmaster Colin Dunlop of Clyde Iron Works was considered as a respected paternalist, a man for his times. He was even the subject of one of Alexander Rodger's poems, 'Colin Dulap' – a wryly ironic but genuinely affectionate composition, in which Dunlop was praised for the constant light shed by his iron furnaces that for miles around made walking home at night 'over burns and the bog-holes, the dubs and the dykes' so much easier. This Rodger considered a more valuable contribution to local society than the learned enlightened tracts written by reform-advocating politicians or Thomas Chalmers, the founder of the Free Church of Scotland. Thomas Harvie, however, was neither a role model nor a recipient of celebratory verse. Harvie was deeply unpopular and became even more so as the decade wore on. He was as stubborn in 1828 as he had been in 1823; if anything, his intransigence became more marked. He conceded nothing and was dismissive of and insulting to everyone he deemed to be socially inferior. Unlike Dunlop, poetic or song effusions that referred to him were positively damning, as in the broadsheet 'The Downfall of the Dyke', already quoted:

> Now pride it is a cursed thing,
> Among Christians or Pagans,
> 'Twas pride, Sir, that sent Lucifer,
> To the infernal regions;
> This thing, call'd pride, I can't abide,
> Since about pride I'm talking,
> 'Twas pride, or the like, that built this dyke,
> To stop the fo'k from walking.

Revising Scottish radicalism

It is commonly assumed that what motivated working people to act collectively was their interest in what have been called 'bread and butter' issues: wages and prices. Their involvement in politics is also attributed to these concerns. Such anxieties were well founded, of course, not least for the handloom weavers. But as we have seen already in this chapter, other matters united the inhabitants of the poorer communities of the east end with the cadre of liberal, educated, better-off citizens of the old town of Glasgow.

Not highlighted so far in this chapter, the most important of these was an appreciation of and love for the natural world. A 'romantic sensibility' – one element of which was a critique of industrial capitalism and the 'unnatural' restrictions it imposed – infused early nineteenth-century radicalism across much of Britain and bled into the Chartism of the 1830s and 1840s.[39] It was a sentiment that was familiar to many Glaswegians. We have already noted the enthusiasm there was for wildlife in the case of George Allan, the Parkhead weaver and self-taught naturalist. Not dissimilar was Robert Drennan, the son of a shoemaker, a Paisley radical who had been involved in the collection of arms prior to the insurgency in

April 1820. He was also known for his love of the hills, glens and running streams of his locality.[40] Celebration of the natural world, sometimes but not always accompanied by critiques of the city, was one of a number of themes associated with Robert Tannahill, Paisley's best-known weaver poet.

In large part the articulation of this appreciation of the natural environment was due to the influence of the mainly English Romantic poets, although as Keith Thomas demonstrated in his pioneering study *Man and the Natural World*, the 'authentic longing' for the countryside and natural objects owed much to the growing distaste there was for life in the rapidly growing towns – no more so than in Scotland from the 1760s – and the encroachments of industry. In Scotland this sentiment was best articulated by the national poet, Robert Burns, whose work was read by all classes, often in cheap anthologies and chapbooks, or heard by word of mouth. Handloom weavers – ubiquitous in Glasgow's east end communities – were among Burns's most avid readers. Burns's *Poems, Chiefly in the Scottish Dialect*, published in 1786, had established him as 'Nature's bard'. This matters: most of the burgeoning population of greater Glasgow had migrated from the countryside, either elsewhere in Scotland or in Ireland. Often such first-generation urban dwellers had been torn by the roots from their former habitations; a world with which they had been familiar was now in the past. Much of Burns's poetry was set in the country, with frequent references to the rural landscape, changing seasons, burns and rivers, fish, the song of birds, delicate flowers and even the tribulations of a mouse.

The immense popularity of Burns in Lowland Scotland in the early nineteenth century owed much to the feelings of nostalgia his poetry induced at a time when manufacturing industry and emboldened owners of property were intruding on the towns' remaining green spaces. These were becoming fewer as industrial buildings and housing engrossed former farms and garden ground and town councils leased or sold off the burghs' common lands. This last was viewed as usurping the rights of ordinary people who had traditionally collected kindling and firewood there, or dug peat, grazed livestock and played games.

Nostalgia, however, had a cutting edge. With the advance of agrarian and industrial capitalism, the relationship between human beings and the natural environment was strained. The potential loss of the latter was both resented and resisted, throughout Britain, often forcibly. The theme of escape from the industrial town to the beauty of the countryside and the urge to retain a connection with and a right to rural pleasures were to become regular tropes for poets in the nineteenth century, notably those with a radical turn whose verse was directed towards engrossing landlords and rights of way restrictions.[41] The 'classless humanism' of Burns's poetry was a major inspiration for radicals, including radically minded poets, and his promotion of liberty and independence was set against oppressive landowners; these were compelling rallying calls against men like Thomas Harvie. True, Harvie was no 'belted knight' decked out in a 'ribband, star and a' that'. But Burns's readers in and around Glasgow might have associated him with the preening 'coof' the poet depicts in one of his most popular productions, the rousing 'For A' That and A' That':

> Ye see yon birkie, ca'd a lord,
> Wha struts, an' stares, an' a' that,
> Tho' hundreds worship at his word,
> He's but a coof for a' that.
> For a' that, an' a' that,
> His ribband, star, an' a' that,
> The man o' independent mind,
> He looks an' laughs at a' that.

By the 1820s this song, with its levelling sentiments that may have come from Thomas Paine's revolutionary *Rights of Man*, had become an integral element in the musical repertoire of Scottish radicalism.

But we can be more specific: Alexander Rodger was one of numerous autodidactic Scots writers who were influenced by, paid tribute to or tried to imitate Burns's poetry, and who had spotted the potential of poetry and song as word weapons. A prime example is his 'Come, Fill a Bumper', written in 1829 in the wake of the House of Lords judgment. Poetry of this kind set in its readers' minds limits on the rights that property owners could legitimately exercise.

The point here is that reformers and radicals in Scotland were interested in more than the standard of living, electoral politics and the constitution. On an everyday basis, fresh air, good health, walking or simply meandering and appreciating the sights and sounds of the natural world were of importance too. The victory of unfettered access along the verdant banks of the river Clyde represents an aesthetic aspect of Scottish radicalism that hitherto has gone unnoticed. This was environmental activism with a radical edge, instigated by the ordinary folk of the east end in alliance with the inhabitants of the older royal burgh of Glasgow. In the words of Alexander Rodger, the banks of the people's beloved river – the

Clyde – were now, once again, 'Throng'd with each class that loves liberty dearly'. The struggle with Thomas Harvie adds a further dimension to working-class endeavour between 1820 and 1832 that sits outside the current two-strand model.

Further binding the Harvie's Dyke campaigners in common cause, whether as leaders or supporters, was commitment to place. Civic pride is something which is normally associated in industrial cities like Glasgow with the mid- and late-Victorian eras. It was when the urban authorities self-consciously embarked on major improvement schemes that included the creation of prestigious civic squares embellished with imposing statuary and the awe-inducing architecture of municipal buildings such as town halls, art galleries and libraries. Key to creating a sense of city-wide harmony was social inclusion. Formal processions mobilised thousands to honour a major benefactor or celebrate a local hero. In the vanguard were landed patrons, civic leaders and members of Parliament, military officers and various officials, followed by members of voluntary associations, trades societies and employees of particular works.

What the campaign against Harvie's intrusive dykes reveals is that affection for Glasgow, above all its chief artery the river Clyde, pre-dates Queen Victoria and the self-conscious attempts of the city fathers to create, partly through architecture, an orderly, morally improving urban environment.[42] It demonstrates that an emerging sense of civic pride, or at the very least an identification with and fondness for the city, was evident among the city's working classes long before the Georgian era (1714 to 1837) had drawn to a close. 'LET GLASGOW FLOURISH!' – the city's motto – was printed prominently, in capitals, on the placards that were posted across the city in the summer of 1823. These were Ferrie's creation and were the main instruments of the campaign committee's initial appeal for funds. The notices specifically targeted working people, evidently on the presumption that the local patriotic flourish would be meaningful for them. It was their mutual interest in access to the Clyde's banks that encouraged the labouring poor from the expanding east end suburbs to join forces with the civic-minded middle-class inhabitants from the old heart of Glasgow. As we saw in Chapter 4, the campaign's originators, James Duncan and Gabriel Neil, were credited with being 'true sons of Nicol Jarvie' who had been used to perambulating the 'banks of their native stream'.[43] Harvie's aggression they interpreted as an attack on *their* liberty but also as having an adverse effect on the rights and privileges of the community at large. Both men, who were immersed in the city's history and traditions, considered the banks of the Clyde as having been public property from time immemorial, or at least since the earliest recollections of the city's oldest inhabitants. They were for the use of all of Glasgow's citizens for all kinds of purposes: as a retreat, for health and recreation 'when the labours of the day had closed', as well as having an aesthetic function.[44] The defence of the Clyde walkway was an epoch-making contest between the city's people in defence of their rights now and for the future against the might and money of the new bourgeois property-owning elite with faux-aristocratic aspirations.

Remembering the heroes of Harvie's Dyke

No memorial stones have been raised for the Harvie's Dyke campaigners, nor are there any statues. The *Narrative* of 1829 was a memorial of a kind and was certainly written as such. Now, though, it is hardly ever consulted. The medals struck in 1829 have not been on public display for over a century. The songs once sung to celebrate the victorious outcome are long forgotten. Perhaps the last was sung in Glasgow as late as 1878. This was 'The Bonny Banks of Clyde', copies of which cost one penny from the Poet's Box in London Street. The words took listeners on a journey from Bothwell in Lanarkshire to Jamaica Bridge in the heart of the city. After dallying at Blantyre and the 'bonny lasses a-working at the loom' and passing Carmyle and then Clyde Iron Works, the singer reflected that Harvie's Dyke was 'a spot we should all remember'. It was where Harvie 'had tried to stop the way, and how he'd to surrender':

> It showed what tyrants they would do, with might on their side,
> And how the people could defend their bonny banks of Clyde.

Memorials, however, need not take a material form, as statues, or monuments or other large-scale artefacts or even something smaller. A *lieu de mémoire*, or memory site, can be an equally potent reminder of what once happened and is worth remembering. For many years after 1829 what remained of the walls and the outbuilding which had been used to watch and fire on intruders at Westthorn performed such a role for interested passers-by.

Parts of the walls are still to be seen, but they are unmarked, and hard to spot, concealed behind wild-growing bushes (see Appendix). More noticeable are graffiti campaigning for more recent causes that cover the fence at what was neighbouring Belvidere estate, immediately to the west.

It is to be hoped that this book will arouse interest in the epic happenings on Clydeside two centuries ago. Perhaps it will even encourage readers to go down to the sweeping bend where the Clyde meanders beneath the tree- and scrub-lined path at Westthorn and there pay silent tribute to the Glaswegians who dared to take on Thomas Harvie: the four working men from Parkhead who were imprisoned for their part in taking down the Westthorn walls, but also those who defied and defeated Harvie in the courts.

The last time anything of this sort was recorded as happening was in July 1933, when the previously mentioned journalist James Cowan visited the spot and registered in his *Glasgow's Treasure Chest* 'mental thanks to the sturdy old citizens who had fought for the right I was now enjoying'. Not far short of a century afterwards, neither should we ignore our ancestors' trials and tribulations in their valiant fight to protect this freedom. Henceforth it is to be hoped that historians will incorporate the story of Harvie's Dyke into their accounts of popular struggles in Scotland. Without it, Scotland's national tale is incomplete.

Appendix: What to See Today

Harvie's Dyke

A small portion of the original dyke is still to be seen. It is a sandstone wall some 2 metres tall and 40 metres in length running north-east to south-west immediately to the east of a modern housing estate, on the site of what was until 1999 Belvidere Infectious Diseases Hospital. This represents the remnants of the high wall – the infamous Dyke – that separated Thomas Harvie's Westthorn estate from Belvidere. Running directly down to the edge of the Clyde, it was this structure which caused such a furore in 1823 and beyond. The wall can be accessed from the west after a roughly three-mile walk along the Clyde Walkway from Glasgow Green. Alternatively, if arriving by car (or from Dalmarnock railway station), there is a short, sometimes muddy, path from the A74 (London Road), opposite Helensea Park in Parkhead. This slopes down to the Clyde walkway and the river Clyde by Thorndyke Lane. Barrowfield Sports Grounds and Westthorn Allotments are on the left and Springbank Gardens are on the right. The guardhouse or watchtower used by Harvie and his employees to observe potential intruders has now been demolished. This was on the east-south-east side of the wall.

Use OS Explorer Map 342 (NS 6264) and refer to the Canmore website (http://canmore.org.uk/event/1029946), although note that some of the date information therein is incorrect.

The commemorative medals (1829)

Two of the bronze commemorative medals made for the members of the committee that led the legal campaign against Thomas Harvie are held by Glasgow Life. Made and presented on behalf of the citizens of Glasgow, they were donated to Glasgow Museums by James McNab and Sergeant Thomas Lang in the early twentieth century. That McNab's donation was made in 1923, the centenary of the Harvie's Dyke riot, may be significant.

The medals can be viewed at Glasgow Museums Resource Centre at Nitshill, by appointment (tel. 0141 276 9300). Opening hours are 10 a.m. until 5 p.m. Monday to Thursday.

Poems and broadsides

Although the three songs written (and performed) by Alexander Rodger, the radical poet, in connection with the Harvie's Dyke campaign date from the 1820s, they were published in *Stray Leaves From the Portfolios of Alisander the Seer, Andrew Whaup, and Humphrey Henkeckle*, edited by Alexander Rodger and published by Charles Rattray, of Glasgow, in 1842. They were reprinted later in Robert Ford (ed.), *Poems and Songs, Humorous, Serious and Satirical by Alexander Rodger* (Paisley and London: Alexander Gardner, 1901). The songs are 'Come to the Banks of the Clyde', 'Roll, Fair Clutha' and 'Come, Fill a Bumper'.

The seven-stanza 'The Downfall of the Dyke' was one of the broadsides written, published and widely distributed in Glasgow to ginger up the campaign against Harvie's obstructive walls. Possibly printed in 1828 but probably earlier, a copy is held by the National Library of Scotland (shelfmark: APS.4.98.6 (1)). A digital version is also available: https://digital.nls.uk>broadsides. This broadsheet was followed by another, the 'Downfall of Harvie's Dyke' (shelfmark APS.4.98.6 (2)), a report of the proceedings that led to the House of Lords ruling in July 1828, and a celebration of the outcome. It concludes, 'HUZZA! – HUZZA! – HUZZA!!!! The Liberty of the Banks of the Clyde for ever'.

Notes

Chapter 1

1 In order not to interrupt the flow of the narrative, endnotes have been kept to a minimum. A full bibliography, listing the sources used, is to be found near the end of the book.

2 The Cameronians were an extreme presbyterian sect formed in the seventeenth century by the followers of the Covenanter Richard Cameron. Later (from 1743) the sect became the Reformed Presbyterian Church of Scotland.

3 National Library of Scotland Map Room, EMS.s.337, Thomas Richardson, 'Map of the Town of Glasgow and seven miles around' (1795).

4 National Records of Scotland [NRS], AD14/23/104, Information & Presentment, George Salmond, Procurator Fiscal against Alexander McPhie and others, 1823. This voluminous bundle of legal papers is the main source of information, including witness statements, for this and the following two chapters. Material taken from it is not referenced.

5 NRS, CS96/1264, Sederunt Book of James Sword, junior, Creditors, 1826.

6 Peter Mackenzie, *Reminiscences of Glasgow, and the West of Scotland* (Glasgow: John Tweed, 1865, 2 vols), II, pp. 432–4. Mackenzie's *Reminiscences* is a principal source for the background to and immediate consequences of the Harvie's Dyke affair.

7 *Glasgow Delineated, in its Institutions, Manufactures, and Commerce* (Glasgow: Wardlaw and Cunninghame, 1826), pp. 87, 226.

8 Information from Dr David Abercrombie, communicated by email, 23 February 2024; NRS, CS38/14/48, J. and T. Harvie agt. Dunbar, 1816, Information for John and Thomas Harvie, spirit dealers in Glasgow, in the Advocation at the Instance of Hugh Dunbar, Change-Keeper at Westmuir, 8 April 1813.

9 John Strang, *Glasgow and its Clubs* (Glasgow: R. Griffen and Co., 1857), p. 216.

10 NRS, CS38/14/48, J. and T. Harvie agt. Dunbar, 15 January 1816, Petition of Hugh Dunbar, 17 July 1811.

11 James R. Anderson (ed.), *The Burgesses and Guild Brethren of Glasgow, 1751–1846* (Edinburgh: Scottish Record Society, 1935), p. 293. I am grateful to Dr Stephen Mullen for drawing my attention to this source.

12 T. M. Devine, *The Tobacco Lords* (Edinburgh: John Donald, 1975), pp. 21–7.

13 John Moore and John R. Hume (eds), *A City Situated for Commerce* (Glasgow: University of Glasgow Library, 2023), pp. 18–30.

14 Quoted in W. Ross Shearer, *Rutherglen Lore* (Paisley: Alexander Gardner, 1922), p. 225.

15 John M'Ure, *Glasghu Facies: History of Glasgow, Ancient and Modern* (Glasgow: John Tweed, 1872, 2 vols), Division 2, p. 794.

16 John Guthrie Smith and John Oswald Mitchell, *The Old Country Houses of the Old Glasgow Gentry* (Glasgow: James MacLehose, 1878), p. 257.

17 NRS, CS96/4216, Sederunt Book of the Creditors of the Glasgow Distillery Co. and Thomas Harvie, Individual Partner thereof, 17 April 1832–17 April 1834.

18 NRS, CS96/1264, Sederunt Book of James Sword, junior, Creditors, 1826.

19 National Library of Scotland [NLS], MS 6260, John Forfar, A Sketch Journey to Glasgow, 1822, pp. 34–5.

20 Taken from 'Colin Dulap', in Robert Ford (ed.), *Poems and Songs, Humorous, Serious and Satirical by Alexander Rodger* (Paisley and London: Alexander Gardner, 1901), pp. 12–14.

21 Alan B. Campbell, *The Lanarkshire Miners: A Social History of their Trade Unions, 1775–1874* (Edinburgh: John Donald, 1979), pp. 36–8.

22 W. Hamish Fraser, *Conflict and Class: Scottish Workers, 1700–1838* (Edinburgh: John Donald, 1988), p. 99.

23 Murray Armstrong, *The Fight for Scottish Democracy: Rebellion & Reform in 1820* (London: Pluto Press, 2020), pp. 167, 190.

24 National Archives, ADM 196/8/67, service record, William Craig.

25 NRS, CS44/79/10, Wardrop agt Craig, 11 March 1825, Representation for William Craig, 1824.

26 NRS, AD14/28/112, Indictment v William Craig etc, Assault and Deforcement, September 1828, Certificate as to the Character of Dr William Craig.

27 NRS, CS44/158/24, Decreet, Thomas Harvie re the sequestration and estate of James Sword, 1828.

28 T. C. Smout, *Nature Contested: Environmental History in Scotland and Northern England Since 1600* (Edinburgh: Edinburgh University Press, 2000), p. 148.

29 *Glasgow Chronicle*, 10 February 1824, p. 2.

30 Kirstie Blair, *Working Verse in Victorian Scotland: Poetry, Press, Community* (Oxford: Oxford University Press, 219), pp. 108–18.

31 John Black, *The Falls of Clyde, or, The Fairies; A Scottish Dramatic Pastoral, in Five Acts, with Three Dissertations* (Edinburgh: William Creech, 1806), p. 10.

32 Hugh MacDonald, *Rambles Round Glasgow* (Glasgow: John Cameron, 1854), p. 31.

33 MacDonald, *Rambles*, p. 29.

34 *Glasgow Past and Present Embracing Loose Memoranda on Glasgow Subjects by Senex and Desultory Sketches by J.B.* (Glasgow: David Robertson and Co., 1856, 3 vols), II, p. 27.

35 *Glasgow Chronicle*, 10 February 1824, p. 3.

36 NLS, AB.1.222.62 (8), *Poetical Miscellanies* (1823).

37 *Glasgow Free Press*, no. 270, 29 July 1826, p. 475.

38 'The Bonnie Walks of Glasgow Green', in Mitchell Library, Special Collections, SR347. *Old Glasgow Street Songs* (1850).

39 *History of Glasgow Green, and of the Various Struggles by the Citizens to Preserve it from Encroachment, Particularly those of 1575–76, 1745 and 1845* (Glasgow: W. C. Pattison, 1845), n.p.

40 *Caledonian Mercury*, 26 June 1823, p. 4.

41 Adam Ferrie, *Autobiography, Late Hon. Adam Ferrie* (n.p., n.d., *c.*1864), p. 17.

42 Hugh Muir, *Reminiscences and Sketches: Being a Topographical History of Rutherglen and Suburbs* (Glasgow: Bell & Bain, 1890), p. 202.

43 *A Narrative of the Proceedings in the Case Rodgers and others, v Harvie, For the Recovery of the Liberty of the Banks of the Clyde* (Glasgow: Hugh Cameron, 1829), p. 4.

44 Mitchell Library, Glasgow City Archives [GCA], RU/3/1/16, Rutherglen Council Book, 1812–1830, 2 July 1814.

45 *Glasgow Herald*, 29 July 1864, p. 5, Letter from 'Young Bridgeton'.

Chapter 2

1 Kenneth Logue, *Popular Disturbances in Scotland, 1780–1815* (Edinburgh: John Donald, 1979); see also Christopher A. Whatley, *Scottish Society 1707–1830: Beyond Jacobitism, Towards Industrialisation* (Manchester: Manchester University Press, 2000), pp. 170–4, 282–7.

2 *Westmorland Gazette*, 5 July 1823, p. 3.

3 *Glasgow Delineated*, p. 47.

4 NLS, L.C.Fol.73 (061), 'The Rights of the Citizens of Glasgow to Walk on the Banks of the Clyde Asserted and Disputed'.

5 E. S. Jackson, *The Inniskilling Dragoons: The Records of an Old Heavy Cavalry Regiment* (East Sussex: Naval & Military Press, n.d.), Chapters I–IX.

6 *The News* (London), 2 July 1815, p. 3.

7 Moore and Hume, *City*, pp. 33–34.

8 Norman Murray, *The Scottish Hand Loom Weavers, 1790–1850: A Social History* (Edinburgh: John Donald, 1978), pp. 183–97.

9 *The Autobiography of Lieutenant-General Sir Harry Smith* (London: John Murray, 1903, 2 vols), I, Chapter 29.

10 Strang, *Glasgow and its Clubs*, p. 410.

11 Gordon Pentland, *The Spirit of the Union* (London: Routledge, 2015 edn), pp. 127–44.

12 T. M. Devine, 'Urbanisation and the Civic Response: Glasgow, 1800–1830', in A. J. G. Cummings and T. M. Devine (eds), *Industry, Business and Society in Scotland Since 1700* (Edinburgh: John Donald, 1994), pp. 189–92; Irene Maver, 'The Guardianship of the Community: Civic Authority Prior to 1833', in T. M. Devine and Gordon Jackson (eds), *Glasgow, Volume I: Beginnings to 1830* (Manchester: Manchester University Press, 1995), p. 254.

13 *Glasgow Chronicle*, 19 April 1823, p. 1.

14 Fraser, *Conflict and Class*, p. 116; Fraser in *Conflict and Class* has suggested (p. 115) that the power loom weavers' dispute may have been linked with the Harvie's Dyke affair. If by this is meant a direct link, this is unlikely, and is partly due to Fraser's assumption that the latter took place in July rather than June. The power loom incident occurred on 22 July. An indirect link cannot be ruled out, however. As this chapter shows, these were troubled times for the inhabitants of Glasgow's east end villages, above all for the weavers and coal workers. And at least one of the central figures involved in the demolition of Harvie's Dyke was also active in the Weavers' Association (see Chapter 3).

15 Elspeth King, *The People's Palace and Glasgow Green* (Edinburgh: W. and R. Chambers, 1991 edn), p. 33.

16 Jackson, *Inniskilling Dragoons*, pp. 280–1.

17 *Glasgow Herald*, 29 July 1864, p. 6.

18 *The Scotsman*, 28 June 1823, p. 7.

19 Quoted in Whatley, *Scottish Society*, p. 325.

20 David Gilmour, *Paisley Weavers of Other Days* (Paisley: Alexander Gardner, 1878), pp. 12–21.

21 *The Topographical Picture of Glasgow in its Ancient and Modern State* (Glasgow: R. Chapman, 1820 edn), p. 109.

22 NRS, JC26/1818/73, Trial Papers of Mary Hutcheson, alias Arrol, Declaration of Mary Hutcheson, 1 April 1818.

23 NRS, JC26/1818/38, Criminal Letters, The Lord Advocate agt Mary Hutcheson, alias Arrol, 1818.

24 See Alex Benchimol, 'Policing the Industrial Order in the West of Scotland', in Gerard Carruthers, Kevin Gallagher, Craig Lamont and George Smith (eds), *1820: Scottish Rebellion. Essays on a Nineteenth Century Insurrection* (Edinburgh: John Donald, 2022).

25 Mitchell Library, GCA, TD164, Diary of John Matheson, 1805–26.

26 NLS, Acc.8100, 145, Gray of Carntyne Papers, R. Gray to John Gray, 9 January, 8 February 1823.

27 North Lanarkshire Archives, Motherwell, W. Mack, Notebook, Weather, Airdrie, 1799–1826, 31 May 1823.

28 W. M. Roach, 'Radical and Reform Movements in Scotland from 1815 to 1820', unpublished PhD thesis (University of Glasgow, 1970), p. 216.

29 Armstrong, *Fight for Scottish Democracy*, p. 187.

30 Fraser, *Conflict and Class*, p. 110.

31 Irene Maver, 'Glasgow's Civic Government', in W. Hamish Fraser and Irene Maver (eds), *Glasgow, Volume II: 1830–1912* (Manchester, 1996), p. 445.

32 Anne-Marie Kilday, 'The Barbarous North? Criminality in Early Modern Scotland', in T. M. Devine and Jenny Wormald (eds), *The Oxford Handbook of Modern Scottish History* (Oxford: Oxford University Press, 2012), pp. 398–9.

33 Anna Clark, *The Struggle for the Breeches: Gender and the Making of the British Working Class* (London: University of California Press, 1995), pp. 25–9.

34 NRS, AD14/24/185, Information and Presentment, George Salmond, PF, against William O'Boyling, James Neilson and Robert Kirkwood, 1824.

35 NRS, AD14/24/199, George Salmond to Adam Rolland, 6 September 1824.

36 NRS, AD14/28/112, 'Certificate as to the Character of Dr William Craig'.

37 NRS, AD14/24/199, Precognition of William Mackenzie.

Chapter 3

1 University of Glasgow, Special Collections [UGSC], Smith Collection, Eph. 310–320, Testimonials from James Hardie in relation to his application to become Superintendent of Police, Glasgow, 1821; Lt Col H G Smith to James Hardie, 29 May 1821.

2 *Autobiography of Lieutenant-General Sir Harry Smith*, Chapter 29.

3 Zachary Garber, 'Tyranny and Liberty, Resistance and Regicide: Political Assassination in John Galt's *The Spaewife*', *English: Journal of the English Association*, 71 (2022), p. 244.

4 Michael Michie, *An Enlightenment Tory in Victorian Scotland: The Career of Sir Archibald Alison* (East Linton: Tuckwell Press, 1997), p. 70.
5 Peter Berresford Ellis and Seumas Mac a' Ghobhainn, *The Scottish Insurrection of 1820* (London: Pluto Press, 1989), p. 252.
6 *Glasgow Medical Journal*, 6 (July 1874), p. 560; I am grateful to Clare Harrison of the Royal College of Physicians and Surgeons of Glasgow for this reference.
7 Royal College of Physicians and Surgeons of Glasgow, RCPSG 2/1/24, William Lyon, 'Remarks on Delirium Tremens', *Medical Essays*, 22 (1834–35).
8 NRS, AD14/23/104, Information and Presentment, ff. 1–8.
9 Emma Griffin, *Liberty's Dawn: A People's History of the Industrial Revolution* (New Haven and London: Yale University Press, 2014 edn), pp. 217–18, 226.
10 David G. Barrie, *Police in the Age of Improvement: Police Development and the Civic Tradition in Scotland, 1775–1865* (Cullompton: Willan Publishing, 2008), pp. 159–60.
11 NRS, AD14/23/104, Petition, George Salmond, writer in Glasgow, Procurator Fiscal of Court, for HM Interest, 23 June 1823.
12 Quoted in Malcolm Chase, *1820: Disorder and Stability in the United Kingdom* (Manchester: Manchester University Press, 2013), p. 117.
13 Peter Mackenzie, *An Exposure of the Spy System Pursued in Glasgow During the Years 1816–17–18–19 and 20* (Glasgow: Muir, Gowans & Co, 1833), pp. 81, 89, 90–2.
14 Irene Maver, *Glasgow* (Edinburgh: Edinburgh University Press, 2000), p. 67.
15 *Glasgow Delineated*, p. 40.
16 T. J. Dowds, *Scotland Free or a Desart: The Radical Insurrection of 1820* (Rothersthorpe: Paragon Publishing, 2020), p. 57.
17 *Caledonian Mercury*, 3 January 1835, p. 4.
18 There is a full transcription of the *Address* in Kenny MacAskill, *Radical Scotland: Uncovering Scotland's Radical History from the French Revolutionary Era to the 1820 Rising* (London: Biteback, 2020), pp. 319–21.
19 Stirling Council Archives, Murray of Polmaise MSS, PD189/1/61, Captain Peter Speirs to Major William Murray, 5 April 1820.
20 *Glasgow Free Press*, no. 40, 1 October 1823, p. 32.
21 M'Ure, *Glasghu Facies*, pp. 785–6.
22 NRS, JC26/1823/122, Indictment, HM Advocate v Alexander M'Phie etc (Mobbing and Rioting).
23 https://doi.org/10.1093/ref:odnb/38005, accessed 23 August 2023.
24 https://www.scottisharchitects.org.uk/architect_full.php?id=200295, accessed 22 August 2023.
25 https://canmore.org.uk/site/44249, accessed 25 August 2023.

26 Sir John Carr, *Caledonian Sketches, or a Tour Through Scotland in 1807* (London: Matthews and Leigh, 1809), p. 537.
27 *Glasgow Free Press*, no. 39, 24 September 1823, p. 307.
28 *Glasgow Free Press*, no. 4, 1 October 1823, p. 1.
29 Mackenzie, *Reminiscences*, vol. II, p. 460.
30 W. W. J. Knox and A. McInlay, 'Crime, Protest and Policing in Nineteenth-Century Scotland', in Griffiths and Morton (eds), *A History of Everyday Life in Scotland, 1800 to 1900* (Edinburgh: Edinburgh University Press, 2010), p. 203.
31 *Caledonian Mercury*, 27 September 1823, p. 4.
32 Ferrie, *Autobiography*, p. 18.
33 NRS, AD14/24/258/14, Precognition against Alexander M'Phie and others, Mobbing and Rioting, 1824.
34 *The Scotsman*, 15 September 1824, p. 681.
35 NRS, JC26/1826/342, Indictment, HM Advocate against Robert Hamilton, Samuel McMenemy and Alexander M'Phie, 1826.
36 *Caledonian Mercury*, 20 July 1826, p. 2.

Chapter 4

1 NLS, APS.4.98.6 (1), 'The Downfall of the Dyke' (n.d., *c.*1826).
2 *Caledonian Mercury*, 26 June 1823, p. 3.
3 NLS, Ry.III.a.2 (010), 'Serious Outrage and Disturbance in Glasgow' (1823).
4 NRS, CS46/1830/5/6, Decreet of Declarator, In Causa, Rodgers v Harvie, 8 June 1826.
5 *Glasgow Free Press*, no. 27, 23 July 1823, p. 211.
6 Mackenzie, *Reminiscences*, vol II, p. 440.
7 James Cowan, *From Glasgow's Treasure Chest: A Miscellany of History, Personalities and Places* (Glasgow: Craig & Wilson, 1951), pp. 260–1.
8 Armstrong, *Fight for Scottish Democracy*, p. 115; Chase, *1820*, p. 72; Fraser, *Conflict and Class*, p. 109.
9 *Glasgow Herald*, 6 July 1821, p. 2.
10 Reproduced in M'Ure, *Glasghu Facies*, pp. 784–5.
11 Mitchell Library, GCA, RU/3/1/16, Rutherglen Council Book, 1812–1830, 24 December 1813, 1 September 1828.
12 Strang, *Glasgow and its Clubs*, pp. 4, 27, 169, 230 and 467.
13 Bob Harris, *The Scottish People and the French Revolution* (London: Pickering & Chatto, 2008), p. 225.
14 UGSC, MS Gen 1059, Gabriel Neil, Notes on Zachary Boyd, MS of Introduction to Four Poems from Zion's Flowers, 1855.

15 John K. M'Dowall, *The People's History of Glasgow* (Glasgow: Hay Nisbet & Co, 1899), pp. 44, 46.

16 NRS, CS46/1830/5/6, Affidavit, Alexander Baxter.

17 Hamish Whyte, 'Motherwell, William (1797–1835), poet and ballad editor', *Oxford Dictionary of National Biography,* 23 September 2004; accessed 10 February 2025: 2025. https://www.oxforddnb.com/view/10.1093/ref:odnb/9780198614128.001.0001/odnb-9780198614128-e-19419.

18 James Coleman, *Remembering the Past in Nineteenth-Century Scotland* (Edinburgh: Edinburgh University Press, 2014), p. 49.

19 *Elgin Courant and Morayshire Advertiser*, 19 August 1859, p. 6.

20 *Glasgow Chronicle*, 10 November 1847, p. 4; *Morning Post*, 6 April 1848, p. 3.

21 Gerald Tulchinsky, 'Adam Ferrie (1777–1863)', in *Dictionary of Canadian Biography*, 9, University of Toronto/Université Laval, accessed 16 October 2023: http://biographi.ca/en/bio/ferrie_adam_1777_1863_9E.html.

22 *Carlisle Journal*, 30 September 1815, p. 1.

23 Mackenzie, *Reminiscences*, vol. II, p. 442.

24 Mackenzie, *Reminiscences*, vol. II, p. 446.

25 Bernard Comment, *The Panorama* (London: Reaktion Books, 1999), pp. 7–8.

26 UGSC, Smith Collection, Eph. E/650, Rotunda, Buchanan Street (n.d., between 1805 and 1820).

27 *Glasgow Herald*, 23 June 1823, p. 3; *Glasgow Free Press*, no. 27, 2 July 1823, p. 211.

28 John Burnett, *Riot, Revelry and Rout: Sport in Lowland Scotland Before 1860* (East Linton: Tuckwell Press, 2000), pp. 150–1.

29 *A Narrative*, p. 7.

30 *A Narrative*, p. 8.

31 *A Narrative*, pp. 14–15.

32 Michael Fry, 'Jeffrey, Francis, Lord Jeffrey (1773–1850), writer and judge', *Oxford Dictionary of National Biography,* 23 September 2004; accessed 10 February 2025: https://www.oxforddnb.com/view/10.1093/ref:odnb/9780198614128.001.0001/odnb-9780198614128-e-14698.

33 David Swinfen, *Moncreiff* (Dundee: Shakenoak Press, 2015), pp. 4–7; Alan Bell (ed.), *Lord Cockburn: Selected Letters* (Edinburgh: John Donald, 2005), pp. 2–3; Elizabeth Elliot, 'Walter Scott's Bannatyne Club, Male Associational Culture, and the Making of Identity', *Review of English Studies*, 67:281 (September 2016), pp. 732–50.

34 Ford, *Poems and Songs*, pp. xv–xvi.

35 Alexander Rodger (ed.), *Stray Leaves from the Portfolios of Alisander the Seer, Andrew Whaup, and Humphrey Henkeckle* (Glasgow: Charles Rattray, 1842), p. vii.

36 *Glasgow Chronicle*, 17 January 1824, p. 4.
37 *Glasgow Free Press*, no. 33, 13 August 1823, p. 263; Christopher A. Whatley, 'Sound and Song in the Ritual of Popular Protest: Continuity and the "Nob Songs" of 1825', in Edward J. Cowan (ed.), *The Ballad in Scottish History* (East Linton: Tuckwell Press, 2000), pp. 142–60.
38 Gerard Carruthers and Norman R. Paton, 'Did Robert Burns write the "Tree of Liberty"?', in Rodger and Carruthers (eds), *Fickle Man*, pp. 253–5.
39 GCA, TD200/75, A Full Report of the Banks of the Clyde, Rodgers and others versus Harvie, Determined in the Jury Court, Edinburgh, 13th Jan. 1826, p. 1.
40 *Glasgow Chronicle*, 17 January 1824, p. 4.
41 NRS, CS46/1830/5/6/3 (23), Decreet of declarator, George Rodgers and others v Thomas Harvie.
42 GCA, TD200/75, *A Full Report*, p. 1.
43 M'Ure, *Glasghu Facies*, p. 810.
44 Ferrie, *Autobiography*, p. 20.
45 GCA, TD200/75, *A Full Report*, pp. 3–4.
46 NLS, L.C.Fol.73 (014), 'Executions', 1820.

Chapter 5

1 M'Ure, *Glasghu Facies*, p. 811.
2 *Glasgow Free Press*, no. 267, 19 July 1826, p. 455.
3 NLS, L.C.179.
4 'Gotham in Alarm: A Farce, in Three Acts' (Glasgow, 1816), in *Chronicles of the Isles*, p. 1.
5 'The Public Meeting, Or Lord Shallow at his Last Gasp' (Glasgow: D. Mackenzie, 2nd edn, 1816), in *Chronicles of the Isles*, p. 13.
6 Whatley, *Scottish Society*, p. 321; W. Aiton, *A History of the Encounter at Drumclog and Battle of Bothwell Bridge, in the month of June, 1679* (Hamilton: W. M. Borthwick & Co., 1821), pp. 123–4.
7 *Glasgow Free Press*, no. 267, 19 July 1826, p. 455.
8 *Perthshire Courier*, 25 August 1825, p. 2; *Glasgow Herald*, 14 April 1826, p. 4.
9 Campbell, *Lanarkshire Miners*, pp. 65–72.
10 *Glasgow Herald*, 14 April 1826, p. 4; *Perthshire Courier*, 20 April 1826, p. 2, taken from the *Glasgow Chronicle*.
11 NRS, AD14/27/161, Precognition against Thomas Cunningham and others, for the crime of assault, Spring 1827.
12 NRS, JC26/1827/239, Criminal Letters against Thomas Cunningham etc, Glasgow Circuit, Spring 1827.

13 NRS, CS13/424, Westthorn, Second Report of Dugald John Bannatyne and State of his Accounts as Judicial Factor in the Estate of Westthorn, 1836.
14 *Morning Chronicle*, 29 December 1827, p. 4.
15 NLS, Advocates Library, *Session Papers*, 178, No. 131 (1829), p. 1.
16 Michael Lobban, 'Henry Peter, first Baron Brougham and Vaux', in *Oxford Dictionary of National Biography*, https://doi.org/10.1093/ref:odnb/3581, accessed 8 December 2023.
17 Ferrie, *Autobiography*, p. 23.
18 Andrea Loux Jarman, 'Customary Rights in Scots Law: Test Cases on Access to Land in the Nineteenth Century', *Journal of Legal History*, 28:2 (2007), p. 229.
19 Ferrie, *Autobiography*, p. 21.
20 William Blackwood (ed.), *Cases Decided in the Court of Session from November 13, 1828 to July 11, 1829* (Vol. VII, 1829), p. 289.
21 NRS, CS46/1830/5/6, Answers, Thomas Harvie to George Rodgers, 12 January 1830.
22 Mitchell Library, GCA, RU/3/1/16, Rutherglen Council Book, 23 March 1829.
23 *Elgin Courant and Morayshire Advertiser*, 2 September 1859, p. 6 (reprinted from the *Glasgow Gazette*).
24 NLS, Advocates Library, *Session Papers*, 204, No 300 (1830), Report from William Kyle, 14 November 1829.
25 Blackwood, *Cases Decided in the Court of Session* (Vol VIII, 1830), pp. 611–12.
26 Mitchell Library, Special Collections, 96975, *Select Pieces Delivered at a Public Meeting held for Promoting the Subscription to Procure Medals, Commemorative of the Triumph of the Citizens of Glasgow in Establishing Their Right to a Path on the Banks of the Clyde* (Glasgow: Robertson & Atkinson, 1829).
27 Sinéad Sturgeon and Frances Clark, 'Knowles, James Sheridan', *Dictionary of Irish Biography* (2009), https://doi.org/10.3318/dib.004602.v1, accessed 17 January 2024.
28 Civic Hampdens: a reference to Hampden Clubs which were first formed in 1812 in London and brought together middle-class reformers and working-class radicals in several English towns who debated and campaigned for constitutional reform. They were named after the seventeenth-century English Presbyterian who died fighting for the parliamentary cause in 1643 in opposition to the absolutism of King Charles I. The writer of the poem may well have been conflating Thomas Harvie with King Charles.
29 Ford, *Poems and Songs*, p. xxii.
30 *Fife Herald*, 2 February 1843, p. 2.

31 *Inverness Courier*, 1 February 1843, p. 2.
32 *The Poetical Works of the Late Hugh Macdonald* (Glasgow: Robert Forrester, 1865), pp. vi–x.
33 MacDonald, *Rambles*, pp. 31–4.
34 Mackenzie, *Reminiscences*, p. 461.
35 Ferrie, *Autobiography*, p. 22.
36 NRS, CS13/424, Westthorn, Second Report of Dugald John Bannatyne and State of his accounts as Judicial Factor in the Estate of Westthorn, 1836.
37 *The Scotsman*, 13 January 1836, p. 1.
38 *Glasgow Sentinel*, 29 May 1858, p. 4; *Elgin Courant and Morayshire Advertiser*, 2 September 1859, p. 6 (reprinted from the *Glasgow Gazette*).
39 Scotland's People, Old Parish Registers – Deaths, OPR ID: 5387559, 18 July 1843, Vol. 560, Ref: 644/1; I am indebted to Dr David Abercrombie for his zealous search through census and other records on my behalf on the Scotland's People website.
40 See, for example, *Northern Whig*, 14 May 1839, p. 2.

Conclusion

1 See T. C. Smout, 'The Highlands and the Roots of Green Consciousness, 1750–1990', in T.C. Smout, *Exploring Environmental History: Selected Essays* (Edinburgh: Edinburgh University Press, 2011 edn), p. 30.
2 Gordon Pentland, 'The Challenge of Radicalism to 1832', in Devine and Wormald (eds), *Oxford Handbook of Modern Scottish History*, p. 451.
3 Catriona M. M. Macdonald, '"The Ebbing of the Old Shallow Tide": The Civil Context of the Radical War (1820)', in Carruthers, Gallagher, Lamont and Smith (eds), *1820*, p. 6.
4 For an informed discussion, see Pentland, *Spirit of the Union*, pp. 109–26; for radicalism of the 1790s, see Harris, *The Scottish People and the French Revolution*, especially pp. 75–113.
5 *Glasgow Herald*, 29 July 1864, p. 6.
6 *North British Daily Mail*, 16 April 1850, p. 2.
7 *North British Daily Mail*, 11 May 1852, p. 4.
8 James Ferguson, *The Law of Roads, Streets, and Rights of Way, Bridges, and Ferries, in Scotland* (Edinburgh: Green & Sons, 1904), pp. 50–2, 99.
9 Mitchell Library, C IX 15, Clyde Navigation Trust, Report as to the Footpath along the South Bank of the Clyde from the Improvement Trust property at Oatlands Eastward to the Municipal Boundary, 5 September 1887.
10 *Glasgow Gazette*, 23 February 1850, p. 4.
11 *Glasgow Sentinel*, 29 May 1858, p. 4.

12 *Glasgow Herald*, 2 July 1864, p. 4.
13 Christopher Smout, 'Introduction: Trees in Scottish Life', in T. C. Smout (ed.), *People and Woods in Scotland: A History* (Edinburgh: Edinburgh University Press, 2003), p. 10.
14 *North British Daily Mail*, 15 June 1891, p. 4.
15 Gordon Pentland, '"Betrayed by Infamous Spies"? The Commemoration of Scotland's "Radical War" of 1820', *Past & Present*, 201 (2008), pp. 152–7.
16 Craig Lamont, 'Remembering the Radical War: Monuments, Markers and Commemorations', in Carruthers, Gallagher, Lamont and Smith (eds), *1820*, pp. 147–8.
17 Pentland, *Spirit of the Union*, pp. 127–44.
18 Pentland, '"Betrayed by Infamous Spies"?', pp. 151–2.
19 Mackenzie, *Exposure of the Spy System*.
20 Maurizio Isabella, *Southern Europe in the Age of Revolutions* (Princeton and Oxford: Princeton University Press, 2023), pp. 428–9.
21 E. P. Thompson, *Customs in Common* (London: Penguin, 1993), pp. 4–10.
22 W. H. Marwick, 'The Beginnings of the Scottish Working-Class Movement in the Nineteenth Century', *International Review for Social History*, 3 (1938), pp. 1–24; Thomas Johnston, *The History of the Working Classes in Scotland* (Wakefield: EP Publishing, 1974 edn), pp. 301–94.
23 Neil Davidson and Jamie Allinson, 'De-provincialising 1820: The West of Scotland General Strike in the Mirror of Uneven and Combined Development (Part 1)', *Scottish Labour History*, 55 (2020), p. 169.
24 Armstrong, *Fight for Scottish Democracy*, p. 207; Dowds, *Scotland Free or a Desart*, p. 169.
25 Dowds, *Scotland Free or a Desart*, p. 169.
26 Neil Davidson and Jamie Allinson, 'De-provincialising 1820: The West of Scotland General Strike in the Mirror of Uneven and Combined Development (Part 2)', *Scottish Labour History*, 57 (2022), p. 129; Fraser, *Conflict and Class*, p. 113.
27 Maver, *Glasgow*, pp. 68–9; Maver does make reference to Harvie's Dyke, but this is unusual.
28 Examples of this approach include chapters in Carruthers, Gallagher, Lamont and Smith, *1820*, and Armstrong, *Fight for Scottish Democracy*, see pp. 266–7; see also Maggie Craig, *One Week in April: The Scottish Radical Rising of 1820* (Edinburgh: Birlinn, 2020), Chapter 27.
29 This paragraph, chosen to highlight the lack of popular support for militant radicalism, is largely based on the account of the poet Janet Hamilton, from Langloan near Coatbridge in Lanarkshire; see Janet Hamilton, *Poems, Essays, and Sketches* (Glasgow: James MacLehose, 1870), pp. 362, 371.

30 T. C. Smout, *A Century of the Scottish People, 1830–1950* (London: Collins, 1986), pp. 28–9, 234.

31 Campbell, *Lanarkshire Miners*, pp. 20–1, 62; see also J. H. Treble, 'The Standard of Living of the Working Class', in T. M. Devine and Rosalind Mitchison (eds), *People and Society in Scotland, Volume 1, 1760–1830* (Edinburgh: John Donald, 1988), pp. 204, 222.

32 Catriona M. M. Macdonald, 'Abandoned and Beastly? The Queen Caroline Affair in Scotland', in Yvonne Galloway Brown and Rona Ferguson (eds), *Twisted Sisters: Women, Crime and Deviance in Scotland Since 1400* (East Linton: Tuckwell Press, 2002), p. 103.

33 Chase, *1820*, p. 125; see also Pentland, 'Challenge of radicalism', p. 440.

34 Macdonald, ' "The ebbing of the old shallow tide" ', in Carruthers, Gallagher, Lamont and Smith, *1820*, p. 15.

35 Whatley, *Scottish Society*, p. 328.

36 *Elgin Courant and Morayshire Advertiser*, 19 August 1959, p. 6 (reprinted from the *Glasgow Gazette*).

37 *A Narrative*, p. 4.

38 For a discussion of 'the People' see Eugenio F. Biagini, *Liberty, Retrenchment and Reform: Popular Liberalism in the Age of Gladstone, 1860–1880* (Cambridge: Cambridge University Press, 1992), pp. 11–12; see also Patrick Joyce, *Visions of the People: Industrial England and the Question of Class, 1848–1914* (Cambridge: Cambridge University Press, 1991), p. 3.

39 Joyce, *Visions*, pp. 34–7.

40 T. J. Dowds, 'The 1820 Rising: Recent Discoveries', *Scottish Local History*, 117 (Spring 2024), pp. 42–3.

41 Blair, *Working Verse*, pp. 108–18.

42 Simon Gunn, *The Public Culture of the Victorian Middle Class: Ritual and Authority in the English Industrial City 1840–1914* (Manchester: Manchester University Press, 2000), pp. 50–3, 163–82; James Smiechen, 'Glasgow of the Imagination: Architecture, Townscape and Society', in Fraser and Maver (eds), *Glasgow, Volume II*, pp. 486–99.

43 Baillie Nicol Jarvie was a character in Sir Walter Scott's novel *Rob Roy*, a merchant and magistrate who embodied the city's commercial values.

44 *A Narrative*, p. 1.

Bibliography

Archival Sources

House of Lords

Appeal Cases, ser 3 – 1828, HL/PO/JO/4/3/55, Thomas Harvie v George Rodgers et al, 1828.

Main Papers, Session 1828, Nos 152–201, HL/PO/JO/10/8/791, Harvie v Rodgers, appellant's petition (195); respondent's petition (197).

Main Papers, Session 1828, Nos 225–270, HL/PO/JO/10/8/795, Petition of both parties to hear cause after Easter recess.

Mitchell Library, Glasgow

C IX 15, Clyde Navigation Trust, Report as to the Footpath along the South Bank of the Clyde from the Improvement Trust property at Oatlands Eastward to the Municipal Boundary, 5 September 1887.

Glasgow City Archives [GCA], RU/3/1/16, Rutherglen Council Book, 1812–1830.

GCA, DTC 6/252–8, Bye Laws as to Bathing in the River Clyde, 1871.

GCA, TD200/75, *A Full Report of the Banks of the Clyde, Rodgers and others versus Harvie, Determined in the Jury Court, Edinburgh, 13th Jan. 1826.*

Glasgow Town Council minutes, 1819–1825.

Special Collections, 96975, *Select Pieces Delivered at a Public Meeting held for Promoting the Subscription to Procure Medals, Commemorative of the Triumph of the Citizens of Glasgow in Establishing Their Right to a Path on the Banks of the Clyde* (Glasgow: Robertson & Atkinson, 1829).

Special Collections, SR347, *Old Glasgow Street Songs* (1850).

TD66/5/8, Plan of lands conveyed by the late John Haig, to Thomas Harvie, 1824.

TD164, Diary of John Matheson, Manager, Messrs Monteith, Bogle & Company, 1805–26.

TD200/75, Full Report of the Banks of Clyde Case, 1826.

T-KF, Kyle and Frew Papers.
UED/35, Clyde Navigation Trust Papers, 1827–1873.

National Archives, London

ADM 196/8/67, Service Record, William Craig.

National Library of Scotland, Edinburgh [NLS]

AB.1.222.62 (8), *Poetical Miscellanies* (1823).
Acc.5381/39, Clyde Iron Works.
Acc.8100 (100), Minute Book of Glasgow Coalmasters, 1813–1817.
Acc.8100, 145, Gray of Carntyne Papers.
Advocates Library, *Session Papers*, 178, No. 131 (1829).
Advocates Library, *Session Papers*, 204, No. 300 (1830), Report from William Kyle, 14 November 1829.
APS.1.88.66, A. Rodger, *Clerical Anecdotes.*
APS.3.94.5, Rights of Way: Bonhill Bridge, *c.*1850.
APS.4.98.6 (1), 'The Downfall of the Dyke' (n.d., *c.*1826).
APS.88.66, *Clerical Anecdotes and Parson's Comic Songster* (Edinburgh: W. and H. Robinson, 1842).
L.C.Fol.73 (014), 'Executions', 1820.
L.C.Fol.73 (061), 'The Rights of the Citizens of Glasgow to Walk on the Banks of the Clyde Asserted and Disputed'.
L.C.179, *The Book of the Chronicles of the Isles, Comprising a Curious and Interesting Record of the Times from the year 1745 to 1826, arranged into Chapters and Verses* (Glasgow: Gabriel Neil and Walter Duncan, 1826).
MS 6260, John Forfar, A Sketch Journey to Glasgow, 1822.
Ry.III.a.2 (010), 'Serious Outrage and Disturbance in Glasgow' (1823).
Stev.271, *Case of the Proprietors and Occupiers of Houses on the North and South Banks of the River Clyde, above the Broomielaw Bridge of Glasgow, with Reference to the two Clyde Navigation Bills* (1825).
Stev.272, *Case of The Proprietors of The Glasgow Water Works* (1825).

National Library of Scotland, Map Room

EMGB.s.34, Great Reform Act Plans and Reports, 1832: Glasgow.
EMS.s.337, Thomas Richardson, 'Map of the Town of Glasgow and seven miles around' (1795).
Roy Military Map of Scotland, 1747–1755.

National Records of Scotland, Edinburgh [NRS]

AD14/23/104, Information & Presentment, George Salmond, Procurator Fiscal against Alexander McPhie and others, 1823.

AD14/24/185, Information and Presentment, George Salmond, PF, against William O'Boyling, James Neilson and Robert Kirkwood, 1824.

AD14/24/199, Precognition against Robert Kirkwood, Dempster Kirkwood for the crime of assaulting officers of the law, 1824.

AD14/24/258/14, Precognition against Robert Reid, Alexander M'Phie and others, for the crime of Mobbing and Rioting, 1824.

AD14/27/161, Precognition against Thomas Cunningham and others, for the crime of assault, Spring 1827.

AD14/28/112, Indictment v William Craig etc, assault and deforcement, September 1828.

CH2/461/3, Old Monkland Kirk Session Minutes, 1800–1823.

CS13/424, Westthorn, Second Report of Dugald John Bannatyne and State of his Accounts as Judicial Factor in the Estate of Westthorn, 1836.

CS38/14/48, J. and T. Harvie agt. Dunbar, 1816.

CS44/79/10, Wardrop agt Craig, 1825

CS44/158/24, Decreet, Thomas Harvie re the sequestration and estate of James Sword, 1828.

CS46/1830/5/6, Decreet of Declarator, In Causa, Rodgers v Harvie, 1830.

CS96/42/6, Sederunt Book of the Creditors of the Glasgow Distillery Company and Thomas Harvie, Individual Partner thereof, 17 April 1832 – 17 April 1834.

CS96/1264, Sederunt Book of James Sword, junior, Creditors, 1826.

CS96/3858, Sederunt Book, Craig's Creditors.

CS96/4216, Sederunt Book of the Creditors of the Glasgow Distillery Co. and Thomas Harvie, Individual Partner thereof, 17 April 1832 – 17 April 1834.

CS271/2026, Answers for the British Linen Company to Bill of Suspension for Adam Ferrie & Coy, 1829.

GD274/6, Inventory of the Machinery and Utensils at Dalmarnock Dye Works, 7 March 1832.

JC26/1818/38, Criminal Letters, The Lord Advocate agt Mary Hutcheson, alias Arrol, 1818.

JC26/1818/73, Trial Papers of Mary Hutcheson, alias Arrol, Declaration of Mary Hutcheson, April 1818.

JC26/1823/122, Indictment, HM Advocate v Alexander M'Phie etc (Mobbing and Rioting).

JC26/1826/342, Indictment, HM Advocate against Robert Hamilton, Samuel McMenemy and Alexander M'Phie, 1826.

JC26/1827/239, Criminal Letters against Thomas Cunningham etc, Glasgow Circuit, Spring 1827.

SC36/48/27, Glasgow Sheriff Court Inventories, Thomas Harvie, Distiller in Glasgow, September 1839.

North Lanarkshire Archives, Motherwell

W. Mack, Notebook, Weather, Airdrie, 1799–1826.

Royal College of Physicians and Surgeons of Glasgow

Glasgow Medical Journal

Medical Essays

Stirling Council Archives

Murray of Polmaise and Touchadam Papers.

University of Glasgow, Special Collections [UGSC]

GB247 MS Murray 636 Barony Parish of Glasgow, by James Hopkirk, 1827.

MS Gen 1059, Gabriel Neil, Notes on Zachary Boyd, MS of Introduction to Four Poems from Zion's Flowers, 1855. (Includes undated copy letters to the *Glasgow Constitutional*.)

Smith Collection

Printed Primary Sources

Newspapers

Belfast Commercial Chronicle

Caledonian Mercury

Carlisle Journal

Christian News

Elgin Courant and Morayshire Advertiser

Fife Herald

Glasgow Chronicle

Glasgow Courier

Glasgow Free Press

Glasgow Gazette

Glasgow Herald
Glasgow Sentinel
Glasgow Weekly Herald
Inverness Courier
Morning Chronicle
Morning Post (London)
News (London)
North British Daily Mail
Northern Whig
Perthshire Courier
Scots Magazine
Scotsman
Star (London)
The Times
Westmorland Gazette

Other printed material

A Narrative of the Proceedings in the Case Rodgers and others, v Harvie, For the Recovery of the Liberty of the Banks of the Clyde (Glasgow: Hugh Cameron, 1829).

Aiton, W., *A History of the Encounter at Drumclog and Battle of Bothwell Bridge, in the month of June, 1679* (Hamilton: W. M. Borthwick & Co., 1821).

Anderson, James R. (ed.), *The Burgesses and Guild Brethren of Glasgow, 1751–1846* (Edinburgh: Scottish Record Society, 1935).

Barony of Glasgow, County of Lanark, *Old Statistical Account*, Vol. XII (1794), pp. 109–26.

Black, John, *The Falls of Clyde, or, The Fairies; A Scottish Dramatic Pastoral, in Five Acts, with Three Dissertations* (Edinburgh: William Creech, 1806).

Blackwood, William (ed.), *Cases Decided in the Court of Session from November 13, 1828 to July 11, 1829*.

Carr, Sir John, *Caledonian Sketches, or a Tour Through Scotland in 1807* (London: Matthews and Leigh, 1809).

Cleland, James, *Annals of Glasgow: comprising an account of the public buildings, charities, and the rise and progress of the city* (Glasgow: J. Hedderwick, 1816).

Cleland, James, *Historical Account of the Steam Engine* (Glasgow: Edward Khull & Son, 1829).

Cleland, James, *Enumeration of the Inhabitants of the City of Glasgow and Lanarkshire* (Glasgow: J. Smith, 1832).

Eadie, John, *The Reign of George Third, for Fifty Years: The Clyde and a Number of Other Poems, Descriptive and Religious* (Glasgow: Young, Gallie & Co., 1818).

Ferguson, James, *The Law of Roads, Streets, and Rights of Way, Bridges, and Ferries, in Scotland* (Edinburgh: Green & Sons, 1904).

Ferrie, Adam, *Autobiography, Late Hon. Adam Ferrie* (n.p., n.d., *c.*1864).

Forbes Gray, W. (ed.), *Memorials of His Time, By Lord Cockburn* (Edinburgh: Robert Grant & Son, 1945 edn).

Ford, Robert (ed.), *Poems and Songs, Humorous, Serious and Satirical by Alexander Rodger* (Paisley and London: Alexander Gardner, 1901).

Gilmour, David, *Paisley Weavers of Other Days* (Paisley: Alex Gardner, 1878).

Glasgow Delineated, in its Institutions, Manufactures, and Commerce (Glasgow: Wardlaw and Cunninghame, 1827).

Glasgow Directory: Containing a List of the Merchants, Manufacturers, Traders etc in the city of Glasgow and Suburbs (Glasgow: W. Lang, 1821).

Glasgow Past and Present Embracing Loose Memoranda on Glasgow Subjects by Senex and Desultory Sketches by J.B. (Glasgow: David Robertson and Co., 1856, 3 vols).

Hamilton, Janet, *Poems, Essays, and Sketches* (Glasgow: James MacLehose, 1870).

Harvie, Wallace, *Chronicles of St Mungo: Or Traditions and Antiquities of Glasgow* (Glasgow: J. Smith, 1843).

History of Glasgow Green, and of the Various Struggles by the Citizens to Preserve it from Encroachment, Particularly those of 1575–76, 1745 and 1845 (Glasgow: W. C. Pattison, 1845).

Hopkirk, Thomas, *Flotta Glottiana: A Catalogue of the Indigenous Plants on the Banks of the River Clyde, and in the Neighbourhood of the City of Glasgow* (Glasgow: John Smith and Son, 1813).

MacDonald, Hugh, *Rambles Round Glasgow* (Glasgow: John Cameron, 1854).

M'Dowall, John K., *The People's History of Glasgow* (Glasgow: Hay Nisbet & Co., 1899).

Mackenzie, Peter, *An Exposure of the Spy System Pursued in Glasgow During the Years 1816–17–18–19 and 20* (Glasgow: Muir, Gowans & Co., 1833).

Mackenzie, Peter, *Reminiscences of Glasgow and the West of Scotland* (Glasgow: John Tweed, 1865, 2 vols).

M'Ure, John, *Glasghu Facies: History of Glasgow, Ancient and Modern* (Glasgow: John Tweed, 1872, 2 vols).

Muir, Hugh, *Reminiscences and Sketches: Being a Topographical History of Rutherglen and Suburbs* (Glasgow: Bell & Bain, 1890).

Leyland, John, *Clyde: A Descriptive Poem by John Wilson* (Edinburgh and London: A. Fullarton & Co., 1803).

Rodger, Alexander (ed.), *Stray Leaves from the Portfolios of Alisander the Seer, Andrew Whaup, and Humphrey Henkeckle* (Glasgow: Charles Rattray, 1842).

Select Pieces Delivered at a Public Meeting held for Promoting the Subscription to Procure Medals, Commemorative of the Triumph of the Citizens of Glasgow in Establishing Their Right to a Path on the Banks of the Clyde (Glasgow: Robertson & Atkinson, 1829).

Shearer, W. Ross, *Rutherglen Lore* (Paisley: Alexander Gardner, 1922).

Smith, John Guthrie and Mitchell, John Oswald, *The Old Country Houses of the Old Glasgow Gentry* (Glasgow: James MacLehose, 1878).

Strang, John, *Glasgow and its Clubs* (Glasgow: R. Griffen and Co., 1857).

The Autobiography of Lieutenant-General Sir Harry Smith (London: John Murray, 1903, 2 vols).

The Poetical Works of the Late Hugh Macdonald (Glasgow: Robert Forrester, 1865).

The Topographical Picture of Glasgow in its Ancient and Modern State (Glasgow: R. Chapman, 1820 edn).

Theses

Livingston, Alistair, 'The Galloway Levellers – A Study of the Origins, Events and Consequences of their Actions', MPhil dissertation (University of Glasgow, 2009).

W. M. Roach, 'Radical and Reform Movements in Scotland from 1815 to 1820', unpublished PhD thesis (University of Glasgow, 1970).

Secondary Works

Alston, David, *Slaves and Highlanders: Silenced Histories of Scotland and the Caribbean* (Edinburgh: Edinburgh University Press, 2021).

Andrews, Cory E., 'Radical Attribution: Robert Burns and the "Liberty Tree"', *Studies in Scottish Literature*, 41:1 (2016), pp. 174–90.

Armstrong, Murray, *The Fight for Scottish Democracy: Rebellion & Reform in 1820* (London: Pluto Press, 2020).

Barrie, David, *Police in the Age of Improvement: Police Development and the Civic Tradition in Scotland, 1775–1865* (Cullompton: Willan Publishing, 2008).

Barrie, David, 'The History of Violence in Scotland Reconsidered: The Culture, Filtering and Treatment of Assault in the Police Courts, c.1829–1890', *Scottish Historical Review*, 103 (2024), pp. 318–53.

Bell, Alan (ed.), *Lord Cockburn: Selected Letters* (Edinburgh: John Donald, 2005).

Benchimol, Alex, 'Policing the Industrial Order in the West of Scotland', in Gerard Carruthers, Kevin Gallagher, Craig Lamont and George Smith (eds), *1820: Scottish Rebellion. Essays on a Nineteenth Century Insurrection* (Edinburgh: John Donald, 2022), pp. 74–92.

Berger, Stefan and Niven, Bill (eds), *Writing the History of Memory* (London and New York: Bloomsbury, 2014).

Berresford Ellis, Peter and Mac a' Ghobhainn, Seumas, *The Scottish Insurrection of 1820* (London: Pluto Press, 1989).

Biagini, Eugenio F., *Liberty, Retrenchment and Reform: Popular Liberalism in the Age of Gladstone, 1860–1880* (Cambridge: Cambridge University Press, 1992).

Blair, Kirsty, *Working Verse in Victorian Scotland: Poetry, Press, Community* (Oxford: Oxford University Press, 2019).

Brown, Callum G., *Religion and Society in Scotland since 1707* (Edinburgh: Edinburgh University Press, 1997).

Burnett, John, *Riot, Revelry and Rout: Sport in Lowland Scotland Before 1860* (East Linton: Tuckwell Press, 2000).

Cairns, John W., '"Famous as a school for Law, as Edinburgh . . . for medicine": Legal Education in Glasgow, 1761–1801', in Andrew Hook and Richard B. Sher (eds), *The Glasgow Enlightenment* (East Linton: Tuckwell Press, 1995), pp. 133–59.

Campbell, Alan B., *The Lanarkshire Miners: A Social History of their Trade Unions, 1775–1874* (Edinburgh: John Donald, 1979).

Campbell, R. H., 'The Making of the Industrial City', in T. M. Devine and Gordon Jackson, *Glasgow, Volume 1: Beginnings to 1830* (Manchester: Manchester University Press, 1995), pp. 184–213.

Carruthers, Gerard (ed.), *The Oxford Handbook of Robert Burns* (Oxford: Oxford University Press, 2024).

Carruthers, Gerard and Gardner, John, 'Finding Alexander Rodger, the Glasgow Poet, in 1820', in Gerard Carruthers, Kevin Gallagher, Craig Lamont and George Smith (eds), *1820: Scottish Rebellion. Essays on a Nineteenth Century Insurrection* (Edinburgh: John Donald, 2022), pp. 144–60.

Carruthers, Gerard and Kidd, Colin (eds), *The International Companion to John Galt* (Glasgow: Scottish Literature International, 2017), pp. 82–97.

Carruthers, Gerard and Paton, Norman R., 'Did Robert Burns write the "Tree of Liberty"?', in Johnny Rodger and Gerard Carruthers (eds), *Fickle Man: Robert Burns in the 21st Century* (Dingwall: Sandstone Press, 2009), pp. 242–56.

Carruthers, Gerard, Gallagher, Kevin, Lamont, Craig and Smith, George (eds), *1820: Scottish Rebellion. Essays on a Nineteenth Century Insurrection* (Edinburgh: John Donald, 2022).

Chase, Malcolm, *1820: Disorder and Stability in the United Kingdom* (Manchester: Manchester University Press, 2013).

Clark, Anna, *The Struggle for the Breeches: Gender and the Making of the British Working Class* (London: University of California Press, 1995).

Clark, Samuel and Donnelly, James S., Jr (eds), *Irish Peasants: Violence and Political Unrest, 1780–1914* (Manchester: Manchester University Press, 1983).

Coleman, James, *Remembering the Past in Nineteenth-Century Scotland* (Edinburgh: Edinburgh University Press, 2014).

Comment, Bernard, *The Panorama* (London: Reaktion Books, 1999).

Cowan, Edward J. (ed.), *The Ballad in Scottish History* (East Linton: Tuckwell Press, 2000).

Cowan, Edward J., *'For Freedom Alone': The Declaration of Arbroath, 1320* (East Linton: Tuckwell Press, 2003).

Cowan, Edward J. and Finlay, Richard J. (eds), *Scottish History: The Power of the Past* (Edinburgh: Edinburgh University Press, 2002).

Cowan, James, *From Glasgow's Treasure Chest: A Miscellany of History, Personalities and Places* (Glasgow: Craig & Wilson, 1951).

Craig, Carol, *The Scots' Crisis of Confidence* (Glendaruel: Argyll Publishing, 2003).

Craig, Maggie, *One Week in April: The Scottish Radical Rising of 1820* (Edinburgh: Birlinn, 2020).

Crownshaw, Richard, 'History and Memorialisation', in Stefan Berger and Bill Niven (eds), *Writing the History of Memory* (London and New York: Bloomsbury, 2014), pp. 219–33.

Cummings, A. J. G. and Devine, T. M. (eds), *Industry, Business and Society in Scotland Since 1700* (Edinburgh: John Donald, 1994).

Cunnison, J. and Gilfillan, J. B. S., *The Third Statistical Account of Scotland: Glasgow* (Glasgow: William Collins, 1959 edn).

Darnton, Robert, *The Revolutionary Temper: Paris, 1748–1787* (London: Penguin, 2023).

Davidson, Neil, *The Origins of Scottish Nationhood* (London: Pluto Press, 2000).

Davidson, Neil and Allinson, Jamie, 'De-provincialising 1820: The West of Scotland General Strike in the Mirror of Uneven and Combined Development (Part 1)', *Scottish Labour History*, 55 (2020), pp. 143–74.

Davidson, Neil and Allinson, Jamie, 'De-provincialising 1820: The West of Scotland General Strike in the Mirror of Uneven and Combined Development (Part 2)', *Scottish Labour History*, 57 (2022), pp. 110–38.

Demson, Michael, 'The Satirical Poetry and Commemorative Contests of Scotland's 1820 Radical War', in Gerard Carruthers, Kevin Gallagher, Craig Lamont and George Smith (eds), *1820: Scottish Rebellion. Essays on a Nineteenth Century Insurrection* (Edinburgh: John Donald, 2022), pp. 179–96.

Dennison, Patricia E., *The Evolution of Scotland's Towns: Creation, Growth and Fragmentation* (Edinburgh, 2018).

Devine, T. M., *The Tobacco Lords* (Edinburgh: John Donald, 1975).

Devine, T. M., 'Urbanisation and the Civic Response: Glasgow, 1800–1830', in A. J. G. Cummings and T. M. Devine (eds), *Industry, Business and Society in Scotland Since 1700* (Edinburgh: John Donald, 1994), pp. 183–96.

Devine, T. M., 'The Golden Age of Tobacco', in T. M. Devine and Gordon Jackson, *Glasgow, Volume 1: Beginnings to 1830* (Manchester: Manchester University Press, 1995), pp. 130–83.

Devine, T. M. and Jackson, Gordon, *Glasgow, Volume I: Beginnings to 1830* (Manchester: Manchester University Press, 1995).

Devine, T. M. and Mitchison, Rosalind (eds), *People and Society in Scotland, Volume 1, 1760–1830* (Edinburgh: John Donald, 1988).

Devine, T. M. and Wormald, Jenny (eds), *The Oxford Handbook of Modern Scottish History* (Oxford: Oxford University Press, 2012).

Dingwall, Helen, 'Illness, Disease and Pain', in Elizabeth Foyster and Christopher A. Whatley (eds), *Everyday Life in Scotland*, pp. 108–36.

Donnachie, Ian L., 'Drink and Society, 1750–1850: Some Aspects of the Scottish Experience', *Scottish Labour History*, 13 (1979), pp. 5–22.

Donnelly, James S., Jr, 'Pastorini and Captain Rock: Millennialism and Sectarianism in the Rockite Movement of 1821–4', in Samuel Clark and James S. Donnelly, Jr (eds), *Irish Peasants: Violence and Political Unrest, 1780–1914* (Manchester: Manchester University Press, 1983), pp. 102–39.

Dowds, T. J., *Scotland Free or a Desart: The Radical Insurrection of 1820* (Rothersthorpe: Paragon Publishing, 2020).

Dowds, T. J., 'The 1820 Rising: Recent Discoveries', *Scottish Local History*, 117 (2024), pp. 42–3.

Duckham, Baron F., *A History of the Scottish Coal Industry, Volume 1: 1700–1815* (Newton Abbott: David & Charles, 1970).

Elliot, Elizabeth, 'Walter Scott's Bannatyne Club, Male Associational Culture, and the Making of Identity', *Review of English Studies*, 67:281 (2016), pp. 732–50.

Esdaile, Charles J., 'The French Revolutionary and Napoleonic Wars, 1793–1815', in Edward M. Speirs, Jeremy A. Crang and Matthew Strickland (eds), *A Military History of Scotland* (Edinburgh: Edinburgh University Press, 2012), pp. 407–35.

Foyster, Elizabeth and Whatley, Christopher A. (eds), *A History of Everyday Life in Scotland, 1600–1800* (Edinburgh: Edinburgh University Press, 2010).

Fraser, W. Hamish, *Conflict and Class: Scottish Workers, 1700–1838* (Edinburgh: John Donald, 1988).

Fraser, W. Hamish, 'Patterns of Protest', in T. M. Devine and Rosalind Mitchison (eds), *People and Society in Scotland, Volume 1, 1760–1830* (Edinburgh: John Donald, 1988), pp. 268–91.

Fraser, W. Hamish, *Chartism in Scotland* (Pontypool: Merlin Press, 2010).

Fraser, W. Hamish and Maver, Irene (eds), *Glasgow, Volume II: 1830 to 1912* (Manchester: Manchester University Press, 1996).

Fraser, W. Hamish and Maver, Irene, 'The Social Problems of the City', in W. Hamish Fraser and Irene Maver (eds), *Glasgow, Volume II: 1830 to 1912* (Manchester: Manchester University Press, 1996), pp. 352–93.

Fry, Michael, 'Jeffrey, Francis, Lord Jeffrey (1773–1850), writer and judge', *Oxford Dictionary of National Biography,* 23 September 2004; accessed 10 February 2025: https://www.oxforddnb.com/view/10.1093/ref:odnb/9780198614128.001.0001/odnb-9780198614128-e-14698.

Garber, Zachary, 'Tyranny and Liberty, Resistance and Regicide: Political Assassination in John Galt's *The Spaewife*', *English: Journal of the English Association*, 71 (2022), pp. 241–63.

Griffin, Emma, *Liberty's Dawn: A People's History of the Industrial Revolution* (New Haven and London: Yale University Press, 2014 edn).

Griffiths, Trevor, 'Work, Leisure and Time in the Nineteenth Century', in Trevor Griffiths and Graeme Morton (eds), *A History of Everyday Life in Scotland, 1800 to 1900* (Edinburgh: Edinburgh University Press, 2010), pp. 170–95.

Griffiths, Trevor and Morton, Graeme (eds), *A History of Everyday Life in Scotland, 1800 to 1900* (Edinburgh: Edinburgh University Press, 2010).

Gunn, Simon, *The Public Culture of the Victorian Middle Class: Ritual and Authority in the English Industrial City 1840–1914* (Manchester: Manchester University Press, 2000).

Harris, Bob (ed.), *Scotland in the Age of the French Revolution* (Edinburgh: John Donald, 2005).

Harris, Bob, *The Scottish People and the French Revolution* (London: Pickering & Chatto, 2008).

Holmes, Richard, 'James Arbuckle's Glotta (1721) and the Poetry of Allusion', *Journal for Eighteenth-Century Studies*, 35:1 (2012), pp. 85–100.

Hook, Andrew and Sher, Richard B. (eds), *The Glasgow Enlightenment* (East Linton: Tuckwell Press, 1995).

Hunter, James, *The Making of the Crofting Community* (Edinburgh: John Donald, 1976).

Hunter, James, *Insurrection: Scotland's Famine Winter* (Edinburgh: Birlinn, 2019).

Isabella, Maurizio, *Southern Europe in the Age of Revolutions* (Princeton and Oxford: Princeton University Press, 2023).

Jackson, E. S., *The Inniskilling Dragoons: The Records of an Old Heavy Cavalry Regiment* (East Sussex: Naval & Military Press, n.d.).

Jarman, Andrea Loux, 'Customary Rights in Scots Law: Test Cases on Access to Land in the Nineteenth Century', *Journal of Legal History*, 28:2 (2007), pp. 207–32.

Johnston, Thomas, *The History of the Working Classes in Scotland* (Wakefield: EP Publishing, 1974 edn).

Joyce, Patrick, *Visions of the People: Industrial England and the Question of Class, 1848–1914* (Cambridge: Cambridge University Press, 1991).

Kilday, Anne-Marie, 'The Barbarous North? Criminality in Early Modern Scotland', in T. M. Devine and Jenny Wormald (eds), *The Oxford Handbook of Modern Scottish History* (Oxford: Oxford University Press, 2012), pp. 386–401.

King, Elspeth, *The People's Palace and Glasgow Green* (Edinburgh: W. and R. Chambers, 1991 edn).

Knox, William W., *Industrial Nation: Work, Culture and Society in Scotland, 1800–Present* (Edinburgh: Edinburgh University Press, 1999).

Knox, William W. J. and McKinlay, A., 'Crime, Protest and Policing in Nineteenth -Century Scotland', in Trevor Griffiths and Graeme Morton (eds), *A History of Everyday Life in Scotland, 1800 to 1900* (Edinburgh: Edinburgh University Press, 2010), pp. 196–224.

Lamont, Craig, *The Cultural Memory of Georgian Glasgow* (Edinburgh: Edinburgh University Press, 2021).

Lamont, Craig, 'Remembering the Radical War: Monuments, Markers and Commemorations', in Gerard Carruthers, Kevin Gallagher, Craig Lamont and George Smith (eds), *1820: Scottish Rebellion. Essays on a Nineteenth Century Insurrection* (Edinburgh: John Donald, 2022), pp. 213–35.

Leonard, Tom (ed.), *Radical Renfrew: Poetry from the French Revolution to the First World War* (Edinburgh, 1990).

Lewis, Anthony, '1820 in the Museum: A Review of Glasgow Museums' Collections of Scottish Radical Political History of the Time', in Gerard Carruthers, Kevin Gallagher, Craig Lamont and George Smith (eds), *1820: Scottish Rebellion. Essays on a Nineteenth Century Insurrection* (Edinburgh: John Donald, 2022), pp. 208–12.

Logue, Kenneth, *Popular Disturbances in Scotland, 1780–1815* (Edinburgh: John Donald, 1979).

MacAskill, Kenny, *Radical Scotland: Uncovering Scotland's Radical History from the French Revolutionary Era to the 1820 Rising* (London: Biteback, 2020).

Macdonald, Catriona M. M., 'Abandoned and Beastly? The Queen Caroline Affair in Scotland', in Yvonne G. Brown and Rona Ferguson (eds), *Twisted*

Sisters: Women, Crime and Deviance in Scotland Since 1400 (East Linton: Tuckwell Press, 2001), pp. 101–13.

Macdonald, Catriona M. M., "'Their Laurels Wither'd, and Their Name Forgot": Women and the Scottish Radical Tradition', in Edward J. Cowan and Richard J. Findlay (eds), *Scottish History: The Power of the Past* (Edinburgh: Edinburgh University Press, 2002), pp. 225–52.

Macdonald, Catriona M. M., "'The Ebbing of the Old Shallow Tide": The Civil Context of the Radical War (1820)', in Gerard Carruthers, Kevin Gallagher, Craig Lamont and George Smith (eds), *1820: Scottish Rebellion. Essays on a Nineteenth Century Insurrection* (Edinburgh: John Donald, 2022), pp. 1–17.

McFarland, Elaine, *Protestants First: Orangeism in 19th Century Scotland* (Edinburgh: Edinburgh University Press, 1990).

McLaren, David J., *David Dale: A Life* (Catrine: Stenlake Publishing, 2015).

Macmillan, Duncan, *Scottish Art 1460–1990* (Edinburgh: Mainstream, 1990).

Maidment, Brian, *The Poorhouse Fugitives: Self-taught Poets and Poetry in Victorian Britain* (Manchester, 1987).

Markus, Thomas, Robinson, Peter and Arneil Walker, Frank, 'The Shape of the City in Space and Stone', in T. M. Devine and Gordon Jackson, *Glasgow, Volume 1: Beginnings to 1830* (Manchester: Manchester University Press, 1995), pp. 106–38.

Marwick, W. H., 'The Beginnings of the Scottish Working-Class Movement in the Nineteenth Century', *International Review for Social History*, 3 (1938), pp. 1–24.

Marwick, W. H., *A Short History of Labour in Scotland* (Edinburgh: W. & R. Chambers, 1967).

Maver, Irene, 'The Guardianship of the Community: Civic Authority Prior to 1833', in T. M. Devine and Gordon Jackson, *Glasgow, Volume 1: Beginnings to 1830* (Manchester: Manchester University Press, 1995), pp. 239–77.

Maver, Irene, 'Glasgow's Civic Government', in W. Hamish Fraser and Irene Maver (eds), *Glasgow, Volume II: 1830 to 1912* (Manchester: Manchester University Press, 1996), pp. 441–85.

Maver, Irene, *Glasgow* (Edinburgh: Edinburgh University Press, 2000).

Michie, Michael, *An Enlightenment Tory in Victorian Scotland: The Career of Sir Archibald Alison* (East Linton: Tuckwell Press, 1997).

Moore, John and Hume, John R. (eds), *A City Situated for Commerce* (Glasgow: University of Glasgow Library, 2023).

Moss, Michael and Hume, John R., *The Making of Scotch Whisky: A History of the Scotch Whisky Distilling Industry* (Edinburgh: Canongate, 2000 edn).

Murray, Norman, *The Scottish Hand Loom Weavers, 1790–1850: A Social History* (Edinburgh: John Donald, 1978).

Nenadic, Stana, 'The Rise of the Urban Middle Class', in T. M. Devine and Rosalind Mitchison (eds), *People and Society in Scotland, Volume 1, 1760–1830* (Edinburgh: John Donald, 1988), pp. 109–26.

Ord, John, *The Story of the Burgh of Calton* (Glasgow: Aird and Coghill, 1912).

Pentland, Gordon, 'Scotland and the Creation of a National Reform Movement', *Historical Journal*, 48 (2005), pp. 999–1023.

Pentland, Gordon, "'Betrayed by Infamous Spies"? The Commemoration of Scotland's "Radical War" of 1820', *Past & Present*, 201 (2008), pp. 141–73.

Pentland, Gordon, 'The Challenge of Radicalism to 1832', in T. M. Devine and Jenny Wormald (eds), *The Oxford Handbook of Modern Scottish History* (Oxford: Oxford University Press, 2012), pp. 439–54.

Pentland, Gordon, *The Spirit of the Union* (London: Routledge, 2015 edn).

Ramsay, A. A. W., 'The Glasgow Outrages, 1820–25', *Quarterly Review*, 429 (1927), pp. 326–38.

Reed, Peter (ed.), *Glasgow: The Forming of the City* (Edinburgh: Edinburgh University Press, 1993).

Reed, Peter, 'The Victorian Suburb', in Peter Reed (ed.), *Glasgow: The Forming of the City* (Edinburgh: Edinburgh University Press, 1993), pp. 57–83.

Robson, Peter and Rodger, Johnny, *The Spaces of Justice: The Architecture of the Scottish Court* (Madison: Fairleigh Dickinson University Press, 2018).

Rodger, Johnny and Carruthers, Gerard (eds), *Fickle Man: Robert Burns in the 21st Century* (Dingwall: Sandstone Press, 2009).

Russell, James B., *The Evolution of the Function of the Public Health Administration as Illustrated by the Sanitary History of Glasgow in the Nineteenth Century* (Glasgow: W. Hodge & Co., 1895).

Sher, Richard B., 'Images of Glasgow in Late Eighteenth Century Popular Poetry', in Andrew Hook and Richard B. Sher (eds), *The Glasgow Enlightenment* (East Linton: Tuckwell Press, 1995), pp. 190–213.

Smiechen, James, 'Glasgow of the Imagination: Architecture, Townscape and Society', in W. Hamish Fraser and Irene Maver (eds), *Glasgow, Volume II: 1830 to 1912* (Manchester: Manchester University Press, 1996), pp. 486–518.

Smout, Christopher, 'Introduction: Trees in Scottish Life', in T. C. Smout (ed.), *People and Woods in Scotland: A History* (Edinburgh: Edinburgh University Press, 2003), pp. 1–13.

Smout, T. C., *A Century of the Scottish People, 1830–1950* (London: Collins, 1986).

Smout, T. C., *Nature Contested: Environmental History in Scotland and Northern England Since 1600* (Edinburgh: Edinburgh University Press, 2000).

Smout, T. C. (ed.), *People and Woods in Scotland: A History* (Edinburgh: Edinburgh University Press, 2003).

Smout, T. C., *Exploring Environmental History: Selected Essays* (Edinburgh: Edinburgh University Press, 2011 edn).

Speirs, Edward M., Crang, Jeremy A. and Strickland, Matthew J. (eds), *A Military History of Scotland* (Edinburgh: Edinburgh University Press, 2012).

Stafford, Fiona, 'Burns and the Natural World', in Gerard Carruthers (ed.), *The Oxford Handbook of Robert Burns* (Oxford: Oxford University Press, 2024), p. 199–215.

Swinfen, David, *Moncreiff* (Dundee: Shakenoak Press, 2015).

Taylor, Harvey, *A Claim on the Countryside: A History of the British Outdoor Movement* (Edinburgh: Edinburgh University Press, 1997).

Thomas, Keith, *Man and the Natural World: Changing Attitudes in England 1500–1800* (London and New York: Penguin, 1984 edn).

Thompson, E. P., *Customs in Common* (London: Penguin, 1993).

Treble, J. H., 'The Standard of Living of the Working Class', in T. M. Devine and Rosalind Mitchison (eds), *People and Society in Scotland, Volume 1, 1760–1830* (Edinburgh: John Donald, 1988), pp. 188–226.

Tuckett, Sally, and Nenadic, Stana, 'Colouring the Nation: A New In-Depth Study of the Turkey Red Pattern Books in the National Museums Scotland', *Textile History*, 43 (2012), pp. 161–82.

Tulchinsky, Gerald, 'Adam Ferrie (1777–1863)', in *Dictionary of Canadian Biography*, 9, University of Toronto/Université Laval, accessed 16 October 2023: http://biographi.ca/en/bio/ferrie_adam_1777_1863_9E.html.

Wallace, Valerie, 'Presbyterian Moral Economy: The Covenanting Tradition and Popular Protest in Lowland Scotland, 1707–c.1746', *Scottish Historical Review*, 89 (2010), pp. 54–72.

Whatley, Christopher A., '"The fettering bonds of brotherhood": Combination and Labour Relations in the Scottish Coal-Mining Industry, *c.*1690–1775', *Social History*, 12:2 (1988), pp. 139–54.

Whatley, Christopher A., *Scottish Society, 1707–1830: Beyond Jacobitism, Towards Industrialisation* (Manchester: Manchester University Press, 2000).

Whatley, Christopher A., 'Sound and Song in the Ritual of Popular Protest: Continuity and the "Nob Songs" of 1825', in Edward J. Cowan (ed.), *The Ballad in Scottish History* (East Linton: Tuckwell Press, 2000), pp. 142–60.

Whatley, Christopher A., *Immortal Memory: Burns and the Scottish People* (Edinburgh: John Donald, 2016).

Whatley, Christopher A., 'The Insider's Eye in the Age of Improvement, Urbanisation and Revolution', in Gerard Carruthers and Colin Kidd (eds), *The International Companion to John Galt* (Glasgow: Scottish Literature International, 2017), pp. 82–97.

Whyte, Hamish, 'Motherwell, William (1797–1835), poet and ballad editor',

Oxford Dictionary of National Biography, 23 September 2004; accessed 10 February 2025:
https://www.oxforddnb.com/view/10.1093/ref:odnb/9780198614128.001.0001/odnb-9780198614128-e-19419.

Wightman, Andy, *The Poor Had No Lawyers: Who Owns Scotland and How They Got It* (Edinburgh: Birlinn, 2011).

Index